Uniting America

Uniting America

Restoring the Vital Center to

American Democracy

Edited by
Norton Garfinkle and Daniel Yankelovich

Yale University Press

New Haven and London

Printed in the United States of America

Library of Congress Cataloging-in-Publication Data
Uniting America : restoring the vital center to American democracy / edited
by Norton Garfinkle and Daniel Yankelovich.
     p. cm
   Includes bibliographical references and index.
   ISBN 0-300-10856-7 (alk. paper)
     1. Democracy—United States. 2. United States—Politics and
government—2001– 3. Political culture—United States. 4. United
States—Social conditions—1980– 5. Social conflict—United States. 6.
Polarization (Social sciences) I. Garfinkle, Norton, 1931– II. Yankelovich,
Daniel.
   JK1726.U564 2005
   320.973—dc22   2005012038

A catalogue record for this book is available from the British Library.

The paper in this book meets the guidelines for permanence and durability of the
Committee on Production Guidelines for Book Longevity of the Council on
Library Resources.

10 9 8 7 6 5 4 3 2 1

Contents

Preface

E. J. Dionne, Jr., has declared that there is a new "revolt of the middle" in American politics—a growing sense among the vast centrist, pragmatic majority of Americans that Washington's ideologically driven "politics of polarization" is increasingly leaving them out. If there is such a quiet revolution afoot today among politically moderate Americans—citizens who do not feel at home with the more extreme positions taken by either side in Washington's ongoing political debates—then such citizens should find *Uniting America* to be a breath of fresh air.

Uniting America is the first of what we hope will be a series of new books, articles, lectures, conferences, and public initiatives— all designed to recover the lost "vital center" in American politics and help Americans to build a shared, sensible, and hopeful vision of our democratic future.

Our work on *Uniting America* inspired us to found a new nonpartisan, nonprofit foundation, The Future of American Democracy Foundation, to sponsor continuing activities aimed at nurturing this new centrist vision.

The Future of American Democracy Foundation is working closely with the Yale Center for International and Area Studies and Yale University Press to develop a research and education agenda designed to renew and sustain the historic vision of American democracy for the future. The Foundation is enlisting some of America's best policy minds to address the full range of domestic and foreign policy issues the United States confronts in the years ahead. The Foundation seeks to develop a new, more balanced paradigm for American policymaking, one that can form the basis of a centrist consensus, uniting citizens around common aims and purposes that will genuinely meet the challenges before us.

Norton Garfinkle chairs The Future of American Democracy Foundation. Daniel Yankelovich chairs the Foundation's Advisory Board. Co-Chairs of the Foundation's Executive Committee include Ian Shapiro, Henry R. Luce, Director of the Yale Center for International and Area Studies, and Jonathan Brent, Editorial Director of Yale University Press. The Foundation's Executive Director is Patrick Glynn. Please visit our Web site—www.futureof americandemocracyfoundation.org—for the latest information on the Foundation's activities.

The editors would like to thank Amitai Etzioni for his help and support in inviting authors to contribute to this volume. The editors also wish to thank Patrick Glynn for his extensive editorial and organizational work in helping to put the book together. Our agent, Frederica Friedman, a consummate publishing professional, worked tirelessly on behalf of this volume. And finally the editors wish to express their gratitude to Jonathan Brent and his excellent editorial and production team at Yale University Press for their superb job in bringing the book to fruition.

Norton Garfinkle
Daniel Yankelovich

Uniting America

Introduction

One of the striking developments of the post–September 11 era has
been the disappearance of the center from American politics. The
U.S. Congress stands polarized as almost never before, with few
moderates in either party attempting to bridge the rancorous divide
between Republicans and Democrats. Backed by Republican majorities in both houses of Congress, the Bush administration has
determinedly pushed U.S. foreign and domestic policy to the right,
while various constituencies have simultaneously pulled the Democratic Party to the left. Both parties seek to claim the center for
electoral purposes, but neither party seems in a mood to build a
genuine bipartisan consensus on crucial policy issues. Pollsters claim
to find the same division among the public at large, pronouncing
America a "50-50 nation," divided culturally and politically between
liberalism and conservatism, city and country, coast and heartland.

None of this is healthy. The current mood stands in sharp contrast to the powerful spirit of national unity that prevailed in the
immediate aftermath of the 2001 attacks on the World Trade Center
and the Pentagon. It also contrasts with the fragile but ultimately

resilient spirit of bipartisanship that helped lead America's democracy to victory in the Cold War.

Democracy is a balancing act. It requires a balance between majority rule and minority rights, between state power and individual liberty, between unity and dissent. At times a democracy can lose its balance, and many today ask whether our era is such a time. In particular, the underlying unity of our democratic society—the sense of common values that binds us together as fellow citizens—appears to be at risk. In the second volume of his famous work *Democracy in America* (1840), Alexis de Tocqueville observed, "Without ideas in common, there is no common action, and without common action, there may still exist human beings but not a social entity. In order for society to exist and, even more to prosper, it is necessary that the spirits of all citizens be assembled and held together by certain leading ideas."

Are Americans bound together today by such "ideas in common"? Or have we instead become a nation irreparably divided? Certainly, there are many signs of political polarization in our national life. Once upon a time one could find many Democrats in Congress who were conservative, and many Republicans who were liberal. In recent years, however, the number of such centrists in each party has declined precipitously. The fight in Congress today is between committed liberal Democrats and committed conservative Republicans, and both sides appear to favor a take-no-prisoners approach. Compromise has become all but impossible. Incivility reigns, especially in the House of Representatives, where, according to a memorable comment by the moderate former Democratic senator John Breaux, "people genuinely hate each other."

The divisions in Congress are mirrored in our increasingly fragmented and politicized media. In the era of twenty-four-hour cable news, the typical "news" program is a political food fight conducted by angry partisans prepared to give no quarter. Bitter ad hominem attacks have become the staple of this brand of news entertainment. Moreover, a significant section of the media is fragmented along political lines. Conservatives tune in to Fox News and Rush Limbaugh. Liberals find solace in "The Daily Show" and Al Franken. Partisans increasingly choose their media outlets according to their politics, and few news organizations speak with equal authority to Americans on both sides of the political divide. Indeed, in an era in which many reporters routinely share their personal opinions in "news analysis" stories and on TV talk shows, the whole notion of objective reporting has been described as old-fashioned, even quaint.

Yet in a sense, "polarization" is a media-spawned fear that may lead us to worry more than we really need to about democracy's future. First, we should remind ourselves that debate is natural—and indeed necessary—in a democracy. Even if cable-news viewers may be overdosing on overheated debate today, if we weren't debating at all, we would have more reason to be concerned. Second, it is by no means clear that the current level of political polarization is excessive by historical standards. The 1960s saw massive demonstrations, violent street confrontations, and even full-scale riots over such issues as civil rights and the war in Vietnam. And once upon a time, this nation fought, and survived, a bloody Civil War. For all of our supposed angry differences, today we see few signs of large-scale political instability.

Some of the polarization we witness is the result of easily understandable historical trends. Perhaps most important is the political realignment of the South. Once a Democratic Party bastion, the South has become a Republican stronghold. The result has been the gradual extinction of the conservative Southern Democrat as a political species. In times past, conservative Democrats from the South were often the glue that held bipartisan coalitions together, particularly when it came to issues of foreign policy. Today, because of the realignment of the parties, ideological differences are generally indistinguisable from partisan differences. The effect is to create the appearance of ideological division among all Americans based on the reality of increasingly sharp divisions between our political parties and their partisan allies.

A second important historical trend has been the transformation in morals and mores brought about by the cultural revolution of the 1960s. Clearly, on a variety of moral questions—many revolving around issues of sexuality and family—there are differences between those with more "progressive" and those with more "traditionalist" views. In many cases, these differences have been transformed into political issues, as can be seen in the ongoing debates over abortion, gay marriage, and stem cell research, which receive extensive media coverage.

Reinforcing the partisan tendencies in Washington has been the rise of "advocacy" think tanks and well-funded activist groups on both the right and the left. The groups now exert an enormous influence on candidates and the political process. As major sources of money, information, and political pressure, these entities make it increasingly difficult for candidates to be responsive to the average voter in the candidate's local district. They provide a further goad to partisan posturing.

The continual media emphasis on these partisan differences has had substantial negative effects. The very notion of a "50-50 nation" seems to have encouraged the growing tendency of our political leaders to cater to their "base" rather than compromise with their opposition. There is little question that the polarization idea has contributed to an atmosphere in which political compromise—and in many cases, sensible, centrist solutions to our policy challenges—has become difficult if not impossible to achieve. There is a certain kind of angry political debate that makes it more difficult, rather than easier, to solve policy problems; the polarization idea has pushed our politicians in that direction.

Yet a more complete survey of contemporary American life—one that looks beyond the confines of the Washington Beltway and the narrow view of America that emanates from TV studios in Washington and New York—reveals a very different picture from the vision of America as a hopelessly polarized nation. Political polarization in Washington is part of the story of contemporary American culture, but arguably not the dominant part. In American culture today there are important countervailing trends, powerful tendencies toward unity that provide hope that we can recover what Arthur Schlesinger once termed the "vital center" of American democracy.

First, we need to put our political food fights into perspective. Politics is a large part of cable TV news, but, for most people, it is a small part of life. One might argue that the abiding affliction of American political culture is not so much political polarization as political apathy. Watching political news remains a distinctly minority pastime. The combined primetime audience for the three major cable news networks on a typical weekday evening ranges from 3 to 4 million, or a tiny fraction of the 109 million TV households. The three major network evening newscasts draw a cumulative audience of 20 to 22 million—still a minor share of the total television viewership. Rush Limbaugh, the most popular of the talk radio hosts, attracts about 20 million listeners daily. And these audiences overlap: the same minority of "news junkies" is soaking up political talk from several different sources. Meanwhile, most Americans, the evidence suggests, are not actively tuning in to the endless partisan debates.

Nor do Americans place themselves at the extreme ends of the political spectrum. In a January 2004 survey by the Pew Research Center for the People and the Press, 45 percent of Americans rated themselves as moderate liberals or moderate conservatives in their approach to politics, while only 26 percent described their views as extremely liberal or extremely conservative.

Moreover, discussion of politics—especially among casual acquaintances or workplace colleagues—is the exception rather than the rule in American life. In 2003, the job search Web site Monster.com asked its visitors how they approach the issue of discussing politics at work. The admittedly unscientific results from 26,000 Internet respondents were suggestive. Some 46 percent said the best strategy regarding discussion of politics in the workplace was to "listen but keep your opinions to yourself." Another 30 percent advocated a policy of "don't ask, don't tell." Only 22 percent thought it was best "to stand up and be heard."

While pundits may delight in take-no-prisoners political argumentation on cable TV, Americans in the sphere of private life are famously nonconfrontational when it comes to the divisive issues of politics—or for that matter, morality and religion. In his many conversations with ordinary middle-class Americans across the country, sociologist Alan Wolfe has found a pervasive posture of "nonjudgmentalism," a widespread live-and-let-live ethic, even among many Americans with strongly held evangelical Christian views. While often disagreeing with the political, moral, or religious choices of others, most ordinary Americans—unlike many of our politicians, ideological interest groups, and cable TV debaters—seem loath to pass judgment on their fellow citizens. While family members may quarrel about controversial questions around the kitchen table, open argument between ordinary Americans over political, moral, or religious questions is the exception rather than the rule outside the sanctum of the family home.

Opinion polls have documented this spirit of toleration. In a 2001 study by the nonprofit organization Public Agenda, nearly all (96 percent) agreed that "one of the greatest things about this country is that people can practice whatever religion they choose." Of those who wished religion to become more influential in American life, the vast majority (76 percent) said that it did not matter which religion it was.

Indeed, as Wolfe's chapter on American religion in this volume suggests, one can see the emergence of an evolving social tolerance at the grassroots level, which is mitigating the effects of the polarization on display in Washington and in the media. It is an understandable and generally healthy response of a society that has exploded over the past thirty years with every kind of diversity: racial, ethnic, cultural, religious, and even moral. At the root of this new mood of social toleration appears to be a deeply held American pragmatism. Instinctively, Americans seem to recognize that, absent a powerful ethic of toleration, citizens of diverse backgrounds and views might spend their entire lives uselessly at each other's throats.

Daniel Yankelovich goes further in his chapter on the emergence of a "new social morality," a cluster of shared values around which strong majorities of Americans seem to be uniting. These values, as Yankelovich describes them, include patriotism, self-confidence, individualism, belief in productive hard work, religious beliefs, child-centeredness, support for community and charity, pragmatism and compromise, acceptance of diversity, desire for cooperation with other countries, and hunger for common ground. Together, Yankelovich argues, these themes provide a basis for a great deal of common ground and point to large areas of everyday life that are mostly unpoisoned by political controversy.

Coupled with these emerging twenty-first-century values is a set of inherited values, some dating from the origins of the American nation in the Declaration of Independence, the Constitution, and the Bill of Rights, and others developed in the course of our shared history. Often unstated but widely assumed, these values include the belief that America should provide its citizens with the opportunity for success through hard work, together with the opportunity for individual self-fulfillment, and that we should conduct our affairs on principles of fairness, justice, and compassion. Included among these core values is the essential idea that the rights of citizens to the benefits of society must be accompanied by an assumption of a certain shared responsibility for building a good society, for creating together, in John Winthrop's famous phrase from long ago, that shining "city on a hill."

The question is whether this cultural soil—old and new—provides support for the rebirth of a spirit of unity and compromise in our larger democracy, and the answer seems to be that it may do so.

In the first place, amid all the chatter about polarization, evidence suggests that the American public's underlying hunger for political compromise remains strong. In June 2004, a CBS News poll asked Americans whether the major political parties should "stick to their principles" or "compromise" to get things done. An overwhelming majority—83 percent—thought they should compromise. Only 12 percent said the parties should stick to their guns. To be sure, the hard-fought 2004 election wore away some of the support for compromise. Still, in the wake of the election early in 2005, nearly three-quarters (74 percent) of those surveyed in a Public Agenda study said they favored compromise on the part of our political leaders.

Indeed, even on the most divisive issues, most Americans will tend to choose a compromise option, if one is available. As Yankelovich shows, when given the choice between accepting abortion under all circumstances, under no circumstances, or under certain circumstances, a majority favors the middle position of "under certain circumstances." Yankelovich also argues that there is more underlying agreement on the hot-button issue of same-sex marriages and civil unions than the headlines suggest. Both consciously and instinctively, the public seems to be searching for common ground.

All this provides us with confidence that many citizens will appreciate the approach to public policy suggested by the contributors to this book. On a range of public policy issues, domestic and foreign, authors here generally try to chart a middle course between conservative and liberal extremes. The chapters provide the beginnings of a blueprint for a new centrist politics, aimed not at serving partisan passions but at finding sensible solutions that serve the common good. We hope these centrist solutions, rooted in core American democratic values, can provide initial steps toward the restoration of the vital center as the compass for our future American democracy.

In Part I, "Restoring the Vital Center," we take up the book's central theme. We begin with Yankelovich's examination of the polarization idea itself (Chapter 1). He argues that a careful and historically minded analysis of survey data tells a more optimistic story: far from splitting asunder, the American public is coalescing around a new shared set of values, gradually reconstructing the "social morality" that eroded in the 1960s. Yankelovich describes a "new social morality" to which policymakers can appeal in shaping practical solutions that unite rather than divide the country.

Norton Garfinkle (Chapter 2) describes the middle-ground consensus that underpinned U.S. economic policy through most of the post–World War II period and argues that recent economic policymaking has marked an unfortunate departure from this long-standing centrist consensus. Over the decades, and especially since World War II, a series of wise and largely minimally bureaucratic government policies—including such programs as Social Security to diminish poverty in old age and tax relief measures designed to foster widespread home ownership and to encourage employers to provide health coverage to employees—helped create an economy and society anchored in the existence of a large and prosperous middle class. Recent economic policies—particularly the steep tax cuts—have undercut our ability to sustain such programs and are ultimately wearing away at the position of the middle class. In time, the American middle class may cease to be able to fulfill its vital role as both the consumer engine of economic growth and the mainstay of American democratic stability. Garfinkle argues that current economic policy appears to be moving toward a "winner-take-all" society marked by ever-growing income inequality—one that promises to be neither prosperous nor stable. To maintain the prosperous American economy that we have known and in particular to sustain the middle class, it will be necessary to find a middle course, based on a more equitable approach to taxation in combination with effective nonbureaucratic government action, to ensure that prosperity is not just the prerogative of the privileged but remains accessible to all.

A longer-term threat to the U.S. economic future arises from what has been called the coming "generational storm," the retirement of the Baby Boom generation, and the related problem of rapidly escalating health care costs. Part II, "Reforming Social Security and Health Care," offers analyses of these issues and suggested policy solutions. As Americans are beginning to understand, retirement of the baby boomers, beginning in 2011, will place enormous stresses on Social Security and Medicare. For years, not to say decades, U.S. political leaders have avoided serious confrontation of these issues. But now the issue is upon us. Will Marshall (Chapter 3) guides us through the ins and outs of Social Security and Medicare reform. He notes that as tough as Social Security reform may be, the future insolvency of Medicare poses a much greater threat. Faulting both political parties for rigidity on the Social Security issue, he outlines a practical bipartisan compromise to save the Social Security system—and offers a series of innovative proposals for fixing Medicare.

Underlying the problems facing Medicare is the wider issue of rapidly escalating health care costs. These costs not only affect the aging; they increasingly pose a major problem for middle-class families. As Tsung-mei Cheng and Uwe E. Reinhardt note (Chapter 4), trends in medical costs make it inevitable that an increasing number of American middle-class families will be priced out of the market for basic health insurance under current policies. Already upwards of 40 million Americans lack health insurance coverage for at least part of each year. The massive annual cost increases in health insurance inevitably mean a growing number of employers will be unable to offer coverage to their employees. Cheng and Reinhardt argue that on this issue the United States, far from pursuing centrist or mainstream solutions, remains an outlier—literally alone among developed countries in failing to offer universal health care to its citizens through some form of government-subsidized insurance. Cheng and Reinhardt are forthright about the costs of such a program, but argue that the alternative will be a world in which even solidly employed, middle-class Americans are denied basic access to medical services. Sooner or later, Cheng and Reinhardt suggest, politicians will have to face up to this problem.

Issues of "values" have played a growing role in politics as we have moved into the twenty-first century. The fault lines in global political life are increasingly defined by issues of religion, culture, and identity. These issues have become ever more prominent within the United States as American society has become more culturally, religiously, racially, and ethnically diverse. Part III, "Diversity and Unity," considers the impact of religion, diversity, and immigration on our sense of national unity.

Alan Wolfe (Chapter 5) attempts to assess the degree to which religion is a force dividing or uniting Americans today. He presents a nuanced picture of the role played by religion in American politics and American life. He argues that while religion has often been a divisive force, the current social schisms over "moral values" may be less sharp than many commentators assume.

A major challenge in uniting the American democracy of the future is the accommodation of our increasingly ethnically diverse population. Sorting through issues of diversity has been one of the great tasks that American society has faced over the past couple of decades. On the one hand, Americans have become more accepting of diversity. For example, the Pew Research Center found that since the late 1980s, the percentage of Americans who approve of interracial dating has risen dramatically, from less than one-half of the population to more than three-fourths. On the other hand, government's response to the diversity question has remained controversial. Peter Schuck (Chapter 6) suggests a middle alternative, distinguishing between the ways government can be helpful and the areas in which government action has proved counterproductive. He argues that the law plays a vital and effective role in protecting individuals from discrimination. But government and law usually prove counterproductive when they try to privilege specific groups under the banner of diversity. Government can often succeed in protecting against discrimination; it usually can do little in a productive way to foster diversity.

One source of diversity, of course, is immigration, which is rapidly changing the face of American society. Peter Skerry (Chapter 7) shows how our pro- versus anti-immigration debate often rests on a confusion. Most Americans are fundamentally accepting of immigration. However, tensions arise when an influx of immigrants is accompanied by an increase in social disorder, especially at the neighborhood level. Skerry points to the need to distinguish between the influx of immigrants, on the one hand, and the presence of social disorder, on the other. While society needs to accept the former, authorities should not hesitate to take firm steps to curb the latter. To brand as discriminatory or anti-immigrant the efforts to enforce the law in immigrant communities, Skerry argues, will not only leave immigrants themselves vulnerable to high crime but will also tend to provoke a backlash among the larger population. Americans should be accepting of immigration, but not of higher crime rates and social disorder that may arise when some immigrants, not yet accustomed to the American way of life, fail to follow the rules that are necessary to maintain stable and peaceful communities.

Religious and cultural conflict has also moved to the fore on the global scene, presenting a new kind of security threat, very different from the dangers America faced during the Cold War. How successful have we been in framing a consensus policy to meet the new threats posed by the post–September 11 world? Part IV, "Security and Liberty," considers the impact of our approach to the war on terrorism both abroad and at home.

In an analysis of the Bush administration's strategy in the war on terrorism, Francis Fukuyama (Chapter 8) argues that U.S. policy needs to achieve a better balance between military and diplomatic means. While giving credit to the Bush administration for its military realism, Fukuyama argues that an effective approach to terrorism cannot rest solely on military force or unilateral action. Agreeing that military action is sometimes necessary—even pre-emptive military action—Fukuyama calls for a greater emphasis on diplomacy. What is needed is outreach to the majority Muslim population to diminish its support for the minority of terrorists. This cannot be achieved, he points out, with a policy based on the iron fist alone. To the degree that our policies arouse anger throughout the Muslim world, they create a hospitable environment, even a breeding ground, for terrorists. While Fukuyama sees the January 2005 Iraq election, the anti-Syrian demonstrations in Lebanon leading to the withdrawal of Syrian forces, and Egypt's announcement of a new presidential election as potentially hopeful signs for democracy, he cautions that the future remains unclear. While such developments may be hopeful, they do not relieve us of the need to match the current U.S. emphasis on military power with an emphasis on outreach to the Muslim world through more effective diplomacy and communication.

What about the impact of the war on terrorism at home? In attempting to combat terrorism, have we maintained a proper constitutional balance between security needs and individual liberties? Michael Vatis, former director of the FBI's center on computer crime, questions the constitutionality of some of the measures undertaken in the wake of September 11 (Chapter 9). In particular, Vatis faults the Congress for providing the administration with a blank check and failing to define limits to the administration's use of such measures as detention without trial. The Founding Fathers recognized, he notes, that in the absence of restraint by the legislature, the executive branch will always tend to favor the pursuit of security over the protection of individual rights. That was why the Framers favored a system of checks and balances. Vatis argues that "checks and balances" alone may not be enough, especially when the executive and legislative branches are controlled by the same political party. Eschewing judicial activism, he calls instead for a new "jurisprudence of constitutional responsibility," whereby the courts would point out where Congress has failed to fulfill its constitutional duty to restrain the executive branch. In such cases, he argues, the courts should call upon the Congress to legislate more specific guidelines to ensure a proper balance between the requirements of domestic security and the protection of fundamental rights.

The survival of American democracy requires more than a defense against external threats. We also must succeed in passing our democratic values on to our children. Part V, "Character, Citizenship, and Values," offers assessments and proposals for meeting this challenge.

In a chapter on the role of education in shaping citizenship, Chester Finn (Chapter 10) shows how the contemporary debates about education make it increasingly difficult for schools, and public schools especially, to perform the vital role of shaping character. In the current "battleground" climate, it is difficult to get agreement even on the essentials of what should be taught in the history classroom, let alone a consensus on values. However, he points to a number of specific steps that can be taken to mitigate the situation and restore the schools to a function that has traditionally been theirs: custodians and transmitters of democratic values.

William Galston (Chapter 11) proposes another solution to the challenge of shaping civic character: national service. He notes that today's U.S. military, based on the All Volunteer Force, draws disproportionately from the lower economic ranks of society. The effect is to reinforce polarization between lower- and higher-income groups. He argues that the obligation of national service should be extended to young citizens of all economic backgrounds and recommends a variety of options—including military service, service in homeland security, or service in Peace Corps–like activities aimed at addressing the root causes of terrorism. A country whose generation of youth has shared the burdens of national service, Galston suggests, is likely to be civic-minded and more united.

Do we have a sufficiently compelling story about our values to infuse our children as well as our adult citizens with a sense of American identity? In a chapter on the concept of "the fair society," Amitai Etzioni (Chapter 12) argues for a greater emphasis on the value of "fairness" in American political dialogue. The idea of fairness, Etzioni suggests, has unusual power to unify. Analyzing data from a poll specially commissioned for the purpose of measuring the force of the "fairness" concept, he shows how casting policy arguments in terms of fairness can give them a universalistic appeal that brings Americans of very different affiliations and outlooks together around consensus policy solutions. The recasting of policy arguments in terms of fairness, he suggests, can move us from a political rhetoric that divides to one that unites.

Part of our legacy to our children will include both our physical environment and our democratic political institutions. Part VI, "Environmental and Electoral Reform," assesses our successes and failures as custodians of these two precious endowments.

On the environment, as on so many other issues, polarized argument prevents us from developing sensible policies—even though a strong public consensus in favor of protecting the environment is known to exist. Mark Sagoff (Chapter 13) criticizes a new group of environmentalists for abandoning the traditional themes of public health and welfare that have sustained the environmental consensus over the past few decades, in favor of new, recondite arguments concerning the "health of ecosystems" that have little public appeal. He cautions that this new environmental paradigm, while all the rage in the academy, is unlikely to translate into practical support for effective environmental policies. By retreating into Ivory Tower language and concepts, these new environmentalists are leaving the field open to economic interests that not only fight new proposals for environmental protection but would also roll back many of the protections put in place over the past forty years.

Finally, democracy depends crucially and obviously on well-functioning electoral institutions. Thomas Mann (Chapter 14) turns our attention to the nation's broken electoral system. Even after the implementation of congressionally mandated reforms following the 2000 election, our system of election administration remains in need of fixing. In 2004, the problem was no longer "dimpled chads" and indecipherable punch-card ballots, but rather unsolved questions about touch-screen voting machines and provisional ballots. In addition, as that presidential contest clearly showed, the McCain-Feingold legislation has provided a less than complete solution to campaign finance reform. Finally, highly politicized redistricting efforts by the two major parties have intensified the political polarization of Congress. Mann outlines a reform agenda, arguing that the world's oldest and greatest democracy deserves an election system that truly works.

It is our hope that these chapters will help to reorient the debate away from the partisan posturing and sloganeering that has dominated our political discussion in recent years and point the way to solutions based on those "ideas in common" that hold our democracy together. Not every reader will agree with every proposal put forth by our authors here. But if this book helps to reawaken the impulse to search for constructive, middle-ground solutions to our toughest policy challenges, it will have performed an important service. It may help us recover a sense of the vital center in American politics, which is so crucial to sustaining the vitality and stability of our democracy in the years ahead.

Part One   **Restoring the Vital Center**

Chapter 1 Overcoming Polarization: The New Social Morality

Daniel Yankelovich

Today's political thinking is colored in tones of red and blue. In the 2000 election, the two coasts and a few states in the Great Lakes region voted Democratic (blue), and the heartland, the South, and most of the Southwest voted Republican (red). In the 2004 election, the red/blue division proved even starker—a sea of red edged in blue. The red/blue theory argues that our nation is being transformed from unity to divisiveness, from pragmatism to ideology, from comity to bitter partisanship, from willingness to compromise to unyielding rigidity. According to the red/blue polarization thesis, we have evolved into a 50-50 nation—50 percent liberal and 50 percent conservative. There is no in-between.

This red/blue dichotomy has become very popular among pundits. Because it is understandable and offers an explanation for the climate of bitterness and frustration in Washington, the red/blue paradigm dominates today's political discourse.

Are we, in fact, becoming a house divided against itself? If this were so, it would signify a radical transformation of our unique American democracy. A careful look at the data, however, shows a far different picture from that presented by the polarization pundits. Opinion polls document too modest a shift in general public attitudes to justify the image of a nation irreconcilably divided; this misleading image masks what is really going on.

HISTORICAL TRENDS

To some extent, the polarization of politicians in Washington reflects a secular trend that has evolved over forty years. It traces back to President Lyndon Johnson's determination, following JFK's assassination in 1963, to pass civil rights legislation even at the cost of losing the "solid South" for the Democratic Party. Between then and now, America's two major political parties have gradually moved away from the "Big Tent" concept whereby each party included liberals, moderates, and conservatives. Our two political parties in Washington are now beginning to look more like European-type parties consisting of people who share the same ideological orientation. The widening spread in Congress between Republicans and Democrats on key issues may be more a matter of like-minded Southerners changing party affiliations than the majority of Americans growing more polarized in their attitudes.

Accentuating this long-term trend in party affiliation is a troubled and anxious public mood relating specifically to the presidency of George W. Bush. George Bush won the presidency in 2000 by promising to be "a uniter, not a divider," to practice "compassionate conservatism," and to pursue a "humble" foreign policy. These promises of a modest and unifying presidency resonated with the electorate. As a candidate, Mr. Bush positioned himself rhetorically close to the center of gravity of American politics— slightly right of center. These "unifying" promises were particularly appropriate for a new president who actually lost the popular vote and won the electoral vote only narrowly, something that has happened only three times before in our history.

It did not take long, however, for the Bush administration to change direction. President Bush has not governed as a centrist. He has governed more from the right than he indicated he would in the 2000 election. He has embraced an aggressive and highly assertive foreign policy, certainly not the humble one that he had advocated in the 2000 campaign. And he has proven himself a divider, not a uniter. He has largely failed to follow through on his promise of compassionate conservative policies for less-well-off Americans. He has catered to the right wing of his party, ignoring the priorities of moderates and liberals. Continuing in this vein, Bush built his victory in the 2004 election on a strategy of maximizing Republican turnout by energizing his conservative base—rather than moving to the political center to capture swing and independent voters, as most successful presidential candidates and incumbents have done in the past. The effect has been to intensify the country's sense of division.

The cultural issues roiling the nation are of a quite different character. Far from being a transitory move, they involve a long-term struggle over the direction of our future social morality.

Traditionally, while the law marks the border between criminal and non-criminal behavior, social norms mark the border between right and wrong. In most societies, the layer of law is relatively thin, while the layer of social morality that sets the standards for how people and institutions should act is much thicker. This largely uncodified body of moral norms is essential to the healthy functioning of society.

One unintended consequence of the American "cultural revolution" of the 1960s was that it caused this thick layer of social morality to erode. The emphasis on individualism—both culturally and economically—has led to the belief in a "live and let live" society bound only by legal requirements. People now unblushingly announce: "I didn't break the law—that proves I didn't do anything wrong." In earlier eras of American life, such a statement would have been met with incredulity. "What," people would ask, "does the law have to do with right and wrong?" Today there are numerous examples of wrong conduct being defined solely on the basis of their legality, and the most notorious of them are found in the business world (Enron, WorldCom, Tyco, HealthSouth, to name a few). But other institutions have fared badly as well, including the American Red Cross and the highly venerated Catholic Church. All of a sudden, what is called the "corporate culture" of any institution acts as if it can ignore social morality in favor of a self-serving code of conduct so long as it stays within legal boundaries.

But all is not lost. The majority of Americans have not become morally obtuse. In private life, most Americans maintain a strong sense of right and wrong for themselves and their families.

DECONSTRUCTING THE POLARIZATION THEME

How polarized are we? Much of the recent discussion of political polarization originated in November 2003, when the Pew Research Center for the People and the Press released a new survey. The Pew Center findings about the political attitudes of Republican and Democrat partisans were summarized in a provocative headline: "Evenly Divided and Increasingly Polarized."

The media immediately picked up the polarization theme. "Across a range of domestic and foreign-policy issues," reported the Associated Press, "the gap between the views of Republican and Democratic partisans is wider than at any point in the last 16 years, a major new survey has found." A spate of such newspaper and magazine stories on the Pew survey heralded a new age of polarization. And the pundits applied the polarization theme to the public at large.

While the Pew poll numbers did show some widening of the divide between partisan Democrats and partisan Republicans—in clear contrast to the unusual sense of national unity that had prevailed in the months immediately following September 11—the new divisions did not polarize the general public as described in many media stories.

A subsequent Pew study released in January 2004 helped clarify the true extent of polarization in the general public (see Table 1.1). Using a 6-point scale, Pew asked respondents to rank themselves on the political spectrum (a score of 1 represented highly conservative and a score of 6 represented highly liberal). The largest two groupings in the Pew scale continued to be the moderates: the "3's" and the "4's," those who rate themselves as moderate conservatives or moderate liberals. Since *Newsweek* and other polling organizations have used the same ranking scale for two decades, Pew was able to get a good handle on the twenty-year trend in popular ideological orientation. In the most recent Pew study, the moderates accounted for 45 percent of the electorate in 2003 compared to 49–50 percent of Americans in the 1980s and 1990s—hardly an earth-shattering change.

To be sure, the constant barrage of polarizing media commentary and Inside-the-Beltway squabbling—combined with the divisive nature of the 2004 election—did have some impact on general public opinion. In the immediate wake of the election, polling by Public Agenda found voters less in a mood for compromise. In 2000, fully 84 percent of Americans thought that the two parties should set aside their convictions to get results in government. After the 2004 election, that majority had dropped to 74 percent.

Table 1.1 Ideological Self-Rating of Respondents in 2003 Pew Study

	More Conservative			More Liberal		
	1	2	3	4	5	6
Percent of Respondents	15	15	27	18	14	11

Among regular churchgoers the decline was slightly larger, from 82 percent to 63 percent. Still, even after the contentious 2004 election, sizeable majorities of both regular churchgoers and Americans as a whole remained committed to the principle of compromise.

Polling data on a variety of other issues in our supposed age of polarization show a similar pattern. While there may be a sharper division today on specific issues between the most committed partisans on the two far ends of the political spectrum, the largest group of voters—a majority or near-majority—still cleaves to the center when given the option to do so.

Abortion is a classic example of what is characterized by pundits as a "50-50" issue, yet polls suggest that the majority of voters seek a centrist position on this divisive question as on most issues. In April 2004, a Fox News/Opinion Dynamics Poll showed Americans split evenly between pro-choice (44 percent) and pro-life (47 percent) positions on abortion—with 6 percent saying they believed in some mixture of the two, while 3 percent said they did not know. But given a choice of taking one of the two extreme positions or occupying a middle ground on abortion, most Americans gravitate to the center. In October 2003, the CNN/USA Today/Gallup poll asked Americans whether abortion should be legal under any circumstances, legal under certain circumstances, or illegal in all circumstances. A majority (55 percent) picked the middle option—legal under certain circumstances—while just 26 percent said abortion should always be legal and 17 percent said it should always be illegal.

We see a similar pattern with same-sex marriage. Much was made of the fact that in exit polling during the 2004 election, a small plurality (22 percent) cited "moral values" as the most important issue on which they voted. It was thought that Republican focus on the gay marriage controversy—particularly among evangelical Christians—had divided the nation based on this hot-button issue. But a closer look at data from the same exit poll suggests that differences on the issue were not as severe as media commentary suggested. A total of 60 percent of voters favored extending rights to same-sex couples (35 percent were in favor of civil unions and 25 percent were in favor of same-sex marriage). Even on such contentious social issues, there is often more underlying agreement than appears on the surface.

Not only does evidence from polls fail to fit the 50-50 polarization mold; there is substantial evidence that the public's allegiances on many issues are not fully formulated and are susceptible to change based on new information and new circumstances. Indeed, there has always been much more dynamism and fluidity in American public opinion than the polarization model implies.

Far from being consistently divided down the middle on critical issues, in 2003 and 2004 the public underwent major shifts in attitude on some key questions. For example, in the thirteen months between the climax of the initial Iraq military campaign and the Abu Ghraib prison scandal, public support for the war in Iraq plummeted. The percentage of those saying it was worth going to war in Iraq fell from a high of 73 percent in April 2003 to 45 percent in May 2004, while the percentage saying it was not worth it rose from 23 percent to 55 percent, according to the Gallup Poll. In the same period, President Bush's approval rating fell from a high of 71 percent to 45 percent, according to Gallup.

Such shifts in opinion do not support the notion that 50 percent of the electorate consistently sided with Bush on all important issues while 50 percent opposed him. The poll data indicate that many in the public change their opinions as developments unfold, in response to more or less pragmatic judgments about events.

THE CULTURAL REVOLUTION AND ITS LEGACY

This is not to deny that there are two very different cultural ideas propounded by those activists who seek to preserve or restore "traditional values" and those who espouse a more relativistic or "progressive" moral outlook deriving from the cultural revolution of the 1960s. These two moral poles still exert a magnetic influence on most Americans. But neither can all citizens be neatly segregated into one camp or another. Most Americans feel the pull of both moral positions at different times and on different questions. It is hard to color the cultural attitudes of most individual Americans as wholly "blue" or wholly "red." Most of us today have a mixture of "blue" and "red" values.

In particular, our culture has been working hard to resolve a crucial dilemma. The cultural revolution of the 1960s—resulting from the Civil Rights movement, the sexual revolution, the drive for women's equality, and the major entry of women into the workplace—has bred a culture with a far greater level of social tolerance on issues of race, gender, sexual orientation, and lifestyle than the America of earlier eras. At the same time, the rise in social tolerance has gone hand in hand with a weakening of social morality.

In almost any society, social morality plays a critical role in guiding and restraining individual conduct. Indeed, in governing most day-to-day conduct, social morality is normally more important than the law. The law for the most part prescribes minimalist standards of conduct—one can act legally and still not act ethically or civilly or politely. Social morality consists of that collection of social norms that, in effect, sits atop the law and fills in the blanks necessarily left by the law, which cannot provide a complete blueprint for how individuals should behave. The relationship is illustrated in Figure 1.1.

In a healthy society, social morality is comparatively "thick." One consequence of the cultural revolution of the 1960s was a weakening, a thinning out, of social morality. The result is that the standards of right and wrong are reduced to the minimalist test of whether a particular action is legal. This is an unthinkable degradation of standards from the America of earlier periods, when society assumed that an individual's moral responsibilities encompassed far more than merely observing the law. The decline in social morality and the rise of legalism are illustrated in Figure 1.2.

This decline has had a real impact on the quality of life in the United States. It has played a role in the economically costly increase in ethical scandals that has plagued American corporate life. It is manifest in the incivility displayed so frequently in public places—aggressive driving, obscenity, violent public confrontations, and so on. It has been a central factor in the proliferation of crudeness and excessive violence and sex in popular culture and entertainment. In general, Americans are unhappy about the decline in social morality, and opinion polls consistently register a public desire for a restoration of moral values in American life.

The dilemma American culture has faced is this: How does one reconstruct absolute social morality without sacrificing the tolerance gained as a result of the 1960s cultural revolution? This is the real struggle going on in American life, hidden beneath the distorted image of a politically polarized America.

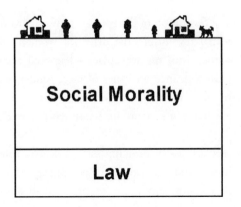

Figure 1.1. Relationship of Social Morality to Law.

TOWARD A NEW SOCIAL MORALITY

What is encouraging is that Americans today seem to be moving, however gradually and uncomfortably, toward a solution to this challenge. That is, today we can detect the emergence of a set of values that constitute an emerging new social morality. This social morality has elements of both traditional and progressive outlooks—indeed, it seems to seek a careful balance between the older requirements of absolute values and the newer demands of tolerance of individual differences.

Annual tracking studies conducted by the DYG public opinion research organization show a trend away from the widespread embrace of the moral relativism that was an immediate consequence of the 1960s cultural revolution. Americans are more likely today than fifteen years ago to insist that there are absolute standards of right and wrong.

When faced with the statement, "It's not for individuals to decide what's right or wrong; we all must live by the same code," 42 percent of Americans in 1988 strongly agreed. By 2003, a majority (52 percent) strongly agreed (Figure 1.3).

Some commentators interpret these data as suggesting a revival of traditional morality. That would only be half right. The new values that are emerging among the American public in fact include a mixture of principles drawn from both traditionalist and progressive perspectives.

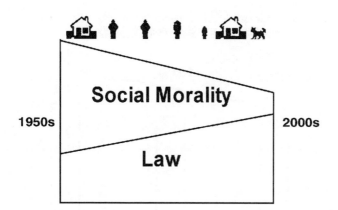

Figure 1.2. Decline in Social Morality.

ELEVEN CORE VALUES

In our analysis of public attitudes, we have identified eleven core values that are consistently embraced by most Americans. They can be summarized as follows:

- Patriotism
- Self-confidence
- Individualism
- Belief in hard work and productivity
- Religious beliefs
- Child-centeredness
- Community and charity
- Pragmatism and compromise
- Acceptance of diversity
- Cooperation with other countries
- Hunger for common ground

What is notable is how many of these values are aimed at ensuring social cohesion while at the same time preserving social tolerance. In particular, acceptance of diversity, hunger for common ground, and a preference for pragmatism and practicality over ideology show a strong yearning for a society that is unified and yet tolerant of differences.

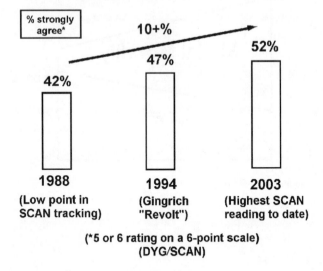

"It's not for individuals to decide what's right or wrong;
we all must live by the same code."

Figure 1.3. Shift Away from Moral Relativism.

The evidence for the preeminence of these values is powerful. All of them represent concepts that strong majorities of the general public—well over 50 percent—say they "strongly agreed" with in the DYG/SCAN tracking study in 2003.

Take patriotism, for example. At the dawn of the twenty-first century, Americans remain a remarkably patriotic people. SCAN shows that two-thirds (66 percent) of Americans describe themselves as strongly patriotic. As many as 68 percent stated that they were "willing to make sacrifices for" their country.

SCAN shows another cluster of values cohering around the concepts of self-confidence, individualism, and hard work. Americans today are unabashedly self-confident. Nearly three-quarters (73 percent) describe themselves as "confident." Similar strong majorities agreed that "no matter what comes my way I can handle it" (69 percent) and that "I am a very self-confident person" (64 percent). Most describe themselves as "smart" (64 percent).

This self-confidence goes hand in hand with a strong penchant for individualism. Nearly two-thirds (65 percent) strongly agreed with the statement that "When making choices, I like to go my own way and not necessarily do what others are doing," while 61 percent said they liked to think of themselves as being "off the beaten path."

A third key personal value represented in the annual SCAN surveys is the work ethic. The vast majority of Americans (82 percent) describe themselves as "hardworking." Three-quarters (75 percent) expressed a preference for active ways of relaxing ("In my spare time, I like to be active and do different things"), while only 27 percent endorsed the proposition that "My way of relaxing is doing as little as possible."

Americans, as is often observed, remain an extraordinarily religious people. Nearly two-thirds (63 percent) describe themselves as "strongly active in church, synagogue, or spiritual group." In 2003, Pew found that fully 69 percent of Americans completely agreed that they had "never doubted the existence of God." Similarly large majorities in the DYG/SCAN studies were in strong agreement with the propositions that "I'm willing to sacrifice . . . for my religious beliefs" (62 percent) and "a person cannot be truly fulfilled without a spiritual aspect to their lives" (64 percent). But there is little desire to impose their beliefs on others. A 2001 Public Agenda study supported by the Pew Charitable Trusts found, "Of those who want religion to become more influential in America, the majority (76 percent) say it does not matter to them which religion it is. Only one in five (21 percent) assume it would be their own religion. Nor is religion the only way to be a moral person—as more than half (58 percent) said it's not necessary to believe in God to be moral and have good values."

If religion remains a powerful force in the emerging new social morality, another key pillar of this new ethical framework is what we would call "child-centeredness." Fully three-fourths (75 percent) strongly agreed with the statement that "once you have a child your own needs come second." Nearly three-fourths (74 percent) of the men said they would describe themselves as a "family man," while 85 percent of women embraced the description "family woman."

Rounding out this social ethic is a strong commitment to charity and concern about the welfare of the poor. In 2003, 81 percent said they had contributed to charity, while 60 percent described themselves as "willing to sacrifice . . . for the poor."

In addition to patriotism, SCAN shows that the political dimension of the new social morality has three core values: a preference for pragmatism and practicality over ideology, an acceptance of diversity, and a hunger for common ground with the world at large.

A generation after the beginning of the cultural revolution, Americans are at home with diversity. When asked which would be a better strategy for the country, "having greater diversity of lifestyles and expressions" or "having greater similarity in the way we all live," 59 percent strongly agreed with the diversity alternative, while only 33 percent opted for the conformist alternative. Acceptance of interracial dating provides a useful index for acceptance of diversity. In 2003, Pew found that fully 77 percent of Americans completely agreed that "it's all right for blacks and whites to date each other." Notably, Democrats and Republicans are closely aligned on this issue (with 78 percent of Democrats and 71 percent of Republicans in complete agreement). The response also represents a marked change from 1987, when only 48 percent of Americans completely agreed with the statement.

At the same time, Americans would like to see their country cooperate with the rest of the world. Nearly three-fourths (74 percent) in the DYG/ SCAN tracking study strongly agreed that the United States should be "working in cooperation with other countries," and nearly two-thirds (66 percent) thought the best strategy for the United States would include "more contact with the rest of the world."

MORE UNITED THAN DIVIDED

Rather than an America divided into irreconcilable camps, therefore, what we see developing is powerful majority support for an emerging set of core values that blend traditional and progressive attitudes into a new social morality. In the end, the values that unite Americans seem far more powerful and compelling than the differences that divide us—even though the divisive issues have captured media attention.

Trend data clearly show that the public is growing ever more concerned with our declining social morality, but even amid the emergence of new consensus values, a measure of uncertainty remains about how exactly social morality is to be reconstructed. It is clear that the country is moving away from moral relativism. Most Americans want to move toward a common social morality. At the same time most Americans want to make sure that the gains of the 1960s, such as cultural pluralism and greater individual freedom, are not undermined by a return to the stifling conformist moral norms of the 1950s. The new values also include some ambivalence.

This kind of struggle is nothing new. In his 1979 book *Life Chances*, social scientist Ralf Dahrendorf pointed out that societies often swing between the poles of moral rigidity and relativism. In the West, the overall direction for 400 years has been toward ever-greater individual freedom and expanded life choices. But within that long secular trend, cycles of moral conservatism have frequently alternated with cycles of moral liberalism.

The present period of struggle may herald greater national unity in the future. While the argument rages, the majority of Americans are united in agreement that our social morality needs to be strengthened and thickened and at the same time the opportunity for individual self-fulfillment also needs to be maintained.

The values that unite us (patriotism, self-confidence, pragmatism, community, child-centeredness, acceptance of diversity, belief in hard work, the hunger for common ground) far outweigh those that divide us. Also, many of the apparent 50-50 splits in the polls are not what they seem. When issues like crime and abortion and school vouchers are ideologically framed, they mask pragmatic attitudes in the general public that demonstrate a traditional American willingness to compromise and find practical solutions.

Both liberals and conservatives have something positive to contribute to the process of renewal. One of the secrets of our success as a democracy is our centrism and grounding in what one might describe as "Chinese menu pragmatism"—political positions comprised of choosing one part from column A (conservative) and one from column B (liberal). For many intellectuals and journalists, Chinese menu thinking represents ideological incoherence. They prefer pure internally consistent positions—pro-life or pro-choice, pro-gun or anti-gun, pro-voucher or anti-voucher. Embracing ideological extremes is actually far more characteristic of our intellectual elites than of the general public. On issues like abortion, crime, and vouchers, the almost invariable pattern among the public is 5 percent to 15 percent on each extreme, leaving the vast 70 percent to 90 percent majority in the muddy middle; for example: opposed to abortion, but not when the mother's life is in danger or when rape has taken place; anti-voucher, but not when there are no public schools of requisite quality available; in favor of strict punishment for crime, but more eager to rehabilitate and prevent crime than to punish people.

If we were to lose this centrist-type pragmatism, our democracy would be jeopardized. Our history has bestowed on us a public voice that is moderate in tone, civil in dialogue, and practical rather than ideological in its approach to problem solving. It is good news that this so-called polarization has not, in fact, taken place among the majority of Americans.

The reality is that, for all our faults and failings, Americans have created a society unprecedented in its tolerance and respect for diversity. At the same time, our culture is moving to correct some of the relativistic excesses that were a by-product of our cultural revolution. There is a powerful desire to combine diversity with basic decency, to recover a moral gyroscope amid the new tolerance.

Political leaders who can tap into these new and emerging attitudes and help Americans implement the values that define their new common ground can unleash a powerful new force for good.

Chapter 2 Nurturing Economic Growth and the Values of American Democracy

Norton Garfinkle

The goals of economic policy in a democratic society are not hard to spell out. Modern democracies need stable economic growth. Democratic governments must also raise sufficient taxes to pay for national defense and for essential services. At times governments can, and have, run deficits, yet in the long run, most sensible economists would agree that unchecked government borrowing will undermine both growth and stability. In addition, since the time of the Great Depression, and especially since the end of World War II, there has been a broad understanding among Americans that government must use its monetary and fiscal tools to encourage economic growth and high employment. In particular, we need to ensure that Americans continue to partake of a shared sense of economic opportunity, and that economic life and the pursuit of wealth do not undermine the core values crucial to maintaining a healthy civic society.

From this perspective, there is much that appears strange and contradictory in the anti-tax philosophy that has come to dominate economic policymaking in recent years. On the one hand, since

2001 we have witnessed a major increase in domestic spending—the biggest such increase since the time of President Lyndon B. Johnson. On the other hand, anti-tax proponents have simultaneously insisted upon enacting major tax cuts. When new threats to national security emerged following September 11, requiring billions in additional federal spending, the anti-tax proponents did not call for adding new revenues, but rather pushed to cut taxes yet again. The effort to shrink the federal revenue base continued even as the United States became involved in a massively expensive war and nation-building campaign in Iraq. Then, Congress approved a major new Medicare entitlement for prescription drugs, without any new funding to pay for it. In a period when income inequality has been on the rise in the United States, the new taxation program has not only drained the federal treasury of resources; it has also fostered increasing income inequality among Americans. Today, in the wake of massive tax cuts, the U.S. government finds itself in the peculiar position of borrowing hundreds of billions of dollars from foreign sources to finance its ongoing operations.

SUPPLY-SIDE MYTHS

The anti-tax ideology emerged in 1980 under then–presidential candidate Ronald Reagan, and it represented a sharp break not only with traditional Republican views of economics but also with Reagan's own previous economic ideas. In 1976, Reagan, running as a challenger against President Gerald Ford, had campaigned as a traditional Republican, advocating fiscal responsibility and a balanced budget. By his 1980 run for the presidency, however, Reagan was championing a wholly new approach. This approach had originated with a small intellectual movement, comprising a handful of economists and conservative political activists, that dubbed itself "supply-side economics."

Supply-side economics was, in truth, part economic theory, part political ideology, and part political strategy. The economic idea at the core of the supply-side view was that cuts in the top marginal tax rate could generate economic growth because the wealthy recipients would invest their tax-cut proceeds in new companies. At the extreme, supply-siders contended that a properly designed cut in marginal tax rates could pay for itself. That is, the tax reduction would result in accelerated growth and increased revenues that would more than make up for the cut in taxes. The supply-side emphasis on tax cuts dovetailed perfectly with the long-standing conservative desire to circumscribe and weaken the powers of "big government" by reducing its annual revenue.

But it was in the realm of political tactics that supply-side theory worked its real magic. It gave conservatives a highly attractive platform (polls consistently show that majorities of both Republicans and Democrats favor lower taxes)—one that was more optimistic and forward-looking than old-fashioned fiscal conservatism. The supply-side approach also functioned to reduce government's revenue base, which in turn could create pressure on Congress to cut government programs. In addition, supply-side tax cuts generated large deficits that made it increasingly difficult for Democrats to put attractive new social welfare programs before the voters. Democrats had typically campaigned on the promise of expanded social welfare benefits, which became difficult to advocate in an atmosphere of budget red ink. Indeed, Democrats increasingly found themselves in the position of advocating tax increases—inevitably an unpopular position with the electorate, and one that led to Democratic presidential challenger Walter Mondale's loss in the 1984 race against Ronald Reagan, the worst Electoral College defeat in history. Finally, like the numerous get-rich-quick schemes and no-pain fad diets that seem to find a limitless market in America, supply-side theory had that attractive aura of a "free lunch."

There was one element of economic truth in the supply-side analysis. Very high top marginal income tax rates do result in counterproductive tax avoidance behavior that reduces economic growth. The enduring legacy of the supply-side movement was the worldwide recognition that very high marginal tax rates can inhibit the growth of an economy. But a key claim of the supply-siders—that tax cuts could more than pay for themselves—was, not surprisingly, never borne out.

One result of Reagan's reduction of the top marginal tax rate from 70 percent to 28 percent was ballooning federal deficits. The reasons were three-fold. First, while the tax cuts did create some pressure for reductions in federal programs, the reductions never proved dramatic enough to cover the shortfalls created by the tax cut. Over the course of his eight years in office, Reagan achieved reductions in nondefense discretionary spending of nearly 10 percent—he has been the only president in the past forty years to do so.[1] But the cuts in nondefense spending went hand in hand with massive increases in defense outlays—as much as a 50 percent increase in defense spending in Reagan's first term. The defense increases—aimed at strengthening America's position vis-à-vis the Soviet Union in the Cold War—

swamped the domestic cutbacks and produced substantial growth in federal government debt. Supply-side prognostications to the contrary, economic growth was never able to keep pace with government spending during the Reagan presidency.

Throughout the 1980s, supply-siders never ceased to predict that the economy would "grow its way" out of the burgeoning deficit, but in truth the promised free lunch never materialized. In 1983, the federal deficit had reached a post–World War II high of 6 percent of the nation's Gross Domestic Product (GDP). Reagan presided over a series of tax increases in 1982, 1984, and 1987, which reduced the deficit to 2.8 percent of GDP by the end of his term.[2] To deal with the remainder of the deficit, Reagan's successor, President George H. W. Bush, signed yet another tax increase in 1990. By finally removing the fiscal drag of the deficit, the elder Bush's action set the stage for the long economic boom under President Bill Clinton, which was sustained even after the top marginal tax rate was raised to 39.6 percent.

DÉJÀ VU ALL OVER AGAIN

Today we see history repeating itself, but apparently with much less fiscal responsibility at the top than exhibited by Reagan, the elder Bush, and Clinton. Interestingly, the George W. Bush administration rejected the need for either tax increases or cuts in government spending. Nondefense discretionary spending was increased by 25.3 percent while spending for defense and homeland security likewise burgeoned.[3] Indeed, at the end of the day, Bush's policies were inconsistent with the fiscally responsible objectives of his father and went even further in the opposite direction from Lyndon Johnson. LBJ tried to wage a major war (Vietnam) and vastly expand social programs (the Great Society) without raising taxes. Bush undertook to wage a major war and expand spending for social programs such as Medicare and education while insisting on tax cuts!

Despite the continuing drive to cut the federal revenue base, the demand for government services continued to increase, fueled by the aging of the Baby Boom generation. Even such a conservative observer as George F. Will acknowledged that the landscape was shifting. "By 2000," he wrote, "conservatives knew that even Americans rhetorically opposed to 'big government' are, when voting, defenders of the welfare state. Social Security and Medicare are the two most popular and biggest components of government." As Will noted, a program that includes support for Social Security and

Medicare is "the only conservatism palatable to a public that expects government to assuage three of life's largest fears: illness, old age, and educational deficits that prevent social mobility."[4] In a sense, the Bush administration's policies have mirrored this popular ambivalence. They have contradictorily tried to satisfy the "anti–big government" and "pro–welfare state" constituencies with simultaneous tax cuts and targeted spending increases.

Even with the troubling trends ahead, there are still those who continue to advocate the free lunch theory. For example, Lawrence Kudlow, a prominent heir of the supply-side school, criticized the Congressional Budget Office for basing its projections for the deficits on what he claims is a too-modest long-term growth estimate (2.8 percent). Under Kudlow's rosy scenario, the American economy is destined to grow at a continuing rate in excess of 4.5 percent. "At this rate," he writes, "budget deficits will evaporate rapidly as the economy quickly marches toward full employment."[5] It is the familiar supply-side refrain—as credible today as it was in the deficit-ridden 1980s.

The reality is that the supply-siders produced a policy completely out of balance with our fiscal commitments. The question to ask is why we needed to get out of balance in the first place. Was it in any sense necessary or logical or helpful to cut taxes for the wealthy at a time when our security needs and costs were clearly increasing? Was it in any sense necessary to increase income inequality by reducing tax rates on the richest Americans—providing them with billions of dollars—after decades during which the gulf between the incomes of the superrich and those of the rest of the population was widening? Why cut taxes and generate deficits when we will have to raise taxes later to restore fiscal stability?

Eventually, somebody is going to have to face up to the mounting deficits and mounting national debt and, like Ronald Reagan and the elder George Bush, increase the federal revenue stream by raising taxes. The only question is when. The effect of supply-side policies has been to shift the responsibility for paying the nation's current bills to our children and grandchildren.

A CENTRIST APPROACH

Sensible people recognize that a certain level of taxation is a necessity to pay for government services that are considered essential by most Americans. Fairness of tax policy is an equally important criterion. Most Americans believe that those who derive the greatest benefit from society should provide commensurate economic support for the community. For this reason, most Americans firmly believe in the necessity of a progressive tax structure.

Tax policy, after all, is not rocket science. The efficacy of taxation policy can be judged by three simple principles:

• To encourage a high-growth economy, there should be a low enough top marginal tax rate to encourage people to engage in maximum economic effort to fulfill their own economic goals—without engaging in counterproductive tax avoidance activity.
• There should be an adequate tax structure to provide funds for legitimate and agreed-upon national goals.
• There should be a progressive tax structure to sustain the general public belief in the fairness of a system where people with higher incomes provide a larger share of tax dollars.

Supply-side tax cut policies are inconsistent with all three of these widely shared objectives. When President Reagan substantially cut the top marginal tax rate down from 70 percent, he reduced counterproductive tax avoidance activities. By contrast, the recent reduction in the top marginal rate from 39.6 to 35 percent had little effect on economic behavior and economic growth. It is also clear from the huge budget deficit, which the Congressional Budget Office estimates at close to $400 billion for 2005, that the new tax structure is insufficient to fund basic government services. Equally important, the supply-side tax changes are regressive, undermining public faith in the fairness of the system. Perhaps the most puzzling aspect of the new tax cuts was their skew in favor of the very rich. Not only did the supply-side approach lower the top marginal rate; it also substantially reduced taxes on dividends and capital gains—measures that disproportionately rewarded the wealthiest taxpayers—and this came in the wake of a steady increase in income inequality over the last two decades. White House documents claimed that the typical family with two children would save $1,600.[6] But they included the wealthiest Americans in this average. In reality, as a result of the 2001 and 2003 tax cuts, households in the top 1 percent (with an average income of nearly 1.2 million) received an average direct tax cut of $40,990 in 2004, while the middle 20 percent, with an average income of $57,430, received an average tax cut of only $1,090 per household. In 2004, fully one-third of the tax cuts on household incomes went to the top 1 percent.[7] These highest-income households have benefited not only from cuts in the top marginal income tax rate, but also from reductions in the estate tax and from increases in the value of their corporate stock holdings thanks to a reduction in taxes on dividends.

The new tax policies are particularly surprising when we consider the growing inequality in incomes that has emerged in American society over the past generation. The trend toward income inequality has been a powerful one. In 2001, the latest year for which figures are available, the share of after-tax income received by the top 5 percent of American households was 35 percent higher than in 1979, while at the lower end of the income distribution, 60 percent of American households had a 14 percent lower share. In fact, over the twenty-two-year period, the top 5 percent of households captured an ever-higher share of after-tax income, while the other 95 percent either lost ground or showed no gain (Table 2.1).

Moreover, the tax cuts have contributed to further inequality since 2001. In 2004, the top 5 percent of households received a rate cut of 17 percent in total federal taxes, compared to the rate they would have paid under previous law, while middle-income households (those in the middle 60 percent of the income distribution) received an average cut of just 13 percent.[8]

But above all, there is no reason that government should be playing political football with the taxation rate. First, there is clearly a level of government services—including homeland security and national defense—that needs to be funded by federal taxes and is not being fully funded under the current tax structure. In 2003, federal taxes fell to just 16.3 percent of GDP, the lowest portion in forty-five years. Not only was this insufficient for Uncle Sam to cover the year's enlarged military and domestic expenses; it was also well below the average of 18.5 percent during the earlier Reagan, Bush, and Clinton administrations.[9] In absolute dollars, this 2.2 percentage point decline amounted to a reduction of $258 billion in 2004.

A sound approach to taxation policy would begin with a consensus on the percentage of GDP the country is willing to devote to federal government expenditures. There is no reason that there could not be agreement on such a figure, which would also remain relatively stable from year to year. Adopting the discipline of specifying a fixed percentage of the GDP as the appropriate level of taxation would prevent politicians from changing the rules with every new annual budget. And growth in the American economy would provide new funds to meet the most important new social requirements of our civic society. Of course, unusual circumstances such as war or depression might require the government to increase the level of expenditures

Table 2.1 Distribution of U.S. Household Income After Federal
Taxes, 1979 and 2001

Income Level	1979	2001	Percent Change
Top 5 percent	18.1	24.5	35
Next 15 percent	24.3	24.4	0
Next 20 percent	22.3	21.3	−4
Lowest 60 percent	35.6	30.7	−14
Total U.S. Income	100%	100%	

Source: Congressional Budget Office, *Effective Federal Tax Rates: 1979–2001,* April 2004.
The CBO study, which covers the years from 1979 to 2001, is widely regarded as the
best available data on U.S. household income and after-tax household income.

in any single year. But these unusual circumstances would be counterbal-
anced in other years so that the fixed level would be maintained over any
extended period. Appropriately, the democratic process would be utilized by
citizens and their governments to set the priorities that would determine
how the fixed percentage of the GDP would be spent to fulfill the identified
objectives of society. This GDP approach could end perennial political argument over the level of taxation. It would provide needed stability to the
tax structure. Such stability would enhance the health of the economy by
providing predictability to businesses and investors.

A final note on taxation. Corporate tax reform could further enhance the
health of our economy. Two essential purposes of our national economic
policy should be to promote higher U.S. business investment and support
the global competitiveness of U.S. firms. Since 1960, revenues from corporate
taxes have declined steadily as a share of total federal revenues and of the
U.S. GDP. This trend is largely due to unproductive special-interest corporate tax breaks, obtained under a wasteful political lobbying system that
encourages unethical behavior in Washington and state capitals all across the
nation. To achieve the goals of maximum business competitiveness, maximum productivity, and minimum lobbying, we would do well to generate
most federal revenues from a well-structured, progressive tax base rather than
attempt to raise revenue from a corporate tax structure that is honored more
in the breach than in practice by the largest American multinational corporations. We should not hobble our innovative smaller corporations with
high corporate tax rates that make them less competitive than the large
American and foreign multinational corporations that have found ways to
pay little, if any, corporate taxes. And a low universal level of corporate

taxation would eliminate all the special "corporate welfare" tax avoidance laws that currently sustain an expensive and counterproductive corporate political lobbying system that violates the fundamental principles of our democracy by buying political influence with campaign contributions.

THE CRITICAL ROLE OF THE MIDDLE CLASS

The issue of fairness and progressivity in taxation remains vital partly because of the central role played in modern democratic economies by the middle class. A core principle of a centrist approach to economics is a commitment to nurturing and sustaining a large, vibrant, educated, self-sufficient, and upwardly mobile middle class. Experience has taught us that a strong middle class is indispensable to a modern democracy, for both economic and political reasons.

From an economic standpoint, the middle-class consumer is the engine driving the modern economy. Consumer spending accounts for two-thirds of U.S. GDP. If middle-class incomes stagnate or decline, aggregate demand for goods and services inevitably suffers. As Henry Ford noted early in the twentieth century, when he doubled the compensation of the workers on his Model T assembly line, "If you don't pay the people enough money, they can't buy the cars."

The core strength of the American economy has sprung from the power and vibrancy of the middle class. Yet for the past twenty years that middle class has been under siege. During this period, incomes of the top 5 percent of the population dramatically increased, even as middle-class wages barely kept pace with inflation. The result has been a major increase in income inequality and a pronounced upward shift in distribution of both income and wealth. Increasingly, we find ourselves in what economists Robert Frank and Philip Cook have called a "winner-take-all" economy.[10] To take just one example: according to *BusinessWeek*, in 1980, CEOs of the largest U.S. corporations received 42 times the pay of the average worker; by 1999, CEO salaries had climbed to 475 times that of the average worker.[11]

The winner-take-all economy threatens to undo the critical social progress of the last hundred years and return us to a quasi–Robber Baron economy, where the rich control an increasing portion of society's wealth and resources, while those who do the lion's share of labor in America increasingly fail to share in the benefits of economic growth. All this threatens the survival of the stable middle-class economy and society that we have known in our lifetimes. A high-growth American economy cannot be sustained if the American middle class lacks sufficient after-tax dollars to support it.

Ultimately, it was the emergence of the middle class that made modern democracy and capitalism sustainable. The first wave of American industrialization in the post–Civil War era gave rise to major inequalities of income, widespread exploitation of industrial workers, and a climate of economic lawlessness. It was the Gilded Age, the era of the Robber Barons. Fortunately, President Theodore Roosevelt—with his "Square Deal," his bold antitrust measures, and his introduction of the first real government regulation of modern economic life—recognized that government must play a more active role in the modern economy if economic and political stability were to be sustained. Roosevelt's reforms were the first to set the country on the road toward a shared middle-class future. Yet sharp divisions between the wealthy and the rest of society persisted through the 1920s and 1930s. It was the Great Depression that finally forced the issue. To save American capitalism, it was necessary for the government to actively encourage the creation of a true middle-class economy. The hallmark New Deal programs of President Franklin D. Roosevelt—such as Social Security—sought to provide a safety net that would lift Americans of ordinary income out of a state of poverty. The final major thrust behind the formation of the American middle class was the economic revival created by World War II and, especially, the postwar G.I. Bill, which gave an entire generation of ordinary Americans a ticket to a college education. That, combined with New Deal legislation that provided strong government support for home ownership and protected the rights of workers to organize, gave birth to a new kind of America, and a new economy in which the vast middle group of wage earners could expect to buy homes and cars, provide education and a good life for their children, and retire securely after a life of hard work.

That America is now under threat; not just the economic consequences but also the political consequences of this development are potentially far-reaching. From a political standpoint, it is the presence of a strong middle class that largely underwrites the social stability of a modern democracy. The middle class acts as the key buffer in the age-old struggle between the haves and the have-nots. It is the middle-class dream that gives the majority of our citizens a strong, shared stake in the country's future. American society continues to be sustained by certain key "dreams" or collective promises— that hard work will enable individuals and families to enjoy a reasonable lifestyle, that harder work will enable individuals to get ahead, that ordinary

incomes will permit people to own their own homes, that educational opportunities will be afforded to every student willing to study hard enough
to achieve them, that a life of hard work will result in a secure retirement.
The reality, however, is that this middle-class dream is becoming less sustainable in the current economy.

That is why, at the end of the day, supply-side economic and taxation
policies have looked so strangely perverse. Why, at a time of increasing
inequality, would government take steps that widen the gulf between the
rich and the rest? Why, at a time when the middle class is under siege, would
government take steps to further erode the middle class's position? What
could possibly have been the rationale to enact "a $1.6 trillion tax cut for
the rich in the midst of the biggest increase in income inequality in modern
history"?[12]

THE COMMUNITARIAN ECONOMIC VISION

Economic arrangements lie at the very heart of our society's unwritten social
contract. The American Dream is essentially an economic vision: if people
work hard, abide by the rules, and develop their skills and capabilities
through education and dedication, they expect to reap the rewards in the
form of an ever-improving standard of living and quality of life. If people's
everyday experience validates this vision, Americans will trust it and believe
in it; if everyday experience violates it, then people grow cynical and mis-
trustful of our institutions. This, in some measure, is the central vision
behind the communitarian approach to economics.

Communitarians believe that with every right there is a responsibility and
that rights and responsibilities can enhance one another if they are in proper
balance. Rights of specific individuals and groups impose demands on all
other community members and are effectively upheld only as long as the
basic needs of all community members are attended to. One consequence
of the current tendency to sever economics from its ethical roots is that the
present economic debate in the United States distorts the central economic
issues facing the nation. On the all-important economic questions of investing for higher levels of economic growth, greater economic mobility, and
a stronger civil society, the arguments presented in the media have little to
offer. Also, the media debates tend to highlight the extremes of both the
liberal and conservative positions, leaving moderate Americans in a quandary.

Communitarian economics has learned the big lessons of the twentieth century: (1) command economies stifle economic vitality; (2) excessively high marginal tax rates and highly bureaucratic government regulation can inhibit economic growth; (3) American society needs to use its government to provide services that are consistent with well-supported, basic American values; and (4) government is most effective when it uses incentive-based systems rather than highly bureaucratic regulation to achieve legitimate economic and social goals.

The evidence is overwhelming that there is no way to allocate the scarce resources of society fairly if certain groups have an automatic and unlimited claim on them. The emphasis on reducing taxes at almost any cost is counterproductive. A certain minimum of revenue is required to sustain necessary expenditures that ensure national welfare and safety, provide education, maintain and expand the national infrastructure, support essential regulating activities, and support the desire of the majority of the American people to "provide every citizen enough to eat and a place to sleep."[13] Reducing revenue from taxes below the necessary minimum impairs our ability to satisfy the legitimate goals of society. And the repeated reduction of taxes for the wealthiest families is an entitlement program for a tiny group of people, which adds to the already troubling problem of increasing income inequality. It is also becoming clear that unlimited entitlements for any single group can only come at the expense of other members of society.

Economic policies depend critically on the common purposes to be achieved. These common purposes must be founded on the core values of the citizens of the community. In the United States the core values of the American people were originally defined by the Declaration of Independence and the Constitution and Bill of Rights, and have since been elaborated by the shared history of the nation. The values that define the American community include the belief that society should provide its citizens with equality of opportunity together with the opportunity for individual self-fulfillment, and that it should operate on the principles of fairness, justice, and compassion. Communitarian economics embraces four core ideas:

1. A growth economy generates positive economic and social benefits:
   • It is to the benefit of society to have a large and growing GDP. Economic abundance can help to diminish many of the problems that arise from conflict over scarce resources. A growth economy provides maximum opportunity to satisfy the legitimate goals of individuals and of the larger society and is conducive to social peace and social order.

- A high-employment economy is a central goal of society not only to provide the satisfaction of work to its members but also to maintain social order and integrity based upon the belief in a fair society.

2. Economic policy must maintain a balance between the common good and the personal objectives of individual citizens. Specifically, economic policy must be based upon the understanding that:

- A command economy is inherently unhealthy. A social and economic structure too constrictive of individual autonomy diminishes both individual effort and overall productivity and, as a consequence, diminishes GDP.

- Insufficient funding of necessary government programs leaves society without the basic infrastructure necessary for the success of the economy and fails to support the safety net necessary to maintain social order and a sense of fairness in society.

- The amount of funding to achieve national goals should be linked to the size of the GDP. The tax structure that supplies this funding should be progressive but should not have a top marginal rate that leads high-income taxpayers to engage in costly and unproductive tax avoidance behavior. Priorities should be established in a democratic way to utilize the limited funds available to achieve the goals most valued by society's members.

3. Economic policies and practices should be designed to minimize bureaucracy and maximize private and voluntary initiatives:

- If the private economy is capable of providing a product or service effectively, the government should not attempt to compete with the private economy. Government interference in matters that can be handled through private or voluntary effort tends to be inefficient and to weaken civic responsibility.

- When the government undertakes an economic task, it should attempt to do so by creating incentives to useful economic behavior that do not require a substantial bureaucracy to implement. Bureaucratic systems tend to utilize command-and-control techniques that are responsive to the idiosyncratic and elitist views of officials and civil servants rather than to the actual needs and responses of the constituencies served by government programs. By contrast, incentives provided directly to individuals and corporations tend to be internalized and to encourage increasing personal and corporate responsibility on an ongoing basis. Examples include programs such as the post–World War II G.I. Bill, where government avoided bureaucracy by providing funds for education directly to veterans returning from military service. This program at once fostered the formation of a skilled workforce and indirectly subsidized the creation of the modern American higher education system. And it included a home loan provision that led to a major increase in home ownership, which now approaches 70 percent of all American households. In the decades since World War II, a series of such nonbureaucratic government policies—including Social Security to diminish poverty in old age and tax deductions for corporations and individuals for expenditures that provide health coverage to employees—have been responsible for creating an economy and society anchored in the existence of a large and prosperous middle class.

4. Acting as agent for the American community, the government in Washington has a distinct role to play in ensuring that economic policy is consistent with national priorities and with building a strong foundation for future economic growth and social stability:

- Government should work to enhance national productivity in three primary areas: providing a legal framework for vigorous competitive efforts that drive innovation and productivity; investment in education to improve the competence and capability of the population; and investment to build the infrastructure necessary for an advanced society.
- Government should support social stability by implementing taxation, social welfare policies, and business regulation policies that are fair to all members of the community.

CONCLUSION

Fortunately, we can expect a high level of public support for the principles and core ideas of communitarian economics, if properly developed and communicated. The public intuitively understands that the goals and performance of the economy are matters of the highest concern. The well-known slogan of the Clinton 1992 presidential campaign still resonates: "It's the economy, stupid." The goals of communitarian economics are very much the same goals that the American public most cherishes. And the public considers these core ideas as passing the test of common sense and fairness.

The beginning of wisdom in economics is the recognition that sound economic policy is mostly about balance: a balance between respect for individual rights and attention to the common good. That is one reason why communitarianism provides an excellent framework for thinking through economic issues. For communitarians, the achievement of the good society requires nurturing economic growth while sustaining the values of a civic society. The two are not mutually exclusive: only a society that provides adequately for the common good can offer genuine opportunities for individual fulfillment. A condition of irresponsible individualism is as inimical to the individual "pursuit of happiness" as a condition of totalitarian tyranny.

Government, as the agent of society, should help to fulfill the economic and social goals of the American community. It should support positive growth in the overall economy, incentives for innovation, thoughtful evaluation and prioritization of the allocation of tax revenues, and a fiscally responsible approach to balancing the benefits of each regulatory and non-regulatory government program against the direct and indirect economic costs of that program. Reforms in taxation policy and methods of allocating government revenues should reduce bureaucracy and maintain incentives to individual productivity. Lower corporate taxation, consistently applied, enables American corporations to charge lower prices, which can help them compete successfully in the U.S. and global marketplaces. Infrastructure investments to support education, transportation, and environmental systems provide benefits across industries, unify the domestic market, and enable American companies to increase their productivity on an international basis. A constant improvement in productivity not only produces a comparative economic advantage for the American economy, but also ensures that American firms can contribute to a growing world economy. And a stable and fair personal income tax system remains critical to the survival of the middle class, the mainstay of our economy and our democratic way of life.

NOTES

1. Veronique de Rugy, "President Reagan, Champion Budget Cutter," paper presented at the American Enterprise Institute for Public Policy Research, June 9, 2004.
2. David R. Francis, "Follow the Leader: Can Bush Live Up to Reagan?" *Christian Science Monitor* (June 14, 2004).
3. Veronique de Rugy, "Reagan's Unheralded Legacy," *Washington Times* (June 14, 2004).
4. George F. Will, "Freedom vs. Equality," *Washington Post* (February 1, 2004).
5. Lawrence Kudlow, "A Boom with Legs," *Washington Times* (May 30, 2004).
6. White House, "The President's Agenda for Tax Relief," available at http://www .whitehouse.gov/news/reports/taxplan.html.
7. Edmund L. Andrews, "Report Finds Tax Cuts Heavily Favor the Wealthy," *New York*

Times (August 13, 2004). See Congressional Budget Office, *Effective Federal Tax Rates Under Current Law, 2001 to 2014*, August 2004; available at http://www.cbo.gov/ showdoc.cfm?index=5746&sequence=0001. See also U.S. Congress, Joint Economic Committee Democrats, "New CBO Analysis Confirms That the Bush Tax Cuts Are Skewed Toward the Rich," *Economic Policy Brief*, August 2004; available at http:// www.jec.senate.gov/democrats/Documents/Reports/CBOtaxcuts13aug2004.pdf.

8. Congressional Budget Office, *Effective Federal Tax Rates Under Current Law, 2001 to 2014*.

9. White House, Office of Management and Budget, *Historical Tables: Budget of the United States Government: 2006* (Washington, DC: GPO, 2005): 33–34.

10. Robert H. Frank and Philip J. Cook, *The Winner-Take-All Society: Why the Few at the Top Get So Much More Than the Rest of Us* (New York: Free Press, 1995).

11. Robert Frank, "Has Rising Inequality Hurt the Middle Class?" *Options Politiques*, March 2001, 64–72; available at http://www.irpp.org/po/archive/mar01/frank.pdf.

12. Ibid., 72.

13. Pew Research Center for the People and the Press, *Evenly Divided and Increasingly Polarized: 2004 Political Landscape* (November 2003): 40.

Part Two Reforming Social Security and Health Care

Chapter 3 Social Security and Medicare
Reform for the Twenty-First Century

Will Marshall

The age wave, a demographic tsunami of unprecedented proportions, is gathering on the horizon. It will break upon America in just six years, when the oldest of the 77 million baby boomers start turning sixty-five. The impact on our country's finances and social insurance systems will be tremendous, yet for years our political leaders have done little to lessen the coming shock. On the contrary, America's deeply polarized politics threatens to turn this big but manageable challenge into a full-blown crisis.

Only now is Washington beginning to confront our demographic dilemmas, beginning with Social Security. Standing in the way of progress, however, is the hyperpartisanship that pervades national politics.

President Bush has made Social Security reform the centerpiece of his second term. Yet his call for using payroll taxes to create private savings accounts has met monolithic opposition from Democrats, who argue that the plan would destroy Social Security's social insurance character without closing its long-term deficit. Even some Republicans have balked at the Bush plan, which would entail more government borrowing at a time when the United States is already running enormous budget deficits. In truth, neither side has been willing to embrace the politically difficult steps necessary to assure Social Security's long-term solvency.

Meanwhile, the more acute problem posed by the graying of America is not Social Security, but exploding health care costs. Unfortunately, Congress missed an opportunity to modernize Medicare in 2003, when Republicans used their slender majority to ram through a bill that made gestures toward reform but that mainly added an expensive new prescription drug benefit. Expected to cost as much as $724 billion over the next ten years—almost twice the Bush administration's original estimate—the bill compounds Medicare's financial woes without addressing the underlying reasons for its rapid cost growth.

Yet as daunting as Social Security and Medicare reform may seem, the age wave need not be just a grim story of rampaging health and retirement costs and hard political choices. It also brings intriguing possibilities for changing what it means to grow old.

THE CHALLENGE OF SUCCESSFUL AGING

If not America's greatest generation, the baby boomers are inarguably its biggest. As they have tramped through the life cycle, they have wrought huge changes in virtually every facet of our nation's life—schools, work, housing, politics, popular culture. Healthier, better educated, and wealthier than previous generations, the boomers now are poised to reinvent retirement. For one thing, they will probably work longer as employers, facing a looming labor shortage and fearing a massive talent drain, try to hold on to older workers. And boomers don't seem as drawn to leisure as previous generations; in a recent survey, nearly 80 percent said they plan to work at least part-time in retirement.[1]

More than the boomers' last act, however, the coming gray revolution will be the beginning of a permanent, structural change in the United States. Not only will there be lots more older people than ever before, but advances in science and medicine will transform aging itself.

In 1900, U.S. life expectancy averaged forty-eight years; now it is seventy-seven years. In just one century, we have added nearly thirty years to our life span—a gain without precedent in human history. For individuals, this means a whole new stage has been added to our lives. For society, it means a huge, sustained increase in the elderly population. Only 4 percent of Americans in 1900 were over sixty-five; by 2030, one in every five Americans will be over sixty-five. Adapting to these realities will require major cultural adjustments. Americans need to revise their mental picture of aging as well as the assumptions on which "old age" institutions were built.

The age wave inevitably will require more fundamental changes in Social Security and Medicare. Reform advocates traditionally have tried to gain political traction simply by sounding alarms about their looming insolvency. There is no doubt that these popular entitlements are growing at unsustainable rates and that the sooner we start to close their long-term deficits, the better. A fresh and more imaginative case for reform, however, also would stress the opportunity to harness these venerable programs to new understandings about how to "optimize aging."

A modernized Social Security system, at a minimum, would fix archaic rules that discriminate against single women and widows. But it should also be the core of a new, twenty-first-century model of social insurance designed to lift all seniors out of poverty, to encourage a more flexible approach to retirement, to boost individual savings, and to give every worker a chance to own wealth.

A better Medicare program needs more than the prescription drug benefit Congress tacked on. It should also tackle the chronic diseases that drive up medical costs, offer seniors a menu of coverage choices, and hold providers accountable for improving the quality of care. Medicare today is a ponderous bureaucracy that pays part of seniors' medical bills. It needs to become a more dynamic, performance-based system that promotes healthy aging. Otherwise, the boomers' retirement will be blighted by preventable illnesses, and future taxpayers will be swamped by unnecessary medical costs.

Unfortunately, a bitter struggle for partisan advantage in Washington stands in the way of such progressive reforms. The Medicare bill offers a prime example. The political logic behind the GOP's newfound enthusiasm for expanding Medicare was obvious: by stealing a traditionally Democratic issue, they hoped to neutralize their opponents' customary advantages on health care, burnish their credentials as "compassionate conservatives," and curry favor among seniors, a potent voting bloc. The result was a deeply flawed bill that had almost no Democratic support, has yet to win favor among seniors (the drug benefit doesn't kick in until 2006), and will make the job of truly modernizing Medicare more difficult.

Today's Social Security debate reveals a similar pattern. President Bush, eager to claim the mantle of reform and flesh out his vision of an "ownership society," has called for adding private savings accounts to Social Security. Young workers like the idea, because they do not think the system will be very generous in the future, and because they want greater personal control of their retirement security. But as White House officials have admitted, individual accounts by themselves will not assure Social Security's long-term solvency. On the contrary, in the short term they dig the system into an even deeper fiscal hole, by diverting nearly a trillion dollars of payroll taxes into personal accounts. Since Social Security uses those tax revenues to pay benefits to current retirees, that money has to be replaced. Given the administration's aversion to raising taxes, it will be forced to borrow to finance these so-called "transition costs."

Democrats have denounced such so-called "privatization" with theological fervor but have yet to coalesce behind alternative reforms of their own. Rejecting a sterile choice between Republican panaceas and Democratic denial, a handful of centrists in both parties are contemplating possible blueprints for bipartisan action. But in today's calm before the demographic storm, there simply has not been enough public pressure to break the partisan stalemate in Washington.

The rumble of distant thunder, however, is getting louder.

THE COMING CRUNCH

The most basic problem facing both Social Security and Medicare is insolvency: The payroll tax that finances both programs will not raise enough money to pay for the benefits promised seniors.[2] The shortfall over the next seventy-five years totals $3.7 trillion for Social Security and a mind-bending $27.8 trillion for Medicare.

For these massive entitlements, demographics are destiny. Thanks to the age wave and falling birth rates, the elderly population will grow much faster than the work force whose taxes support them. The ratio of workers to retirees, 16:1 in 1950, will fall to 2:1 by 2030. In the past, we have compensated for a dwindling ratio by bringing more occupations into the system, but today more than 90 percent of working Americans are covered by Social Security.

So why not just hike payroll taxes? Because we have gone to that well too often. Just 6 percent in 1960, the payroll tax rate was bumped up seven times in the 1980s alone. Today it stands at 15.3 percent (of which 12.4

percent goes to Social Security and 2.9 percent to Medicare). In fact, it takes a bigger bite out of most workers' paychecks than the federal income tax. The conditions that since 1940 have allowed each generation of retirees to take more from Social Security than they put in—a fast-growing workforce and public willingness to accept higher payroll taxes—no longer exist. Former Congressional Budget Office director Rudy Penner put the matter succinctly at a 1998 White House conference: "The golden age of Social Security is over."

Social Security's seventy-five-year deficit amounts to nearly 2 percent of payroll. Once the trust fund is drained in 2042, say the trustees, the system will only raise enough revenue to cover 73 percent of promised benefits. Closing the gap would require either raising the 12.4 Social Security tax by 2 points, cutting benefits by 13 percent, or doing some combination of the two. And that is the price tag if changes happen today; delay only makes the long-term chasm between income and spending—and therefore the costs of restoring solvency—grow.

Medicare, meanwhile, is in far worse financial shape than Social Security. According to the 2004 trustees' report, the Hospital Insurance (HI) trust fund will be exhausted by 2019. Medicare spending is growing faster too, and is expected to overtake Social Security's by 2024. To make the HI trust fund solvent, we would need either to raise the Medicare portion of the payroll tax from 2.9 percent to 6 percent, to cut benefits by 48 percent, or to enact some combination of the two.

In addition, another Medicare trust fund that pays for doctors' services and the new prescription drug benefit "will require substantial increases over time in both general revenue transfers and premium charges," the trustees warn. In addition to a fast-aging population, Medicare's problems stem from double-digit increases in overall health care costs, propelled especially by an unrestrained appetite for new technology, underuse of cheaper preventive and chronic health care, paper-based medical and administrative record keeping, and high malpractice insurance premiums.

Keep in mind too that the Social Security and Medicare trust funds are accounting devices that tell us little about the real economic impact of the boomers' retirement. Take Social Security: the real fiscal crunch comes not in 2042 when the trust fund is depleted, but in 2018, when payroll tax revenues fall below what is needed to pay benefits. To plug the gap, Social Security will have to start redeeming Treasury bonds it holds because it has been lending surplus revenue to the U.S. government. Had the federal government not been borrowing from the trust fund—more invidiously known as "raiding Social Security"—its budget deficits would have been even larger.

In other words, the trust funds' "assets" are also the federal government's liabilities. When Social Security starts to redeem those IOUs, the Treasury will have to pay them off with interest, either by raising taxes, cutting programs, or borrowing more money. Most likely, this means that between 2018 and 2042, for the first time since Social Security's inception, lawmakers will start tapping general revenues to make up the difference between payroll taxes and benefit checks. After that, how the system meets its obligations to older Americans is anyone's guess.

In short, the compact embedded in Social Security and Medicare's "pay as you go" (hereafter called "paygo") structure is breaking down. In that compact, today's workers and their employers pay a special tax dedicated to paying retirement and health benefits for their retired parents and grandparents. But as the ratio of workers to retirees shrinks, the payroll tax will not raise enough to finance benefits. So both systems are drifting toward greater reliance on general revenues.

This is why doing nothing to fix the programs' financial problems is actually a policy choice. It is a tacit vote for raising taxes at some point in the not-too-distant future, because Washington already is running stratospheric budget deficits, and because lawmakers are unlikely to slash everything else government does to pay for automatic increases in the big entitlements. Moreover, it is the worst possible remedy, because higher taxes put the entire burden of "saving" Social Security and Medicare on young working families, violating the principle of intergenerational equity that lies at the heart of our social insurance compact.

And even if we jacked up taxes, we would still be left with the core dilemma: Social Security and Medicare are growing at unsustainable rates. If we allow them to gobble up an ever-growing share of our national budget, we will have very little left over for education, universal health care, homeland defense, research, the environment, transportation, anti-poverty initiatives, or anything else.

The trustees project that Medicare and Social Security spending will more than double from 7 percent of gross domestic product (GDP) today to 15 percent of GDP by 2040 as the boomers retire, then rise to 20 percent of GDP in 2078 because of increases in longevity. That is more than the federal government's entire yearly haul in taxes, which historically has averaged about 19 percent of GDP. Unless we slow the growth in entitlement spending, Washington would have to double federal taxes or devote every penny it collects to the needs of older Americans.

The coming squeeze on federal revenues and spending poses a particularly acute dilemma for liberals who oppose changes in the original paygo architecture of Social Security and Medicare. Without a fundamental rebalancing of the costs and benefits of Social Security and Medicare, their ballooning cost growth will crowd out spending for progressive public investments of every kind. As former Senator Bob Kerrey has warned, the federal government eventually would become little more than an ATM machine for the nation's seniors.

UPDATING SOCIAL SECURITY

Social Security, which sends checks to 47 million beneficiaries each month and covers 156 million workers, touches more lives than any other government program. The system unquestionably has succeeded in its basic mission of reducing poverty in old age and insuring Americans against losses stemming from disabling accidents or the death of a working spouse or parent.

No "reform" that threatens to undo these historic achievements will get very far. As Peter Diamond and Peter Orszag note in their book *Saving Social Security: A Balanced Approach,*[3] the system offers an insurance package that no private company can match. Unlike private pensions, savings plans, and annuities, Social Security benefits are protected from the risk of inflation, the risk of outliving your assets, and the risk that bad investments or bad luck will erode your retirement nest egg.

Moreover, at a time of growing economic disparities, Social Security remains one of the few great equalizing forces in our market-oriented society. Its progressive benefit formula enables low-wage workers to collect retirement benefits that are a higher proportion of the taxes they paid than higher-wage workers.

But now the paygo system is breaking down under the strain of demographic changes, longevity, and Social Security's own past generosity. The challenge is to figure out a way of paying for Social Security that is equitable across generations (between young workers and retirees) and within generations (between low-income and affluent workers), that enhances its anti-poverty effects, and that adapts the system to the new realities of work and family life in the twenty-first century.

Instead of grappling with these challenges in a pragmatic and comprehensive way, our political leaders are locked in a narrow ideological struggle over "privatization." At issue is whether workers should be allowed to divert a portion of their payroll taxes (in President Bush's proposal, 4 points of the 12.4 percent tax dedicated to Social Security) into personal savings accounts invested in financial markets. To liberals, privatization is an assault on the ethos of mutual dependence and socialized risk that underpins Social Security's paygo architecture. They fear that subjecting workers to financial market fluctuations will make them less secure, and that a growing clamor from affluent workers to be allowed to invest more of their payroll taxes in the market will make the system less social.

Conservatives insist that, thanks to the magic of compound interest, workers could reap much higher returns by investing in stocks than they will get from a lifetime of contributions to Social Security. As workers earned more from market investments, they say, lawmakers could cut paygo benefits and thereby help restore the system's long-term fiscal integrity.

For President Bush, private accounts are integral to creating an "ownership society." As he promised in his second inaugural address: "We will widen the ownership of homes and businesses, retirement savings and health insurance. By making every citizen an agent of his or her own destiny, we will give our fellow Americans greater freedom from want and fear, and make our society more prosperous and just and equal."

Where does the public stand on Social Security reform? According to the Pew Research Center, 67 percent of Americans think that Social Security will run low on money in the future. Similarly large majorities say changes should be made now or in the next few years. Yet even as President Bush stumped the country to promote his plan last spring, support for personal savings accounts plummeted, from a high of 70 percent in 2000 to just 46 percent as of February 2005.[4]

On closer inspection, public attitudes toward Social Security generally and personal accounts in particular diverge strikingly by age. Younger voters, more skeptical about the system's future, express the strongest support for personal accounts, while older Americans are strongly opposed to anything that looks like an attempt to change the system's rules just as they are about to retire.

This generational split explains why then-candidate George Bush, who made personal savings accounts a key campaign pledge in 2000 and 2004, could step on the proverbial "third rail" of American politics and not get electrocuted. However much liberals may inveigh against the bugaboo of privatization, there appears to be a growing constituency among younger voters for reinventing Social Security to reflect trends in the rest of society toward greater individual choice and responsibility for retirement security. Over the last two decades, for example, there has been a dramatic shift away from private pensions that offer "defined benefits" (like Social Security) toward "defined contribution" plans like 401k pensions or IRAs that enable workers to invest in financial markets. A 2001 Federal Reserve study found that nearly half of families with a worker were covered by a defined contribution plan, while only 25 percent of families were covered by a defined benefit plan that guarantees a fixed monthly payment for life.

The debate over personal accounts and investing raises basic questions about the philosophical underpinnings of social insurance. Liberals say Social Security's system of intergenerational transfers fosters sentiments of social solidarity and collective responsibility that lean against the excessive individualism and economic disparities bred by market competition. Opening the door to private investments in markets would undermine such sentiments, shift risks from the government to individuals, and create greater economic disparities among seniors. Ultimately, liberals fear, it could lead the wealthy to secede from Social Security altogether, destroying its universal character and undermining public support for redistribution.

Conservatives believe the top-down distribution of public goods through universal entitlements like Medicare and Social Security deprives people of the freedom to make choices about their own lives and weakens individual responsibility by severing the link between effort and reward. Libertarians bridle at what they regard as the paternalistic assumption that government needs to protect people from market risks as well as the consequences of their own actions. In a more practical vein, Republicans bemoan Social Security's dwindling benefits and say that workers would get a much better deal from market investing.

It is important to note that many Democrats do not oppose personal accounts per se. What they really object to is diverting payroll tax contributions into private accounts. After all, President Bill Clinton proposed a new system of "universal savings accounts" paid for by general revenues. This "add on" approach may be the best hope for breaking the current political impasse, since it offers a way around liberals' vehement objections to "carving out" payroll taxes to fund accounts.

Even so, it is hard to see why liberals should regard one form of financing personal accounts as ideologically taboo, and another as perfectly fine. Once you accept the principle that government should enable all workers to save more and own personal assets, the question of how you fund personal accounts should be more mechanical than theological. After all, countries with much stronger social democratic pedigrees than our own, such as Sweden and Britain, have embraced personal savings accounts and investment without peril to their progressive souls. They have rightly viewed these changes not as an assault on the welfare state, but as a bid to assure its financial sustainability.

FIVE SIMPLE RULES FOR REFORM

Sooner or later, Americans will have to break the partisan stalemate in Washington and undertake reforms that can ensure Social Security's financial viability well into the twenty-first century. Here are five simple rules for progressive Social Security reform:

1. Close the Social Security deficit.
2. End old-age poverty as we know it.
3. Let workers decide when to retire.
4. Restrain the growth of retirement costs.
5. Enable workers to save and own financial assets.

Close the deficit.   President Bush's plan fails the most fundamental test of Social Security reform: it does not guarantee the system's long-term solvency. In fact, it makes matters worse in the near term by diverting a third of payroll tax revenues into private accounts. While the administration says these transition costs eventually will be offset by benefit cuts down the road, the president's personal accounts will not earn enough both to pay for themselves and to close the system's nearly $4 trillion deficit over the next seventy-five years. The system needs more money; where will it come from?

The federal government could borrow it, but Washington already is running huge budget deficits that Federal Reserve chairman Alan Greenspan has warned are unsustainable. We should also rule out hiking the payroll tax, a regressive levy that penalizes work, makes labor more expensive, and puts a special burden on the small businesses which generate most of the new jobs. To plug the financial gaps in Social Security and Medicare, and to finance personal accounts—whether added on or carved out—we will need to tap other sources of revenue.

One idea popular among Democrats and the public is to raise the cap (currently set at $90,000) on income exposed to the payroll tax. This would mean a stiff tax increase for relatively high earners, whose benefits would rise only modestly. Diamond and Orszag offer an intriguing idea: instead of phasing out the estate tax, as the Bush administration intends, use its revenues to shore up Social Security. This step, which would affect only the wealthiest Americans, would close about a fifth of Social Security's seventy-five-year deficit. Pollution taxes are another potential source of revenue. The Progressive Policy Institute, for example, has proposed a "cap and trade" system for reducing carbon emissions. By auctioning off tradable emissions permits, we could raise substantial amounts of money that could be dedicated either to cutting the federal government's swollen deficits or to keeping Social Security and Medicare solvent. Not only does it make sense to raise taxes on activities we want to discourage (polluting the air) rather than those we want to encourage (work), but this approach would have the added benefit of reducing America's dependence on oil and speeding the development of clean energy sources and technologies.

In the meantime, we can take a modest step toward broadening Social Security's revenue base by bringing in 4 million state and local government workers, the last major group of workers who remain outside the system. In any event, there is no credible plan to modernize our retirement policies that does not include a significant infusion of new revenues, from whatever combination of sources.

End old-age poverty. Although the poverty rate among retired Social Security beneficiaries is low (around 9 percent when all sources of income are factored in), the system is not especially generous to low-wage workers, even those who worked their entire adult lives. Reform should make the program more progressive by raising the minimum Social Security benefit enough to lift all longtime workers out of poverty. Diamond and Orszag, for example, propose boosting the minimum benefit to 100 percent of poverty for those who have worked thirty-five years.

Conceived at a time when divorces were relatively rare and when far fewer married women worked, Social Security's benefit formulas tend to be skewed against divorced women (whose earnings often ranged from low to nonexistent) and two-earner couples. Widows, whose living standards often plunge when their husbands die, have a poverty rate three times higher (15 percent) than that for retired married couples. To rectify these archaic inequities, we need to raise the "survivor replacement rate"—the percentage of a couples' former benefit that a surviving spouse gets when the other spouse dies.

By weaving a wider and stronger safety net, these progressive measures would have the added benefit of mitigating the risks of market investing if the United States follows other countries in adopting a "two-tiered" retirement policy that combines personal savings accounts and paygo benefits.

Let workers decide when to retire.   Given the improved health and longevity of boomers and successor generations, and the coming dearth of workers, it no longer makes sense to encourage people to retire as early as age sixty-two. An alternative to raising the retirement age, however, would be to abolish a legal retirement age altogether and index benefits by longevity. We should adjust benefit formulas to discourage early retirement (say, before sixty-five) and thereafter let seniors decide for themselves when to quit working, knowing that the longer they worked, the bigger their monthly benefit checks would be. Hardship exemptions could be made for manual workers in physically demanding occupations.

Restrain the growth of retirement costs.   The right way to pay for extra help for workers with modest incomes is to ask more affluent retirees to provide for more of their own retirement needs. But it is essential, as well, that we curb Social Security's rate of growth, lest the big entitlements squeeze out other vital public programs. There are several ways to cut future benefits:

- Adopt a progressive system of wage and price indexing for Social Security benefits. Low-income workers would continue to have their benefits adjusted upwards to reflect the overall growth of wages in the economy, while wealthier workers would have their benefits adjusted by inflation, which traditionally lags wage growth. In effect, progressive indexing trims future benefits for wealthier retirees who rely less on Social Security, while ensuring that workers with modest incomes will see their benefits grow along with the economy. In contrast, a complete shift from wage to inflation indexing, as some Republicans have proposed, would result in a 30 percent cut in benefits for low-wage workers who depend most on Social Security.
- Adopt a new inflation adjustment for cost-of-living increases for Social Security benefits. The current measure, the Consumer Price Index, slightly overstates inflation. Adopting a new measure developed by the Bureau of

Labor Statistics, according to Social Security actuaries, could close nearly one-fifth of Social Security's long-term financing shortfall.

Promote saving and ownership. Progressives should view Social Security reform as an opportunity to shift U.S. retirement policy from a paygo system of wealth transfers to a two-tiered system that also promotes national saving and individual wealth creation. If they deem President Bush's approach to personal savings accounts too risky, they need to offer an alternative that enables working Americans to save for their own retirement and acquire financial assets of their own.

Stock market returns average about 8 percent after inflation, or roughly four times more than what the paygo system offers. Savings accounts would give every worker a chance to boost his or her retirement savings, harness the power of compound interest over four decades of work, and accumulate personal financial assets that they would own and, assuming they did not use them all up, could pass on to their heirs. Some advocates also believe they could boost the nation's savings rate, although that would depend on how we financed the transition from a paygo system to one that is partially prefunded by personal savings. And to the extent that individuals earn higher returns from market investing, we could reduce their scheduled paygo benefits without a net loss in their living standard.

Of course, there are considerable risks and costs associated with personal savings accounts. Some workers might squander their money in rash investments, while others might earn lower returns through excessive caution. Some age cohorts will have the bad luck to retire during a bear market. Administrative costs for personal savings accounts could eat deeply into earnings, especially for low-income workers with modest accounts. Workers who fail to buy annuities on retiring could outlive their assets.

Progressives should insist that workers' retirement security is too important to be left entirely to the vagaries of markets. Government needs to create a framework of rules that mitigate the risks of personal investing. For example, many reformers have called for an approach modeled on the federal government's Thrift Savings Plan, which has low administrative costs and offers a choice of relatively safe investment vehicles, chiefly stock market index funds.

By embracing "add on" accounts to supplement Social Security, progressives could match president Bush's appeal to younger voters without worsening the system's financial woes. In contrast to the president's fiscally irresponsible plan to finance his accounts through more government borrowing, they should pay for theirs by tapping the estate tax or other sources of general revenue. And they should make it clear that as personal accounts grow, they stand ready to cut paygo benefits not only to put Social Security back on a sound financial footing, but also to ensure a decent balance between what we as a society spend on the needs of the elderly and what we invest in working families and children.

Finally, progressives should embrace modernizing Social Security as an opportunity to expand capital ownership and thereby create a more vibrant, democratic capitalism. While over half of all American households report holding some stocks or bonds, the top 10 percent own more than half of all financial assets, while the bottom 40 percent hold only 5 percent. By adding personal accounts to Social Security, we can reduce asset inequality, which is greater than income inequality, and give every U.S. worker an ownership stake in the nation's economy.

MODERNIZING MEDICARE

The cornerstone of Lyndon Johnson's Great Society, the enactment of Medicare in 1965, was hailed as the greatest progressive achievement since the creation of Social Security thirty years earlier. Not only did it give all seniors basic protection against medical emergencies, it also proved popular with their children, who otherwise would have had to worry about their parents' ability to pay their medical bills.

Nearly four decades later, however, Medicare is utterly unprepared to meet the challenges, financial and medical, of the boomers' retirement.

The program, which serves 41 million Americans, is based on the private health insurance models of the 1960s and earlier. In those days, insurance was mainly intended to shield people from ruinous hospital bills. Both health care and health insurance were "after the fact" in that they kicked in only after a crisis, such as a heart attack or stroke, had already occurred.

Over the last century, we have made tremendous progress against acute or life-threatening illnesses. Americans today survive conditions—strokes, heart attacks, even cancer—that routinely caused quick death. Health insurance still covers doctor and hospital bills, but the actual practice of medicine is gradually switching to an emphasis on early diagnosis, monitoring, and treatment of chronic illnesses, such as arthritis, Alzheimer's, heart disease, diabetes, osteoporosis, and breast and prostate cancers. Three-fourths of the elderly population suffers from one or more chronic condition. In less than twenty years, caring for chronic conditions is projected to account for 80 percent of the nation's health care spending.

Markets have responded more swiftly to these changes than government health care programs. Some private health plans have created "disease management" or "care management" programs that help people with chronic ailments monitor their conditions and avoid severe crises. Such programs pay health care providers to help patients care for themselves through jointly developed treatment plans; self-monitoring and reporting to identify problems or trends early so they can be tackled before hospitalization becomes necessary; assessment of risk factors and ways of reducing risks; better drug therapy (especially for patients with multiple prescriptions); and improved diets and proper exercise.

Medicare has not kept pace with the movement toward care management. In fact, its traditional fee-for-service program is constrained by decades of regulations that have locked in old, inefficient ways of paying for care. Consider this absurdity: Medicare will pay for an amputation, but will not pay doctors for the education, continuous monitoring, and coordination of care that can prevent people with diabetes from losing limbs.

The debate over Medicare reform, however, has dwelt more on expanding benefits than improving the quality of care. It is true that prescription drugs have become integral to the practice of modern medicine and that Medicare needed to catch up with private health care plans, which have long offered drug coverage. But absent other reforms, adding a costly new drug benefit worsens Medicare's funding woes without ensuring commensurate improvements in seniors' health. It is ironic that the Republicans have claimed bragging rights for delivering the new drug entitlement, given their traditional hostility to Medicare as the entering wedge of "socialized medicine" in the United States. But it is also true that, left to their own devices, liberal Democrats might have added an even more expensive drug benefit without tackling the more difficult challenges of structural reform.

America urgently needs a "third way" on Medicare reform. The first step is to define Medicare's mission clearly as enabling healthy aging, which entails a major focus on the prevention and treatment of chronic illnesses. Step two is to convert Medicare from a bill-paying regime into a performance-based system that produces measurable improvements in seniors' health.

The Progressive Policy Institute has proposed a health care version of the

"CompStat" system that New York police have used to dramatically cut crime rates. Just as CompStat holds precinct commanders responsible for reporting and reducing crime in their sectors, Medicare should require its local administrators to hire medical directors and collect information on treatment outcomes of the most frequently occurring chronic diseases, morbidity and mortality rates, emergency room admissions, access to and use of preventative care, patient satisfaction, availability of care management programs, cost trends, and other measures of the performance of Medicare within their jurisdiction. Medicare needs the flexibility to reward good performance and penalize bad, to develop a health information-sharing network that will support continuous improvement of all services, and help patients choose health care services on the basis of highest quality, fewest errors, and best outcomes. In turn, local administrators and medical directors need the budgetary and regulatory flexibility to offer services critical for treating chronic diseases, including patient self-management, telephone and e-mail communication between doctors and patients, management of multiple prescriptions, care coordination among specialists and caregivers, and electronic medical record keeping.

The third step is to expand coverage choices for seniors. Like any large public bureaucracy, Medicare evolves slowly. Its benefits, fixed in law by Congress, have lagged behind those provided most Americans in private insurance plans. How can we build into the system the capacity for continuous innovation and improvement that Americans increasingly demand from the public as well as private sectors? One way is to give all Medicare beneficiaries a genuine choice between the traditional fee-for-service system and private health insurance plans. For example, we could convert Medicare into a "premium support" system, modeled on the Federal Employees Health Benefit system, which provides federal employees with a menu of private health care options. In this approach, Medicare will pay a certain percentage of the premium and let seniors decide between the traditional fee-for-service system and private plans.

Liberals, as Medicare's traditional defenders, are deeply wary of competition. They fear that private plans will find ways to exclude the sickest seniors, undermining Medicare's ability to spread risks across the elderly population and driving up costs in the fee-for-service system. Conservatives, in a cynical rush to claim credit for bestowing a new drug benefit on seniors, have all but abandoned their previous demands for more choice and competition within Medicare.

Before resorting to more drastic measures to rein in Medicare's galloping costs, such as rationing care, we should test the power of patient choice and competition to help seniors get the best care at the best cost. Most important, a healthy rivalry between private and public health plans will force Medicare's benefits and systems to evolve by more quickly spotlighting the sorts of benefits seniors need and the methods of health insurance and health care that work.

Progressives ought to be defenders of seniors' health security, not the price-fixing bureaucracy that is struggling to provide it. Through these reforms, we can make Medicare a national leader for health insurance quality, efficiency, and effectiveness as we steer the program toward treating chronic illnesses and healthy aging.

CONCLUSION

Reforming Social Security and Medicare should be more than a dull, dry exercise in actuarial accounting. Our task is not just to close deficits, but to keep our nation's commitments to the old and young in decent balance as the age wave dramatically swells America's elderly population. Our goal should not be to preserve Social Security and Medicare as we have known them, but to adapt old social insurance models to the changing needs of new generations of Americans.

What progressives should defend is not, as the left contends, the existing structure of Social Security and Medicare, but the commitment to universal retirement and health security that those programs embody. At the same time, we should oppose the push to replace the two programs with purely private alternatives. This course would deny Americans the right to voluntarily agree to pool risks and insure themselves against certain vicissitudes of life. It would worsen social inequality, make life for many harsher, and shrivel the spirit of mutual responsibility on which any civil society worthy of the name depends.

The reforms outlined here entail a re-imagining of American social insurance. They would inject new elements of choice and competition into top-down government monopolies. They would harness the power of markets to discipline health insurance costs and to boost savings and retirement income. While retaining Social Security and Medicare's vital insurance functions, they would shift decision-making power from government to individuals. These changes reflect not so much a radical leap into the unknown as an evolutionary progression from the welfare state model of the twentieth century to the new paradigm of the "enabling state," which empowers individuals to take greater control of their own security. As Neil and Barbara Gilbert, leading analysts of comparative social policy have observed, the enabling state model is based on the new principle of public support for personal responsibility.[5]

These reforms seek to renegotiate, not abandon, the social compact implicit in Medicare and Social Security. They would offer working Americans new opportunities to build personal wealth and take advantage of modern medicine while asking them to take greater responsibility for financing their retirement and managing their health. They would convert Social Security from an entitlement based on the false promise that everyone can consume more than they produce to a system that promotes savings, investment, and greater economic self-reliance. And they would embody a new approach to governing based on a modern understanding that government's role is not to take care of us, but to give us the tools we need to take care of ourselves and each other.

NOTES

1. AARP, "Baby Boomers Envision Retirement II: Survey of Baby Boomers' Expectations for Retirement, Prepared for AARP by Roper ASW," May 2004; available at http://research.aarp.org/econ/boomers_envision.html.
2. Data in this section are drawn from the 2004 trustees' reports for Social Security and Medicare: The Board of Trustees, Federal Old-Age and Survivors Insurance and Disability Insurance Trust Funds, *The 2004 Annual Report of the Board of Trustees of the Federal Old-Age and Survivors Insurance and Disability Insurance Trust Funds* (Washington, DC: GPO, 2004); available at http://www.ssa.gov/OACT/TR/TR04/tr04.pdf; and The Boards of Trustees, Federal Hospital Insurance and Federal Supplementary Medical Insurance Trust Funds, *The 2004 Annual Report of the Boards of Trustees of the Federal Hospital Insurance and Federal Supplementary Medical Insurance Trust Funds* (Washington, DC: GPO, 2004); available at http://www.cms.hhs.gov/publications/trusteesreport/2004/tr.pdf.
3. Peter Diamond and Peter Orszag, *Saving Social Security: A Balanced Approach* (Washington, DC: Brookings Institution Press, 2003).
4. Pew Research Center for the People and the Press, "Bush Failing in Social Security Push," Press Release, March 2, 2005; available at http://people-press.org/reports/pdf/238.pdf.
5. Neil Gilbert and Barbara Gilbert, *The Enabling State: Modern Welfare Capitalism in America* (New York: Oxford University Press, 1989).

Chapter 4 The Ethics of America's Health

Care Debate

Tsung-mei Cheng and Uwe E. Reinhardt

In the wake of the demise of the Clinton Health Security Plan, one of the present authors asked readers of the *Journal of the American Medical Association* the following fundamental question: "As a matter of national policy, and to the extent that a nation's health system can make it possible, should the child of a poor American family have the same chance of avoiding preventable illness or being cured from a given illness as does the child of a rich American family?"[1]

The question triggered a number of letters, none of them answering it in the affirmative. Physicians responding to the journal did not address the question at all but merely wrote it off, variously, as "socialist propaganda," replete with "the ancient propagandistic use of children," or "an effete ploy at class warfare."[2]

One physician proposed that instead of using government to assure the nation of equitable universal health insurance, "each physician must cherish and practice the sacred duty to care for all patients with dignity and compassion irrespective of ability to pay."[3] That felicitous rhetoric has seduced the rest of American society, particularly its politicians, into believing that America's uninsured have access to appropriate health care when they need it. The belief is at variance with the facts portrayed in the research literature, well summarized in the Institute of Medicine's recent report *Care Without Coverage: Too Little, Too Late*.[4] Indeed, a health policy based on the premise that physicians and other providers of care can absorb the cost of modern American health care for the millions of uninsured Americans—including time-consuming and technically sophisticated surgical interventions—is a romantic notion that was bound to fail, at the expense of the uninsured. That policy also is particularly unfair to physicians, who have devoted more than a decade of their lives to arduous training, at little or low pay, and many of whom have emerged from that training deeply indebted.

Another physician brushed aside the question with allusions to the "fierce sense of rugged individualism, independence, and self-reliance that have been and still are the hallmarks of the American ethos."[5] To raise the politically and economically disenfranchised infant of, say, a lowly paid waitress to the status of a self-reliant, rugged American individualist, however, is a highly romantic notion as well. In fact, one may call it cruel.

Only one letter writer, University of Chicago Distinguished Law Professor Richard E. Epstein, had the temerity to address the question forthrightly, with a crisp "The correct answer is no." Esptein argued that "[Reinhardt's] proposal for equal medical treatment [of children] *perversely* requires more care to children of poor parents than to children of rich ones, precisely because the rich families can more easily avoid injury and illness and can better pick up any slack in health care delivery" [emphasis added].[6] Presumably, by "perverse" Epstein has in mind the dictionary definition of that word, that is, "deviating from what is considered right and acceptable." Is that how Americans feel about the proposition that, in a nation that aspires to give all citizens an equal opportunity to prosper, all children, rich and poor, ought to have access to appropriate health care, on equal terms?

In his letter Epstein goes on to write: "Worse, programmatic success [of public policies that assure children egalitarian access to health care] depends not just on offering carrots but on wielding sticks by overriding parental judgments on children's food, lifestyle and education." Is that really so objectionable to Americans? Most societies, including American society, routinely use both the persuasive and the coercive power of government to override parental choices on the food, lifestyle, and education experienced by the nation's children. They do so on the theory that children are more than pets, kept for the owners' enjoyment, whose upkeep is their owners' fiscal responsibility. Most societies, even America, view parents as the agents of the larger community, entrusted with nourishing and educating what the community regards as its most precious resource, the next generation. On that notion, public subsidies for the intellectual and physical development of children, and community control over the parental supervision of children, have long been regarded as "right and acceptable."

The preceding sampling of responses to a straightforward question on social ethics is symptomatic of the manner in which Americans debate this fundamental issue. For some reasons, Americans have been extremely reluctant to debate the issue head-on. More typically, if they debate it at all, they do so in camouflaged language, for example, seemingly technical jargon such as "consumer choice," "market solutions versus rationing," "efficiency," and so on. Other nations are far less reluctant to commit to paper the "rights to health care" they envision, and to be openly constrained by these presumed rights in the forging of their health policies. Thus in Europe, policymakers make frequent reference to their cherished "principle of solidarity." Canadians, too, have no difficulty expressing the social ethic that underlies Canada's approach to health policy.[7]

The reluctance of Americans to debate social ethics head-on can explain the chronic confusion that drives American health policy, which embraces truly remarkable generosity—for example, the Americans with Disabilities Act of 1990—side by side with callous neglect of hard-working, low-income American families, including those of poorly paid soldiers.[8] As a distinguished scholar of health law summed up his thirty years of research on American health policy: "[American] national health policy has become mostly incoherent, just as health care law remains a mass of anomalies and fundamental contradictions that reflect a high degree of cognitive dissonance both in public attitudes toward health care and in health policy itself."[9]

The overarching question here is whether, in their partisan fight over health policy, Americans will eventually muster the courage to address forthrightly the ethic that ought to govern that policy, or whether they will continue to dance deftly around that issue and muddle through incrementally and incoherently, as they have for over half a century.

HEALTH SPENDING AND GDP

Figure 4.1 shows the trend in health spending per capita in the United States in constant dollars during the nearly four decades from 1965 to 2003. The

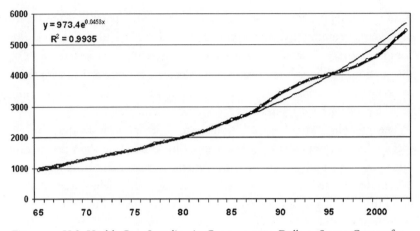

Figure 4.1. U.S. Health Care Spending in Constant 2000 Dollars. *Source:* Centers for Medicare and Medicaid Services.

dotted regression trend line in that graph suggests that, over the long haul, American health care costs per capita have risen at an average of 4.5 percent per year. The major deviation from this average occurred in the decade from 1988 to about 1998, when the annual growth in U.S. health care spending first increased in the later 1980s and then abated during the 1990s, presumably because of the rise of managed care.

During the same period U.S. gross domestic product (GDP) grew at an average annual compound rate of about 2 percent. Together, the two trends suggest the following actuarial rule for American health care: over the long haul, the American health care sector expects that its slice of the nation's GDP will grow about 2.5 percentage points faster than the rest of the GDP.

It may be mentioned in passing that no other industrialized nation spends anywhere near as much on health care as does the United States, whether the measurement used is per capita health spending or the percentage of gross domestic product devoted to health care. Even Switzerland, with a much older population than America's, spent only $3,445 on health care per capita in 2002, versus $5,267 by the United States. The corresponding percentages of GDP spent on health care in the two countries were 11.2 percent and 14.6 percent, respectively. All other industrialized nations, including neighboring Canada, spent even less than Switzerland on health care.[10] Remarkably, all of these nations—including Switzerland—have comprehensive, universal health insurance coverage, and they usually rank higher than the

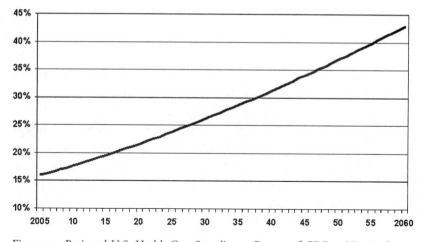

Figure 4.2. Projected U.S. Health Care Spending as Percent of GDP at Historical Trends, 2005–2060.

United States on health status indicators, such as infant mortality, life expectancy, and premature death.

Figure 4.2 projects the implications of the 2.5 percent faster-than-GDP growth rule of American health spending for the next half century. Health spending is projected to be between 18 and 19 percent of GDP a decade hence. That projection coincides with the current official forecast of the actuaries of the U.S. Department of Health and Human Services.[11] If this trend continues, health spending will grow to 40 percent of GDP by mid-century.

The question arises whether the U.S. economy can actually absorb these large projected outlays in health spending. The answer to that question is different for the short run and the long run. From the perspective of individual American families, it also depends on their socioeconomic status.

In the short run of a decade or two, from a purely macroeconomic perspective, the currently projected health spending can easily be absorbed by our steadily growing GDP. To illustrate, in 2001 the United States devoted about 14 percent ($1.4 trillion) of its $10 trillion GDP to health care. Current projections are that, by 2013, the United States will spend 18.4 percent ($3.4 trillion) of its projected $18.2 trillion GDP on health care. On the basis of these projections, even after health spending, the nonhealth GDP available to Americans in 2013 is projected to be $14.8 trillion, versus $8.6 trillion in

2001. After adjustment for projected general price inflation and population growth, these numbers imply that constant-dollar nonhealth GDP per capita will be about 20 percent larger in 2013 than it was in 2001. Indeed, not until three decades hence would health spending begin to actually lower the constant-dollar nonhealth GDP per capita in the United States, in spite of the impending retirement of the baby boomers.[12]

Yet long before the impact of rapid health-spending growth would be felt at the macroeconomic level, the roughly one-third of American families at the bottom of the nation's distribution of family incomes will find access to the ever more costly modern American health care financially out of reach. This problem will arise within the coming decade. The question, then, is how the rest of America will respond to this ominous development.

GROWTH AND DISTRIBUTION OF EARNINGS
AND INCOME

Figure 4.3 shows hourly earnings of male workers in the United States with different income levels, in constant 2001 dollars, over the period 1980–2001. The hourly earnings for each income level have been indexed to 1 for 1980.

In constant 2001 dollars, only the top 30 percent or so of the wage dis-

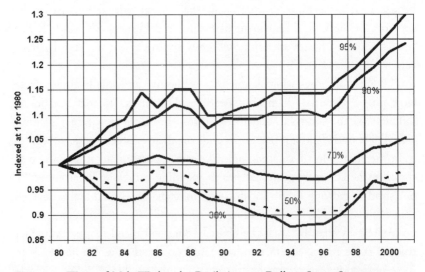

Figure 4.3. Wages of Male Workers by Decile in 2001 Dollars. *Source:* Lawrence Mishel, Jared Bernstein, and Heather Boushey, *The State of Working in America 2002/2003*, Ithaca, NY: Cornell University Press, 2003: table 2.7.

tribution has experienced an increase in hourly earnings since 1980. The bottom 30 percent of male wage earners actually earned less in 2001 than in 1980. In May 2004, for example, *BusinessWeek* reported that "one in four [American] workers earns $18,800 or less."[13]

This dispersion of the wage distribution has important implications for American health policy, because it will make an equitable approach to the distribution of health care ever more politically challenging.

It is worth noting, moreover, that even the median hourly wage for male wage earners (the dashed line near the bottom of Figure 4.3) has not grown at all over the past two decades. U.S. Bureau of the Census data indicate that the median annual earnings for full-time, year-round male workers fifteen years or older undulated narrowly below $40,000 over the entire period 1973–2002. The comparable median for female workers did rise over the period, but from $25,000 in 1973 to only $30,000 in 2002.[14]

Finally, Figure 4.4 shows the distribution of U.S. family income in 2002. In that year, close to a third of American families had an annual income below $35,000 and almost half had an annual income of less than $50,000. The Federal Poverty Level in 2001 was defined for a family of three as $14,128. It is for these families that the inexorable growth in the per capita cost of American health care, which far exceeds the growth in family income, will become a perfect storm in the decade ahead.

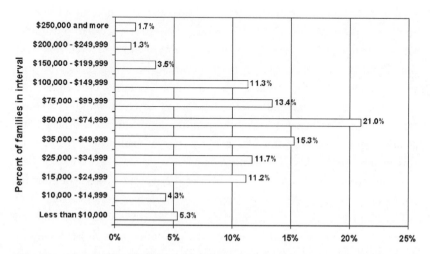

Figure 4.4. Income Distribution of U.S. Families, 2002. *Source:* U.S. Census Bureau, Current Population Survey, Income Distribution to $250,000 or More for Families: 2002.

PREMIUMS FOR PRIVATE HEALTH INSURANCE

Except for families and individuals covered by the government-run Medicare program for the elderly—or by the Medicaid/S-Chip program for very-low-income families and for the disabled and the pauperized elderly—Americans typically obtain health insurance coverage through their employers. Employers usually pay the lion's share of premiums, while employees usually cover 10 to 20 percent. Only a small minority of Americans under age 65 (about 10 percent of that cohort) purchase private coverage on their own. Finally, some 15 percent of Americans, about 44 million in 2004, did not have any health insurance at the point in time when surveys on health insurance coverage were made.[15] That percentage is likely to grow in the decade ahead.

In 2003, average per capita health spending in the United States was in excess of $5,200. In that year, the total premium for a family policy purchased—and mostly paid for—by employers averaged $9,068. That premium for the same policy exceeded $10,000 in 2004. Between 2000 and 2001, the premiums for employer-paid insurance grew at 10.9 percent. Between 2001 and 2002, that growth rate had increased to 12.9 percent. It was 13.9 percent between 2002 and 2003.[16] At this point, premium growth of "only" 10 percent per year would bring sighs of relief.

For low-income American families, these are ominous trends. Consider, for example, a hypothetical American worker for whom an employer paid a total of $35,000 in salary and benefits in 2004. Let us assume that from the employer's point of view, $35,000 is the upper limit that it can afford to pay for this particular employee, given the worker's job and skill level; that is, if the employer paid more than $35,000, it would be losing money on this worker. Included in this $35,000 total, of course, is not only the employee's take-home pay, but also the employer's share of payroll taxes and expenses for the employee's benefits, including pension contributions and health insurance premiums. For want of a better term, we shall henceforth refer to this total as the worker's "gross wage base."

If we assume that the gross wage base of the typical worker will grow by about 3.5 percent per year for the next decade, this worker's gross wage base will amount to about $50,000 ten years from now. Now suppose that the average health insurance premium for a family policy grew from its current level of $10,000 a year by "only" 8 percent per year for the next decade (rather than the actual current rates of between 12 and 18 percent). In ten years, that premium will have grown to $21,600. Regardless of whether the employer or the employee formally paid that premium, it would have to come out of the worker's gross wage base of $50,000. In other words, ten years from now, fully 43 percent of that worker's gross wage base would have to be allocated to health insurance alone. If, on the other hand, health insurance premiums grew by as much 10 percent per year (still much below current levels of growth), then over half (52 percent) of the gross wage base would be absorbed by health insurance alone ten years hence.

It may be objected that many families are headed by more than one earner and that the full cost to employers of insuring a particular worker may not be fully shifted back to that worker's paycheck. These objections are valid, but they do not impair the basic message emerging from the preceding calculations, namely, that for many low-income Americans with commensurately low pay, their gross wage base (as defined above) sooner or later will be too small a donkey to carry the load of the ever more expensive private health insurance for modern American health care.

Employers will initially try to manage this problem, from their perspective, by shifting more and more of the cost of employment-based health insurance into the employees' paychecks. That approach, however, will not solve the problem of rising health care costs as a percentage of the employee's wage base; it will merely reallocate it from the employer to the employee. One much-discussed version of this cost shifting, for example, is the so-called "consumer-direct-health-plan" under which employers would provide employees with only a so-called catastrophic health insurance policy with a high deductible of, say, $4,000 per year. To help employees meet that high deductible, employers might deposit $1,500 or so into a medical savings account (also known as a "health savings account") opened for the employee, leaving the employee's family, however, to pay the remainder of the deductible out of the family's own budget. Once again, this extreme version of cost sharing would not substantially reduce the overall cost of health care for the family. Whether directly paid by the employer or the employee, that cost would still have to come out of the employee's gross wage base.

Caught between the vise of rapidly rising premiums for employee health insurance and revenues per employee that grow much less rapidly or consistently, many employers in the decade ahead will be likely to rethink the merit of offering their employees health insurance at all, especially in establishments with predominantly low-skilled workers with commensurately low gross wage bases. Left on their own, however, these employees are unlikely to be able to afford the procurement of health insurance in the individual insurance market, where premiums are much higher than they would be, for the same coverage, as part of a group policy purchased by the employer.

Almost inevitably, then, rapidly rising health insurance premiums, in the face of a much less rapidly growing payroll base, will flush millions more currently insured Americans into the ranks of the uninsured. It already happened during the 1990s. Even as the economy boomed during that decade, and the unemployment rate plummeted, the number of uninsured in the United States grew from about 35 million in 1990 to about 44 million in 2004, in spite of the fact that the State Children's Health Insurance Plan (S-CHIP) enacted by Congress in 1996 covered millions of hitherto uninsured children.

THE NUMBER OF UNINSURED

Describing the phenomenon of the uninsured in America is a challenge, because they are an economically heterogeneous group, some of whom drop in and out of health insurance over time.

In a recent publication, the Congressional Budget Office (CBO) provided a variety of estimates on the number of uninsured in 1998, using different surveys and definitions of the term "uninsured."[17] The CBO estimated that between 56.8 and 59 million were without health insurance at some point in 1998. Of these, the CBO estimated that 21 to 31 million were uninsured for the entire year. Separate "snapshot" surveys taken at specific points in time during 1998 found that the number of uninsured at any given point ranged from 39 to 42.6 million. The latter number is the one most commonly used in the literature and in the media to describe the health insurance status of Americans. In these surveys, about 80 percent, or more than 30 million, were estimated by the CBO to have been uninsured for more than twelve months.

It is well known that lack of health insurance falls as income rises. Some 17 percent of nonelderly people in the United States lacked health insurance in 2001. But among households with incomes below the Federal Poverty Level (FPL), 37 percent lacked coverage. Among households with incomes between poverty and up to two times the FPL, 27 percent lacked coverage.[18] By contrast, among households with incomes three times the FPL and higher, only 6 percent were without health insurance. In 2001 the FPL was defined as $14,128 for a family of three.

Of the 39 to 42 million or so Americans estimated by snapshot surveys to be uninsured at the time of the survey, only 19 percent were estimated to belong to families with an income three times the FPL or above. Most of these individuals or families probably could have afforded to procure with their own resources at least a catastrophic health insurance policy, if it were offered to them in the marketplace at premiums comparable to those paid for group policies.

However, families with incomes below 300 percent of the FPL will find it increasingly difficult a decade from now to afford health insurance coverage with their own resources, unless they are subsidized through employer-provided health insurance. Furthermore, as noted, employers of relatively low-skill, low-wage workers who currently provide health insurance for their employees also will find it increasingly difficult to do so.

HEALTH CARE FOR THE UNINSURED

To be uninsured in the United States does not mean that one goes without health care altogether. First, the uninsured sometimes procure needed health care with their own resources. Alternatively, when they are critically ill, they may succeed in obtaining health care on a charitable basis or, if they fail in that endeavor, they may simply not pay all or any of the charges they were billed by health care providers. The latter tendency is all the more common because, lacking any market power, the uninsured typically are charged the highest prices that any patients pay in hospitals and at the pharmacy. Failing to pay hospital bills, however, can expose uninsured Americans to harsh methods by collection agencies, including the garnishing of wages, the forfeiture of savings accounts or other assets, arrests for failing to make court-ordered payments[19] and, ultimately, family bankruptcy. A history of unpaid medical bills also may lead to the outright denial of health care by providers in subsequent episodes of illness among uninsured families.

Remarkably, in spite of the nation's wealth—and the huge allocation of GDP granted to the American health system—these untoward events occur year after year only in the U.S. health system. They are unheard of in other nations in the industrialized world. In Taiwan, for example, which established universal, national health insurance in 1995, the Supreme Court ruled explicitly in 2002 that no Taiwanese can be denied health care for lack of ability to pay.[20]

It is generally agreed that, even though the uninsured do receive needed health care when critically ill, they typically do not receive the timely, early interventions that can help avoid catastrophic illness or premature death. In their paper "Covering the Uninsured: What Is It Worth?" Miller et al. estimate that the GDP cost of postponing medical interventions for the uninsured—and the loss of social value due to their poorer health and earlier deaths—may range between $65 and $130 billion a year.[21] Even from the strictly economic view of social welfare theory—leaving aside other humanitarian considerations—society as a whole would be better off if it could provide universal coverage at a cost below the price ultimately paid for the lack of timely and preventive care for the uninsured. The question therefore arises: how much would a move to universal coverage cost?

In a paper entitled "How Much Health Care Do the Uninsured Use, and Who Pays for It?" Jack Hadley and John Holahan estimate that in 2003 the uninsured did receive health care costing about $100 billion, an estimate also accepted as valid in a volume on the uninsured published by the Institute of Medicine. These costs were covered by a variety of sources, including the uninsured themselves, along with hospitals and physicians who did not receive direct payments for these services. In a second paper entitled "Covering the Uninsured: How Much Would It Cost?" Hadley and Holahan present two alternative estimates of the increase in annual total national health spending (NHE) that would be triggered by the additional health care that the currently uninsured would be likely to use if they had health insurance. Assuming that the insurance were the typical private coverage now provided to middle- and low-income American families, the authors estimate that the additional use of health care would add about $70 billion a year to total NHE. On the other hand, if the uninsured were folded instead into public insurance programs (Medicaid, S-CHIP) that pay providers substantially lower fees, the additional health care then likely to be used by the uninsured is estimated to add only $34 billion to annual NHE. A major problem with this last approach is that a large number of physicians refuse to treat Medicaid patients at these low fees.[22]

Depending on which approach would had been chosen—private or public insurance—the impact on total NHE in 2001 would have been to increase NHE in 2003 between 3 and 6 percent. Either approach would have raised the percentage of GDP absorbed by health care by less than one percentage point. These costs, of course, would have been offset by the $65 to $130 billion in social benefits estimated by Miller et al. This estimate, however, indicates only what the additional health care likely to be used by the now uninsured would add to total national health spending, if these uninsured had health insurance in the future. That additional spending is not to be confused with the additional government spending such a policy would entail. The latter figure would be higher, because universal coverage presumably would shift some of the costs already borne in 2003 by the low-income uninsured (or by providers of health care) to the federal or state government budgets.

As a rough rule of thumb, additional government spending to achieve universal coverage in 2003 therefore might be in the neighborhood of $100 billion a year. On that assumption, and the further assumption that health spending per capita in the next decade will increase by an average annual compound rate of 6 percent in the ensuing decade, the additional ten-year budget outlay occasioned by a move to full-fledged universal health insurance might be $1.3 trillion,[23] or $1.6 trillion if health spending per capita rose by 10 percent per year over the decade. Although these seem like large numbers, they appear less so when compared to the roughly $130 trillion of GDP likely to be generated over the same time span if GDP grows at an average compound growth rate of 5 percent over the next decade.[24]

Even so, in thinking about the prospect for universal health insurance in America and the plight of the uninsured, the fundamental question is whether American taxpayers would be willing to shoulder the taxes and transfers implied in the estimates presented above. That question brings us back to the matter of social ethics.

THE SOCIAL DIMENSIONS OF GOODS
AND SERVICES

In the debate on health policy, it is sometimes proposed that health care, like education, is a "social good" that should be made available to all who need it without regard to the recipient's ability to pay for it. This notion implies substantial or full collective financing of the consumption of health care, through some private or public health insurance mechanism, with premiums that are related strictly to ability to pay, rather than on a per capita basis or the actuarially expected cost of health care for the individually insured.

The stated purpose of financing health care collectively is twofold. First, it is to assure the individual timely access to appropriate health care. That desideratum is both humane and efficient, because timely health care can avoid costly critical illness. A second—and sometimes overlooked—purpose is to protect the individual from financial destitution as a result of illness. Most modern societies have come to view it as ethically unacceptable that a family should be driven to bankruptcy because one of its members has fallen seriously ill. Remarkably, in the United States such bankruptcies are not uncommon.[25]

Unfortunately, it is not a straightforward matter to categorize the goods and services produced in an economy into (a) purely private consumption goods whose financing is wholly the recipient's responsibility and (b) purely social goods that should be collectively financed. There are many shades in between, rooted in a characteristic economists call "externalities."

Every good and service available to individuals has attributes that matter to the individual who receives them or contemplates their acquisition. The value the individual attributes to specific goods and services, however, may be smaller or larger than the value the community at large would impute to them, because certain attributes of some goods and services have wider social implications. It is these attributes that economists call "externalities" or "spillover effects," so called because they matter to individuals other than the recipient of the good or service in question.

Economists distinguish between positive and negative externalities, and those associated with production or with consumption. A production externality occurs when the process of production itself is associated with spillover benefits or costs. A consumption externality occurs when one person's consumption of a good or service makes other persons either happy (altruism) or unhappy (social envy). Whether or not a good or service exhibits externalities often is a purely subjective matter that lies in the eyes and mind of the beholder. Two rational observers may differ on the issue. These differences in the subjective assessment of externalities drive the sharp ideological differences in American health policy.

In the literature of economics, goods and services that are characterized by positive externalities have long been known as "merit goods" (rather than the more common "social goods") and those with negative externalities as "demerit goods."[26] A market economy based purely on individual choice as the engine of resource allocation will produce insufficient amounts of merit goods and excessive amounts of demerit goods, unless government intervenes to subsidize the production and consumption of merit goods and to penalize the production of demerit goods.

In theory, the magnitudes of the subsidies or penalties depend strictly on the magnitudes of the underlying externalities. Some merit goods may qualify for full subsidization (for example, clean air or national defense) while others are only partially subsidized (for instance, college education). Similarly, some demerit goods may be outlawed outright (for instance, the consumption of heroin or pollution with lethal substances) while others may be merely taxed to discourage use to efficient or socially approved levels (for instance, the gasoline used by automobiles). Getting these subsidies and penalties right is a challenge even in theory. Getting them right in practice, and in the political arena, is nearly impossible. All nations muddle through as best they can in this area.

Much of the political debate on public policy in general, and on health policy in particular, revolves around different perceptions concerning the degree to which particular goods and services warrant public subsidies or penalties, that is, on the nature of the externalities inherent in these goods and services.

EXTERNALITIES IN HEALTH CARE

Health care is riddled with externalities of various types. The most obvious example is immunizations against communicable diseases, which bestows benefits not only on the individual recipient but also on society at large. It is an externality in the production of better health, as is the bulk of what are known as public health services.

A positive externality in the consumption of health care occurs when individual A derives happiness from knowing that individual B receives health care of a given type—for example, preventive or curative care. The health care of children, in particular, tends to trigger such positive consumption externalities in modern societies.

Social envy, on the other hand, can trigger negative externalities in the consumption of health care. For example, one can easily imagine situations in which individual A is unhappy to see individual B receive a health service (for example, an organ transplant or a very expensive drug) that individual A cannot afford to purchase and that is not collectively financed for him or her. Such negative externalities in consumptions can easily lead to social tension within societies.

To overlook the political implications of negative externalities in health care would be to miss many of the issues that drive the current debate on health policy, in the United States and abroad. Along with altruism, social envy is a force that drives the preferred ethic for health care toward equal availability in many societies. Canada, for example, is currently in the midst of a national debate on the idea to allow Canadian families with the means to do so to purchase health care not readily available under Canada's government-run health system from private health care providers on Canadian soil. So far, that idea has been rejected on egalitarian grounds. It could be inferred from this political posture that the majority of Canadians would impute a negative consumption externality to the emergence of a privately financed, upper-tier health care system in Canada.

HEALTH CARE AS A "MERIT GOOD" (OR "SOCIAL GOOD")

A major problem with the phrase "health care," of course, is that the term spans an incredibly wide collection of goods and services, each with different endowments of externalities.

Modern societies treat certain types of health care as social goods that are to be made available to all who need them, on equal terms, and without regard to the recipient's ability to pay. Health care for critically ill or injured individuals typically qualifies for that label. The provision and distribution of social goods typically involves collective financing—either through private insurance based on heterogeneous risk pools or through tax-financed public schemes.

There are other types of health care that few people would deem worthy of collective financing. Injections with Botox, cosmetic surgery, and cosmetic orthodontics fall into that category. These commodities, then, are viewed as purely private consumption goods whose financing is wholly the recipient's responsibility.

In between, however, are a myriad of health care goods and services that some societies treat as social goods while others do not. Drugs to overcome erectile dysfunction may fall into this category, or birth control, or treatments for infertility.

Debates over the social ethic that should guide the financing and the delivery of health care in modern societies basically revolve around the extent to which particular types of health care are thought to be social goods, which, as noted earlier, is really a debate over the magnitude of the externalities inherent in particular health care goods and services. At the practical level, the debates have led to arguments over the benefits package to which everyone in society should have unfettered access in case of need, regardless of his or her ability to pay for it. These debates also involve arguments over the financing of the basic benefit package—whether it should be financed by progressive income taxes, by more regressive payroll taxes, by even more regressive per capita premiums, or by "actuarially fair" premiums based on the health status of the individual insured. Finally, these debates involve arguments over the degree to which patients should be made to share in the cost of health care at the time they receive it, through either deductibles or copayments or both.

HEALTH AS A SOCIAL GOOD IN THE EYES OF NATIONS

In most nations in the industrialized world, there has long been a political consensus to define the guaranteed package of health care benefits very broadly, and to finance that comprehensive benefit package with progressive, income-related premiums or taxes. The central ethical tenet is that all elements of the basic benefit package are to be treated as social goods to be made available to all who need them, on roughly equal terms, regardless of the recipient's ability to pay for them. Canada furnishes an extreme example of this approach.

It is not necessary, of course, to produce goods and services in this basic package collectively. To treat health care as a social good it suffices to organize the financing of the covered health care through social insurance. That term is not to be confused with socialized medicine, under which government owns and operates the delivery of care, as has long been the case for hospital care in the British National Health Services (NHS) or in the U.S. health system operated by the U.S. Department of Veterans Affairs.[27] Most nations in the industrialized world, including Canada and Taiwan, seek more or less egalitarian health systems mainly through social insurance, rather than through socialized medicine.

Naturally, to keep such social insurance systems financially sustainable, some goods and services must be excluded from the nationally financed benefit package, and some level of superior quality and amenity must be excluded as well. Because these exclusions tend to vex members of the upper-income strata who could easily afford them on their own, almost all nations permit this segment of the population to opt out of the social health insurance system. In most countries, however, less than 10 percent of the population takes advantage of this option, although by law the Netherlands literally forces about a third of its population to do so. As noted, Canada does not offer its well-to-do citizens that option at all on their home turf. On the other hand, well-to-do Canadians enjoy the option nevertheless, simply by procuring whatever health care or quality they cannot have on preferred terms in Canada from providers in the United States. As a general rule, then, most modern nations do operate health care systems with at least two tiers.

HEALTH CARE AS A SOCIAL GOOD IN THE UNITED STATES

Unlike other nations with broad social insurance systems and uniform national standards, the U.S. health insurance system is a highly complex mosaic of different social contracts that vary by distinct population groups segmented by age, work status, income, and region.

First, there are the elderly, who are insured through the federal Medicare program. This program, however, covers only about 50 percent of the total cost of health care used by the elderly. To assist the poorest of the elderly in meeting the remaining costs, there are five more distinct, categorical, federal programs for low-income Medicare enrollees, each of which offers a distinct set of federal subsidies.

For younger, very-low-income families (mainly single mothers and children) and for the disabled there are the federal-state Medicaid and S-CHIP programs. The truly pauperized elderly—the so-called "dual eligibles"—are entitled to a combination of Medicare and Medicaid and basically receive all needed health care free of charge. The federal government pays for more than half of the cost of the states' Medicaid programs and, therefore, has the right to impose on it some uniform federal guidelines. Even so, eligibility levels for the program, and many other parameters—including the fees paid the providers of care—are the states' prerogative, which means that there are really fifty distinct health insurance programs for the poor and the disabled. Furthermore, in many states, the fees paid to providers by Medicaid are so low that many physicians do not accept Medicaid patients for treatment.

Employed Americans and their families are covered by whatever insurance policies are provided at the place of work by their employers. These policies vary from extremely comprehensive to bare-bones, minimal coverage. The self-employed either purchase health insurance on their own, in the costly market for individual coverage, or they join the ranks of the millions of uninsured Americans who, as noted, are left to fend for themselves in the health care market and are often subject to harsh rationing of timely health care by income and price.

WHITHER AMERICA'S SOCIAL ETHIC FOR HEALTH CARE?

Clearly, the United States today lacks a political consensus on the social ethic that ought to govern American health care. The crazy quilt of private, federal, and state health insurance products for Americans—and the large number of uninsured—reflects this lack of consensus.

Many Americans impute to health care much the same externalities as are imputed to it in the rest of the industrialized world—in neighboring Canada, in Europe, and in Asia. These Americans would like to see the United States embrace universal health insurance coverage on the social insurance model, even at the expense of higher taxation and regulation of the health care system.

Many other Americans, however, have come to impute fewer and fewer externalities to more and more health care goods and services. That tendency may be a reaction to the ever-rising cost of health care, which has made bestowing a coronary artery bypass graft on a poor person the monetary equivalent of bestowing on him or her a fully loaded Mercedes-Benz. This view is fueled by the increasingly popular thesis that many illnesses in modern society are the product of improvident lifestyles more so than of infelicitous genetics or other bad luck.

It is fair to assert that the politically dominant policymaking elite in the United States increasingly has embraced the second view of health care, namely, that for the most part health care is basically a private consumption good. That policymaking elite now favors the "consumer-directed health care" described earlier in this chapter and would accompany that approach with tax preferences in the form of medical savings accounts that, on an after-tax basis, effectively makes health care cheaper in dollar terms for high-income families in high-marginal tax brackets than for low-income Americans in low-marginal tax brackets. This tax preference rests on a peculiar social ethic that is, once again, rarely discussed.

Finally, no clearer ethical statement on the plight of the uninsured could have been made by America's policymaking elite than the federal budgets of

2001 and 2003. In 2001, the administration and the Congress faced a pro-jected ten-year budget surplus of $5.6 trillion, of which $2.5 trillion were cumulative prospective surpluses in the Social Security and Medicare trust funds, and $3.1 trillion were available for general government spending, in-cluding health programs. Even though these surpluses were subsequently diminished somewhat by more pessimistic assumptions about the economy, the remainder would have been more than ample to finance a move toward genuine universal health insurance in the United States. The administration and the Congress chose instead to devote that surplus to two massive tax cuts, one in 2001 and a subsequent one in 2003. The implied signal on social ethics vis-à-vis America's uninsured was unmistakable. As one of the authors has argued recently, it signaled that, for the foreseeable future, there is little hope for America's uninsured.[28]

As to the question raised at the outset of this chapter, namely, whether Americans will ever forthrightly debate the social ethic that ought to guide their health system, it can be doubted that such a debate will be forthcoming soon. Instead, that ethic will continue to be forged and reshaped piecemeal, over time, as a mere by-product of incremental policy changes that will be rationalized mainly with appeals to economic jargon such as "market vs. regulation," "market vs. rationing," "efficiency," and "consumer empower-ment." As one of the present authors has argued elsewhere, this camouflage jargon is the economics profession's peculiar contribution to America's health policy debate.[29]

Only when we begin to move beyond such euphemisms, and face the real human costs imposed on our fellow citizens by the confusion and neglect inherent in America's high-cost health care system, can we start on the long road to remedying what can be viewed as our ethically impoverished ap-proach to addressing this vital human need. In the meantime, one can only hope that Winston Churchill was right when, during World War II, he remarked that "In the long run, Americans will always do the right thing—after exploring all other alternatives."

NOTES

1. Uwe E. Reinhardt, "Wanted: A Clearly Articulated Social Ethic for American Health Care," *Journal of the American Medical Association* 278, no. 17 (1997): 1446–1447.
2. Donald G. Lindsay, MD and James F. Lally, MD, in *Journal of the American Medical Association* 279, no. 10 (1998): 745–746.

3. Lindsay, Letters, *Journal of the American Medical Association* 279, no. 10 (1998).

4. Institute of Medicine, *Care Without Coverage: Too Little, Too Late* (Washington, DC: Institute of Medicine, 2002).

5. Lally, Letters, *Journal of the American Medical Association* 279, no. 10 (1998).

6. Richard E. Epstein, Letters, *Journal of the American Medical Association* 279, no. 10 (1998): 745.

7. See, for example, Terrence Sullivan and Patricia M. Baranek, *First Do No Harm: Making Sense of Canadian Health Reform* (Vancouver, BC: UBC Press, 2002).

8. Drew E. Altman and Robert J. Blendon, "Perpetual War Hits Military Families Hard," *Boston Globe* (June 13, 2004).

9. Clark C. Havighurst, "I've Seen Enough! My Life and Times in Health Care Law and Policy," *Health Matrix: Journal of Law-Medicine* 14, no. 1 (2004): 107–130. See also Clark C. Havighurst, "American Health Care and the Law—We Need to Talk!" *Health Affairs* 19, no. 4 (2000): 84–106.

10. OECD data for 2004.

11. Stephen Heffler, Sheila Smith, Sean Keehan, M. Kent Clemens, Mark Zezza, and Christopher Truffer, "Health Spending Projections Through 2013," *Health Affairs* ("Web Exclusive"), February 11, 2004; available at http://content.healthaffairs.org/cgi/reprint/hlthaff.w4.79v1?maxtoshow=&HITS=10&hits=10&RESULTFORMAT=&author1=Heffler&andorexactfulltext=and&searchid=1110398360815_3675&stored_search=&FIRSTINDEX=0&resourcetype=1&journalcode=healthaff.

12. Michael E. Chernew, Richard A. Hirth, and David M. Cutler, "Increased Spending on Health Care: How Much Can the United States Afford?" *Health Affairs* 22, no. 4 (2003): 15–25, Exhibit 1.

13. "The Working Poor: We Can Do Better," *BusinessWeek* (March 31, 2004).

14. Carmen DeNavas-Walt, Robert Cleveland, and Bruce H. Webster, Jr., U.S. Census Bureau, Current Population Reports, P60-221, *Income in the United States: 2002* (Washington, DC: GPO, 2003), 9 (Table 3).

15. Congressional Budget Office, *How Many People Lack Health Insurance and for How Long?* (Washington, DC: Congressional Budget Office, 2003).

16. Hefler et al., "Health Spending Projections"; Kaiser Family Foundation and Health Research and Educational Trust, *Employer Health Benefits—2003 Annual Survey*, Exhibit 1.12; available at http://www.kff.org/insurance/loader.cfm?url=/commonspot/security/getfile.cfm&PageID=20672; Kaiser Family Foundation, *Employer Health Benefits*, Exhibit 1.1.

17. Congressional Budget Office, *How Many People Lack Health Insurance and for How Long?*

18. Presentation by Diane Rowland, Kaiser Commission on Medicaid and the Uninsured, "Briefing on Health Policy Issues," New York, NY, June 3, 2003.

19. Lucette Lagnado, "Hospitals Try Extreme Measures to Collect Their Overdue Debts," *Wall Street Journal* (October 30, 2003), A1.

20. Tsung-mei Cheng, "Taiwan's New National Health Insurance Program: Genesis and Experience So Far," *Health Affairs* 22, no. 3 (2003): 61–76.

21. Institute of Medicine, *Hidden Costs, Value Lost: Uninsurance in America* (Washington,

DC.: National Academy Press, June 2003); Wilhelmine Miller, Elizabeth Richardson Vigdor, and Willard G. Manning, "Covering the Uninsured: What Is It Worth?" *Health Affairs* ("Web Exclusive"), March 31, 2004: W4-157-67; available at http:// content.healthaffairs.org/cgi/reprint/hlthaff.w4.157vi?maxtoshow=&HITS=10& hits=10&RESULTFORMAT=&author1=vigdor&andorexactfulltext=and&search id=111040106165_4027&stored_search=&FIRSTINDEX=0&resourcetype=1& journalcode=healthaff.

22. J. Hadley and J. Holahan, "How Much Medical Care Do the Uninsured Use, and Who Pays for It?" *Health Affairs* ("Web Exclusive"), February 12, 2002, Exhibit 1; available at http://content.healthaffairs.org/cgi/reprint/hlthaff.w3.66vi?maxtoshow =&HITS=10&hits=10&RESULTFORMAT=&author1=hadley&andorexactfull text=and&searchid=111040120041_4062&stored_search=&FIRSTINDEX=0& resourcetype=1&journalcode=healthaff; Institute of Medicine, *Care Without Coverage*, 3–4; J. Hadley and J. Holahan, "Covering the Uninsured": How Much Would It Cost?" *Health Affairs* ("Web Exclusive"), June 4, 2003; available at http://content .healthaffairs.org/cgi/reprint/hlthaff.w3.250vi?maxtoshow=&HITS=10&hits=10& RESULTFORMAT=&author1=hadley&andorexactfulltext=and&searchid=111040 120041_4062&stored_search=&FIRSTINDEX=0&resourcetype=1&journalcode =healthaff.

23. Calculated using the equation $H = X[(1+g)^N -1]/g$, where H is total additional health spending over the future period of N years, X is the incremental spending in the first year, and g is the annual growth in spending.

24. In 2001, the U.S. GDP was $10.02 trillion. It is estimated to be $17.4 trillion by 2012, which implies an average annual compound growth rate of about 5 percent. See S. Hefler, S. Smith, S. Keehan, M. K. Clemens, G. Won, and M. Zezza, "Health Spending Projections for 2002–2012," *Health Affairs* ("Web Exclusive"), February 7, 2003, Exhibit 1; available at http://content.healthaffairs.org/cgi/reprint/hlthaff.w3 .54vi?maxtoshow=&HITS=10&hits=10&RESULTFORMAT=&author1=zezza& andorexactfulltext=and&searchid=111040183357_4111&stored_search=&FIRSTIN DEX=0&resourcetype=1&journalcode=healthaff. Applying the equation given in the previous note to these numbers implies a total GDP over the period 2002–2012 of about $131 trillion.

25. Elizabeth Warren, T. A. Sullivan, and M. B. Jacoby, "Medical Problems and Bankruptcy Filings," Harvard Law School, Public Law Working Paper No. 008; and University of Texas Law, Public Law Research Paper No. 09, April 2000.

26. M. B. Jacoby, T. A. Sullivan, and E. Warren, "Rethinking the Debate over Health Care Financing: Evidence from the Bankruptcy Courts," *New York University Law Review* 76, no. 2 (2001): 375–418.

27. Curiously, although some politicians in the United States routinely condemn "socialized medicine," they tend to be highly protective of the socialized medicine system reserved for American veterans.

28. Uwe E. Reinhardt, "Is there Hope for the Uninsured?" *Health Affairs* ("Web Exclusive"), August 27, 2003, W3-376-90; http://content.healthaffairs.org/cgi/reprint/hlth aff.w3.376vi?maxtoshow=&HITS=10&hits=10&RESULTFORMAT=&author1

= Reinhardt & andorexactfulltext = and & searchid = 1116534952645_2872 & stored_
search = &FIRSTINDEX=0&resourcetype=1&journalcode=healthaff.

29. Uwe E. Reinhardt, "Economics," *Journal of the American Medical Association* 275, no.
23 (1996): 1802–1804; available at http://content.healthaffairs.org/cgi/reprint/hlthaff
.w3.376v1?maxtoshow = &HITS = 10 & hits = 10 & RESULTFORMAT = &author1 =
reinhardt&andorexactfulltext=and&searchid=1110402224583_4133&stored_search=
&FIRSTINDEX=0&resourcetype=1&journalcode=healthaff.

Part Three   **Diversity and Unity**

Chapter 5 Religion as Unifier and Divider

Alan Wolfe

It has been a long time since religion was thought of as a unifying force. The moment to which such a description perhaps best applies occurred during the height of Christendom, in, say, the fourteenth or fifteenth century, when at least one of the world's great monotheistic religions, Catholicism, could claim something like universal status. That, of course, changed with the Protestant Reformation, but even after that epochal event, when Latin remained the lingua franca of the intellectuals and the Tridentine Mass became an unchanging liturgy for ordinary Catholic believers, Catholicism was hardly universal, even in its own bailiwick. Eastern Orthodox Catholics had their own rituals. Many Roman Catholics had a less-than-faithful relationship to their church, and their church borrowed from so many traditions that its practices approached syncretism. The universal church was universal in name only.

Whatever unifying potential Catholicism once possessed, the rise of Protestantism was synonymous with the rise of sectarianism. Martin Luther's great contribution was not only to reform the corruption of the church, but to create a German religion, tied, forever after, to the language and history of one particular country, even as other countries, such as those in Scandinavia, became Lutheran as well. Nationalism gave Protestant sects their strength, but at the cost of contributing to, rather than abating, the cultural forces that were dividing the world. And even within the nations that committed themselves to a particular Protestant sect, unity proved to be illusive; before long, there would be many different varieties of Dutch Calvinists or German Lutherans, each claiming a monopoly of a particular truth and identifying as the infidel those closest in cultural affinity, rather than some distant target.

RELIGION AND AMERICAN IDENTITY

Religious conflict was one of the many aspects of European culture brought across the Atlantic as colonists, most of whom were Protestants, settled in what would become the United States. Significant voices hoped that the new country could avoid the sectarianism that had been associated with religion in Europe. "Providence," wrote John Jay in *The Federalist Papers*, "has been pleased to give this one connected country to one united people—a people descended from the same ancestors, speaking the same language, professing the same religion, attached to the same principles of government, very similar in their manners and customs, and who, by their joint counsels, arms, and efforts, fighting side by side throughout a long and bloody war, have nobly established general liberty and independence."[1] Even at the time he wrote these words, however, Jay's words reflected more a wish for than an accurate description of his country. In fact, the reason for writing *The Federalist Papers* in the first place was that national unity was so problematic. Due in part to the heroic efforts of Jay, Madison, and Hamilton, the Constitution was (just barely) ratified, but it would take a Civil War and the overcoming of entrenched sectional resistance after that, before anything like unity was achieved. Neither a common language nor the presumption of a common religion proved powerful enough in their own right to overcome American disunity.

This has not, however, stopped commentators from continuing to look to religion as a source of national identity. The latest inheritor of John Jay's position is the Harvard political scientist Samuel P. Huntington. In his recent book *Who Are We?*, Huntington claims to find a common Anglo-Protestant culture in the United States, one particularly marked by the dissenting or evangelical approach to Jesus. This, as I argue in my review of his book in

Foreign Affairs, is not an accurate picture of religion in the United States, either at the founding or at the present time.[2] At least two of our original religions were established rather than dissenting: Presbyterianism, once the state church of Scotland, and Episcopalianism, which was the American off-shoot of the Church of England. The Dutch, who are not Anglo (and who offered the Puritans a home before they came to the United States), were disproportionately strong in New York and New Jersey. Maryland was founded by Catholics; within one hundred years they would become the largest denomination in America. Rhode Island was settled by Baptists, many of whom were Anglo-Protestant dissenters, but the religion itself had its origins in the German Reformation.

As Huntington's choice of an example inadvertently shows, if we look to religion to find a force for unity, based on the premise that a society needs a common culture in order to flourish, American history does not offer it. We have had so many different cultural imperatives because we have had so many different religions. The fact that nearly all of them, at least until the second half of the nineteenth century, called themselves Protestant does not mean that they shared the same views about biblical authority, the role of the clergy, the place of women, the significance of race, the nature of the liturgy, or the necessity of mission. Northerners and Southerners who shared the same religion went to war against each other. Urban and rural differences persisted despite belief in the same God. Long before we were a religiously diverse nation we were a politically and economically divided one. Indeed, if one compares the era of the Civil War to the era of affirmative action, we were more divided when we shared a common faith than now when we no longer do.

True, in the past most Americans shared at least the two testaments of the Hebrew and Christian Bible; the inability of faith to serve as a force for unity is even more noticeable now that we have so many religions and sacred texts flourishing in the United States.[3] Just to offer one illustration of our diversity, an organization formed in 1927 to promote interreligious cooperation was called the National Conference of Christians and Jews. Formation of this organization was something of a daring act; before we started calling ourselves Judeo-Christian (that would only come about during World War II in response to Hitler's attacks on the Jews[4]), the founders of this group believed that the cause of inclusion would best be served by giving Jews equality with Christians in the name of their organization. In 1998, the NCCJ—in a move to keep at least the same initials—changed its name to the National Conference for Community and Justice. Its former title, once a symbol of inclusion, had become a mark of exclusion, for kept outside the range of the organization's name were Muslims and Buddhists, both of whom probably outnumber Jews in the U.S. population, as well as numerous other religions that arrived on these shores in response to the Immigration Act of 1965. So diverse is the state of American religion at this time that we no longer have a name capable of characterizing ourselves. After the passing of the term "Judeo-Christian," some have proposed "Abrahamic," for that would include Muslims. But even that term would not include many of the Asian religions and would therefore be obsolete the moment it was adopted.

It is common to speak about race as a divisive force in America, but the number of races is far smaller than the number of religions. And while it is difficult to find people who have no race, there are people who have no religion. Because nonbelievers are a significant and perhaps growing percentage of the American population, even if we were to find a way of unifying all our diverse believers, those who do not believe would still be left out. There are, in fact, reasons to believe that the conflict between religion and nonreligion is far more divisive in American life than the conflict between religions; conservative Catholics, Protestants, and Jews are more likely to find a common enemy in secular humanism than they are to struggle with each other over fine points of theology.[5] Our first culture war—the battle over public schools in cities like Boston or the battles over admissions to Ivy League universities—were fought between religions. Our current culture, as in the Pledge of Allegiance case, is being fought between believers and nonbelievers. Whether from within or without, in short, religion has a way of polarizing people that makes one wonder whether unity can ever be possible the moment God comes into the picture.

RELIGION IN THEORY VERSUS PRACTICE

Despite this history of division, however, there is one way in which religion can serve as a force for unity in American society. A widespread gap exists between religion as it is supposed to exist in theory and religion as it actually exists in practice. Much of the discussion about religion has concerned the former. But in recent years sociologists, especially those trained in ethnographic methods, have been examining in detail what religion actually means to believers in the course of their worship.[6] The focus on practice, or, as it is frequently called, "lived religion," tends to demonstrate how similar people of faith are, even when the religions in which they believe are very different.

Take, to begin, the term "belief" itself. Beliefs have been at the core of religion's history of strife and conflict. Religious creeds have traditionally been efforts to codify the truths that define one religion, and that make it distinct from others. The sociological reality of many religions combined with an epistemological assumption of one exclusive truth for each of them is a formula for discord. For if my truth is, so to speak, true, another's is, by definition, false, and if religion is central to the salvation of the soul, as many believe it is, then my obligation is to do whatever is in my power to persuade another of his or her false understandings. Religion would hardly be worth dying for, let alone requiring considerable investments of time and money, if its truth claims were not taken seriously.

Yet Americans tend to become a bit uncomfortable around strong epistemological claims. As I demonstrated in my book *One Nation, After All*, there is a strong current of nonjudgmentalism in the attitudes and opinions of ordinary Americans.[7] It is not just that Americans are averse to conflict, although, in general, they are. It is also that they are quite aware of the history of religious sectarianism and do not want to see it repeated. Catholics, for example, generally know that their faith has been defined as that of the one true church. They, or at least many of them, would insist, moreover, that their religion is true. But they tend to draw the line at suggesting that it is the only true church, with the corresponding conclusion that people who hold to another faith adhere to false beliefs. "For me and for my children and my family, it's the one true church," as one believer put it. "But to God, I don't think it is the one true church. . . . I really believe that the God that I think is out there isn't really going to care that the Episcopalians do things one way and Catholics do it another."[8] This is not an attitude, needless to say, exclusive to Catholicism. A study of reform Jews found that many of them worry about believing in a God who is "too Jewish," for the notion of a commanding and distant figure is not what attracts them to their religion in the first place.[9] And the much-noticed rise of evangelical and fundamentalist forms of Protestantism is not only a move from liberalism to conservatism but is often a move from denomination to nondenomination. Conservative Protestants often look with suspicion at doctrinal differences in favor of a personal relationship with Jesus that transcends

considerations of creed; indeed, the largest evangelical Protestant denomination, the Baptists, consider themselves anti-creedal, as if formal confessions
of the faith are too Catholic for Baptist sensibilities.

The presence of nonjudgmentalism among religious believers has religious
origins; many of those I have interviewed cite scripture as their authority for
judging not. But nonjudgmentalism also has a secular dimension; it is one
of those legacies of the 1960s that seems to have engulfed the entire culture
and not just flower children and anti-war protestors. Like grade inflation or
social promotion, nonjudgmentalism reflects an unwillingness to be cruel, a
sense that society may have gone too far in stigmatizing people whose differences from the rest of society may not represent moral failings but are
reflective of the fact that people come with different abilities—and different
beliefs. Even though religious nonjudgmentalism comes closer to laissez-faire
indifference than pure liberal tolerance—"I won't judge you if you don't
judge me" is the way the ideal is usually expressed—it does contrast sharply
with a period in which religious believers fought, sometimes to the point of
violence, over creed. What unifies Americans, in short, is not specific beliefs
but the belief that specific beliefs should not divide us. This is not a robust
form of communitarianism; it focuses on what we should not do rather than
on what we share. But it does provide more for unity than for division and
in that sense possesses some communitarian benefits.

THE RISE OF GENERIC TRADITIONALISM

Much the same is true of another dimension of religious practice: tradition.
Religion and tradition are so closely intertwined that the two terms become
synonymous. No wonder, then, that those who find religion a source of
conflict discover the same result when tradition is an issue. An example is
offered by the political commentator Michael Barone, who wrote of the 2000
election that "the single greatest divide in American politics is that the Bush
coalition consists of people who are religious and respect traditional morality
while the Gore coalition consists of people who are not traditionally religious
and favor a more relativistic morality."[10] In the Red States/Blue States meta-
phor of American politics, it is an accepted fact that half of the country
believes in the importance of tradition while the other half is modern or
even, these days, postmodern.

Not only are Americans divided over tradition, we are frequently told,
they are also divided among them. Barone's formulation, for example, would

include among the traditionalists people whose actual traditions vary greatly, Orthodox Jews and pre–Vatican II Catholics can both call themselves traditionalists, but their respective traditions include considerable distrust of each other. What we now call traditional Catholics were once convinced that the Jews killed Christ and evangelical Protestants, despite their lack of interest in creeds, were typically united in viewing Catholics as the anti-Christ. The more we evoke tradition, it would seem, the more divided we will be.

Yet Americans evoke tradition in ways that do not always fit the role that tradition is expected to play. Tradition in American life has qualities much like ethnicity in American life. As sociologists study the dynamics of ethnicity, they often find that while Italians, Poles, or Chinese speak with great pride about their customs, they speak in very similar ways about closeness of family, the importance of food, or clothing, music, and other distinguishing rituals. As sociologist Mary Waters has observed, it is as if there is a generic form of ethnicity into which all specific ethnicities can fit; what matters is that you are ethnic, not which ethnicity you are.[11]

As generic ethnicity exists in the social sphere, generic traditionalism exists in the religious sphere, as the anthropologist Melinda Bollar Wagner has pointed out.[12] Obviously, religions have different traditions and honor them in different ways; Jews consider tradition more important than belief, which evangelical Protestants do not, and the traditions honored by Jews are different from those honored by Christians. But one thing unites all religious traditionalists in America: they are striving to hold onto the old in a society that worships the new. The constant process of adjusting traditions to fit new realities unifies them even as their specific traditions divide them.

Numerous examples of this generic traditionalism exist in American life. One of the most interesting concerned the reaction to the movie *The Passion of the Christ*. Although the film relied on historical sources that had anti-Semitic overtones, a number of conservative Jews praised the film because it evoked a sense of religious traditionalism. In a similar way, evangelicals— who not only have had a history of anti-Catholicism but who also typically do not identify with Jesus suffering in favor of Jesus the redeemer—flocked to an explicitly Catholic treatment of the Passion for the same reason. In America we welcome tradition even if we tend to gloss over the details of the traditions we welcome.

An even more striking example of generic traditionalism is offered by the experience of Muslims and Jews in America. Jews constitute a majority in Israel and Muslims are a majority in Saudi Arabia or Pakistan, but in the

United States, both are minority religions. No minority religion can experience tradition the way it can when it is in the majority; so long as both Islam and Judaism exist in a primarily Christian society, their respective religious laws can never become the secular law. Minority status gives both religions something in common. Despite the fact that Jews and Muslims kill each other in the Middle East, in the United States they both face the question of how to interpret their dietary laws, deal with feminism, send their children to school, and contemplate the possibility of intermarriage.[13] When Muslims decide that in the absence of a halal butcher it is appropriate to opt for a kosher one instead, American culture has made its mark on religious traditionalism.

TO PROSELYTIZE OR NOT?

No aspect of religion is more conducive to disunity than the fact that some religions consider it a duty of faith to spread the word to others. Proselytizing has been the core of many of the U.S. Supreme Court decisions dealing with religious conflict, since those who are the object of another religion's efforts to convert them nearly always view such efforts as invasions of their privacy or violations of their own religious freedom.[14] Aware of the dangers posed to unity by aggressive efforts at evangelization, the U.S. Supreme Court has tried to define various tests that distinguish between the freedom of a religion to advocate its beliefs and the rights of religious minorities. The most famous of such tests is the one that says that public funds should be denied to those faiths that are "pervasively sectarian."[15]

It is certainly true that evangelical Protestants in particular insist on the importance of witnessing their faith; in the evangelical world, the term "Christian" is often used to indicate another evangelical, not a Catholic or mainline Protestant, and when evangelicals are in the majority, say in small towns in Texas, their public manifestations of their faith can seem offensive to other Christians, Jews, Muslims, and nonbelievers. For this reason, witnessing the faith can hardly be considered a force for communal unity. Yet it may also be the case that witnessing is not as disunifying as commonly believed. To understand why, it is important to consider the acute dilemma in which evangelicals find themselves in the United States. If they reject the culture in favor of a fundamentalist purity, few will be converted. On the other hand, if they want to spread the word effectively, they have to join, rather than marginalize themselves from, the culture around them. Most evangelicals take the second path. Because they do, evangelicalism is a growing faith but it is not the sectarian faith it once was, since, in adapting to the culture, evangelicalism will inevitably be shaped by it. It is difficult, in fact, to be sectarian in American life since sects tend to die out and what flourishes typically becomes inclusive.

Although the literature on social capital and the literature on evangelization are rarely related to each other, the much-lamented tendency of Americans to "bowl alone" also has had a significant impact on the way Christians spread the message of the gospel. Ensconced in exurban developments with few spaces for public interaction, afraid of knocking on doors for fear of crime, harassed by the demands of dual-income families and over-scheduled children, Americans who bring Jesus into their lives often seek creative methods of witnessing their faith. One of the most popular has been called "lifestyle evangelism" by the sociologist Joseph Tamney.[16] The idea is to live as best you can according to your religious principles, for if you do, the theory goes, you will glow as a result and others will notice you and ask you about it, offering you a nonconfrontational and friendly way to share your convictions. Compared to "cold calling" methods of evangelizing such as knocking on doors or handing out pamphlets, methods that generally do not work in any case,[17] lifestyle evangelism constitutes a sharp break with the conflictual history of Christian proselytizing. And since Americans share lifestyles even as they adhere to different religions, lifestyle evangelism becomes one more force downplaying divisiveness in favor of unity.

At the same time as evangelicals bend their practices to meet the expectations of American culture, nonevangelicals develop a personal relationship with the deity that overlaps with the way evangelicals typically approach their faith. Especially since Vatican II, American Catholicism, forced to compete with evangelical churches for members, has relied less on an authoritative clergy and more on emphasizing a close and personal God to keep the faith.[18] Even Jews, as one study of moderately affiliated modern Jews discovered, want a more personal relationship with God.[19] American religions engage in less conflict with each other at least in part because they are becoming more like each other, as each finds ways to respond to a widespread desire among believers for a faith that speaks to their needs. Paradoxically, the one thing Americans have in common is their individualism, and it is to such individualism that most religions find themselves appealing.

SIN AND SECULARIZATION

One final example can be used to illustrate the proposition that religion in practice tends to be more unifying than religion in theory: sin. Religion typically acts in good Durkheimian fashion as a form of the collective conscience, insisting that some forms of behavior, especially those of an antisocial nature, ought to be prohibited because they violate God's moral teachings. Yet while the main Abrahamic religions emphasize the ubiquity of sin and the need to seek redemption, they all do so in different ways. Catholics have tended to emphasize the power of reconciliation more than some Protestant sects, while Jews (and Muslims) have typically been more legalistic in their approach to sin. No wonder, then, that in a multireligious society there have been multiple sins, as well as a variety of paths to salvation. Under such circumstances, religiously pluralistic societies lack common agreement on the behaviors to be prohibited as sinful, and societies that commit to the separation of church and state cannot make what religion deems as sinful automatically illegal under civil codes.

In practice, however, religions of all kinds in the United States have increasingly adopted therapeutic methods and psychological language when dealing with the problem of sin.[20] Sin is more likely to be viewed as behavior that harms the self rather than as conduct that violates the collective conscience. Focused on the bottom line of church growth, clergy are reluctant to insist on the ubiquity of sin for fear of turning off potential congregants in a highly competitive market for souls. Upbeat language tends to be more popular among churchgoers of all faiths than dark and brooding views of human nature.[21] Critics frequently point out the shallowness of a therapeutic faith; one conservative Protestant views trends like these as the triumph of the "culture of narcissism" in the religious community.[22] And indeed there is much truth in the charge. The best-selling books in Christian bookstores are not those that explicate the Bible but those that offer religious approaches to dieting, personal problem solving, and even business success.[23]

As problematic as narcissism may be for traditional religious teachings, however, it is a force for unity in the culture. Unlike strict religious approaches to sin, therapeutic ones emphasize the problems that all people have in common and seek solutions that cut across the denominations and creeds that characterize a religiously pluralistic society. Although psychology focuses on individual selves, the self is something that all Americans can understand, whatever their religious upbringing and current convictions. In a way not fully appreciated by those who proclaim the existence of a culture war in the United States, the new rules that Daniel Yankelovich sees coming out of the 1960s and 1970s have influenced everyone in America, not just adherents to the counterculture, but religious believers, including conservative ones, as well.[24]

For all of religion's history of sectarianism and division, culture is generally a force for unity. This is as true for American culture as it is for any other society's common beliefs and practices; our culture may not be as deep as some others, but it is widespread, appealing, and inclusive. American culture influences just about all of America's institutions and practices, from entertainment and sports to education. No wonder, then, that it influences religion as well, and in turn, religion will shape itself to the culture. Whether or not this is good for religion, it is good for America, for it gives all believers, whatever the specifics of their faith, the common language, symbols, and identities with which to overcome some of their differences.

BEYOND THE DIVIDE OVER FAITH

Religion has been at the core of the culture war that has engaged so many pundits and politicians since the *Roe v. Wade* abortion decision in 1973. Some of the issues involved in the culture war, such as affirmative action, do not have an explicitly religious basis. But nearly all of the others do, from abortion itself, which lives on in controversies over late-term procedures and overseas family planning policy, to debates over the Pledge of Allegiance and faith-based initiatives. Especially with the election of George W. Bush in 2000 and again in 2004, religion has been especially prominent in American public debate. Two highly publicized decisions have focused attention on the potentially divisive role of religion: stem cell research and gay marriage. President Bush, clearly determined to appeal to his core voters in the religious right, has taken positions on both of these issues, reflecting a strategy which holds that mobilizing the base can be more important than appealing to the center.

This persistence of religious-based issues that divide Americans into camps comes as no surprise to many on both sides of the faith divide. Those such as Susan Jacoby view religion's entry into politics as hostile to civil liberty and equality; for her, the Bush administration's policies confirm her conviction that believers are intolerant and unwilling to accord respect to their adversaries.[25] On the other side of the spectrum, defenders of the faithful frequently admire religious people for their uncompromising stands; they do not make good liberal citizens, an admirable quality from this point of view, because they believe in prophecy more than in politics.[26]

Yet a funny thing has happened to the role of religion in the culture just at the point when, in theory, Americans ought to be most divided from each other. None of the wedge issues involving religion seem to be dividing Americans as much as they were expected to.

This is especially the case with stem cell research. No doubt to the shock and surprise of President Bush, former First Lady Nancy Reagan has taken a very public position in favor of using stem cells to help find cures for diseases such as the one that afflicted her husband, even if such cells may originate from human embryos. And she is not the only conservative advocating such a position. Senator Orin Hatch of Utah has said that being pro-life includes attempts to prevent human suffering and to extend life where possible and ethical. Across the spectrum, the idea of human cloning has almost no supporters. But the notion of using therapeutic cloning as potential cures for dreadful diseases has united more than divided those Americans who pay attention to this issue. As an issue in the culture war, stem cell research is a nonstarter.

Gay marriage is an even more interesting test case of the ability of religion to serve as a force for disunity. If one went out searching for an issue that would expose divisions over faith, gay marriage would appear to be the choice. For devout evangelicals and Catholics, homosexuality is a sin that should, in the view of some, be punished or, at the very least, not be explicitly sanctioned. Conservative clergy will cite homosexuality as a cause for the breakdown of traditional family values and will find support for this view in scripture. For some religious conservatives, gay marriage is, as a political issue, almost too good to be true, since the state that legalized it, Massachusetts, was the home of both the 2004 Democratic convention and and John F. Kerry, who ran against President Bush in 2004. As with abortion and race, gay marriage ought to be a way of uniting the conservative base of the Republican Party while dividing the Democrats.

Yet gay marriage never turned out to be quite the divisive issue that many had predicted. True, the issue was on the ballot in eleven states in 2004 and in all cases, voters expressed hostility to gay rights. In addition, the presence of the initiative on the Ohio ballot may have helped swing that state, and therefore the electoral college, in the direction of the Republicans. Still, despite initial exit polling demonstrating the importance of "moral values," later analysis proved that the major reason for the Republican victory in 2004 had more to do with foreign policy—President Bush was perceived as a strong leader in the war against terrorism—than they did with religious issues per se.[27] A surprising number of conservative intellectuals argued on behalf of gay marriage, pointing out that since homosexuality is real and unlikely ever to disappear, conservatives ought to want to see gay people in strong relationships and not as promiscuous free floaters.[28] Although the clergy of mainline and liberal Protestant churches were divided over the issue, other clergy were the ones officiating at gay marriages once they became legal. The issue, in short, turned out to be gray more than it was black and white, and as a result, neither party rushed to take advantage of it; even President Bush endorsed a constitutional amendment to ban gay marriage late and then did not make it a central issue in his campaign.

After their victory in 2004, Republicans also tried to use the case of Terri Schiavo, a brain-damaged woman kept alive by a feeding tube, as an effort to rally religious voters to their cause, but even more than gay marriage, this failed to ignite divisions in the country and even seemed to backfire on the Republicans. The failure of religious divisions to emerge on issues such as these may have something to do with the difference between religion in theory and religion in practice that I have tried to address in this chapter. In theory, homosexuality is a sin, and life is sacred. In practice, it is difficult for even the most devout believers to watch gay people engaged in a marriage ceremony and not come away at least a bit moved, just as it is not that hard to identify with the difficulty of dealing with people in Terri Schiavo's condition. In theory, marriage is traditionally defined as permanent union between a man and a woman. In practice, there are so many varieties of heterosexual marriage—second marriages, childless marriages, step-children, artificially conceived children—that adding one more nontraditional form of marriage does not seem so big a deal. In theory, homosexuality violates scripture. In practice, religion is a powerful force for the satisfaction of needs, including the need for companionship and security. In theory, life is sacred and to be protected at all costs. In reality, being kept alive by a feeding tube is not a life most people recognize. In their religious lives as in their secular lives, Americans tend to be more experimental and pragmatic than ideological, and as uncomfortable as gay marriage makes many Americans, they can also respond to the idea that if it works, perhaps it ought to be tried.

Only time will tell whether differences over such issues as gay marriage will become as polarizing as divisions over abortion were for a previous generation of Americans. But given that young people tend to be more sympathetic to gay marriage than older Americans, there are grounds for believing that this issue will not lead to a replay of the backlash against *Roe v. Wade*. If so, then gay marriage, the issue that in theory was supposed to have kept the culture war alive, will instead become the last battle in the struggle, for if Americans are not to be all divided over this religious-based issue, it is hard to imagine any other playing the same role.

None of the analysis in this chapter should be taken to suggest that we can now count on religion to be a source of unity for otherwise divided societies; the history of religious sectarianism, as well as the ongoing conflict between believers and nonbelievers, is not about to die out anytime soon. Nor has the point of my analysis been to suggest that either conflicts over faith or among them have easy solutions; we can expect that U.S. Supreme Court litigation over these kinds of issues will continue unabated. The more religions there are in the United States, including various forms of spirituality that reject organized faiths as well as people who insist that they are not religious at all, the more we can expect suspicion and hostility from all sides in these never-ending controversies.

At the same time, however, religion is not the permanent force, the rock of ages, it is sometimes said to be. As Catholics know after Vatican II, as Jews experience when they intermarry, as Protestants discover when they attend a new megachurch, and as Muslims find out when they move to London or Detroit, religion is a dynamic force constantly adapting itself to new situations. There is no reason why such a process of adaptation cannot include the building of bridges between believers as they discover that, whatever their differences in doctrine and tradition, they are practicing their faiths in remarkably similar ways.

NOTES

1. *Federalist* 2.
2. Samuel P. Huntington, *Who Are We?: The Cultural Core of American National Identity* (New York: Simon and Schuster, 2004); Alan Wolfe, "Native Son," *Foreign Affairs* 83, no. 3 (May/June 2004): 120–125.
3. For accounts of American religious diversity, see Diana Eck, *A New Religious America: How a "Christian Country" Has Now Become the World's Most Religiously Diverse Nation* (San Francisco: Harper, 2001); and Peter H. Schuck, *Diversity in America: Keeping Government at a Safe Distance* (Cambridge, MA: Harvard University Press, 2003).

4. Mark Silk, *Spiritual Politics: Religion and America Since World War II* (New York: Simon and Schuster, 1988).

5. Robert Wuthnow, *The Restructuring of American Religion: Society and Faith Since World War II* (Princeton, NJ: Princeton University Press, 1988).

6. Efforts to offer overviews of this approach can be found in David D. Hall, ed., *Lived Religion in America: Toward a History of Practice* (Princeton, NJ: Princeton University Press, 1997); and Colleen MacDannell, ed., *Religions of the United States in Practice*, 2 vols. (Princeton, NJ: Princeton University Press, 2001).

7. Alan Wolfe, *One Nation, After All: What Middle Class Americans Think about God, Country, Family, Poverty, Work, Immigration, the Right, the Left, and Each Other* (New York: Viking/Penguin, 1998).

8. Cited in Dean R. Hoge, William D. Dinges, Mary Johnson, and Juan L. Gonzales, *Young American Catholics: Religion in the Culture of Choice* (Notre Dame, IN: University of Notre Dame Press, 2001): 223–224.

9. Steven M. Cohen and Arnold M. Eisen, *The Jew Within: Self, Family, and Community in America* (Bloomington: Indiana University Press, 2000): 155.

10. Cited in Adrian Wooldridge, "As Labor Lost Ideology, U. S. Parties Found It," *New York Times* (July 22, 2001), D4.

11. Mary C. Waters, *Ethnic Options: Choosing Identities in America* (Berkeley: University of California Press, 1990).

12. Melinda Bollar Wagner, "Generic Conservative Christianity: The Demise of Denominationalism in Christian Schools," *Journal for the Scientific Study of Religion* 36 (1997): 13–24.

13. For examples of how this works, see Etan Diamond, *And I Will Dwell in Their Midst: Orthodox Jews in Suburbia* (Chapel Hill: University of North Carolina Press, 2000); and Elise Goldwasser, "Economic Security and Muslim Identity: A Study of the Muslim Community in Durham, North Carolina," in Yvonne Yazbeck Haddad and John L. Esposito, eds., *Muslims on the Americanization Path?* (New York: Oxford University Press, 2000).

14. For helpful overviews of the issues involved, see John Witte, Jr., *Religion and the American Constitutional Experiment: Essential Rights and Liberties* (Boulder, CO: Westview, 2000).

15. *Hunt v. McNair*, 413 U.S. 734 (1973). See also Stephen V. Monsma, "The 'Pervasively Sectarian' Standard in Theory and Practice," *Notre Dame Journal of Law, Ethics, and Public Policy* 13 (1999): 321–340.

16. Joseph Tamney, *The Resilience of Conservative Religion: The Case of Popular, Conservative, Protestant Congregations* (New York: Cambridge University Press, 2002).

17. Rodney Stark and Roger Finke, *Acts of Faith: Exploring the Human Side of Religion* (Berkeley: University of California Press, 2000): 135.

18. See, for example, Bernard J. Lee, SM, with William V. D'Antonio, *The Catholic Experience of Small Christian Communities* (New York: Paulist Press, 2000).

19. Cohen and Eisen, *The Jew Within*.

20. James Davison Hunter, *The Death of Character: Moral Education in an Age Without Good or Evil* (New York: Basic Books, 2000).

21. Marsha Witten, *All Is Forgiven: The Secular Message in American Protestantism* (Princeton, NJ: Princeton University Press, 1993).
22. Marva J. Dawn, *Reaching Out Without Dumbing Down: A Theology of Worship for the Turn-of-the-Century Culture* (Grand Rapids, MI: Eerdmans, 1995).
23. See, for example, Michelle Mary Lelwica, *Starving for Salvation: The Spiritual Dimensions of Eating Problems among American Girls and Women* (New York: Oxford University Press, 1999); and R. Marie Griffith, *Born Again Bodies: Flesh and Spirit in American Christianity* (Berkeley: University of California Press, 2004).
24. Daniel Yankelovich, *New Rules: Searching for Self-Fulfillment in a World Turned Upside Down* (New York: Random House, 1981).
25. Susan Jacoby, *Freethinkers: A History of American Secularism* (New York: Metropolitan Books, 2004).
26. See, for example, Stanley Hauerwas and William Willimon, *Resident Aliens: A Provocative Christian Assessment of Culture and Ministry for People Who Know that Something Is Wrong* (Nashville, TN: Abington Press, 1989).
27. D. Sunshine Hillygus and Todd G. Shields, "Moral Issues and Voter Decision Making in the 2004 Presidential Election," *PS: Political Science and Politics* 37 (April 2005): 201.
28. See Jonathan Rauch, *Gay Marriage: Why It's Good for Gays, Good for Straights, and Good for America* (New York: Times Books, 2004).

Chapter 6 Diversity, Community, and Government

Peter H. Schuck

American society has always been diverse—regardless of how one defines or measures diversity. This remarkable heterogeneity dates from the very beginnings of the republic. Historian Jon Butler has documented the strikingly ethnically varied nature of American colonial society as early as the late seventeenth century.[1] Jill Lepore notes that the proportion of non-English speakers in the United States was actually greater in 1790 than in the highly diverse society of 1990.[2] Language being a good proxy for culture, it is evident that we were from the outset, and are today, a polyglot society, a nation of nations.

What have we made of this diversity? What meanings have we taken from it? What will we make of it in the future?

Political scientist Rogers Smith, among others, shows that ethno-racial diversity has engendered social anxiety and bitter conflict in American life. The struggle for toleration, Smith finds, has been episodic, hard-fought, hard-won, and punctuated by backlash movements driven by animus, ideology, and interests seeking to sustain social hierarchy and prevent integration. Historically, American communities have defined themselves, at least in part, by the particular groups they have chosen to exclude.[3]

History provides little reason to expect these communal animosities to have morphed into a tolerant, inclusive, cohesive society. Throughout history, after all, relatively few instances of successful social integration of ethno-racial diversities can be found. Today, almost all diverse nation-states, including many liberal democracies, are at serious risk of fracturing into ethnic shards. (Australia and Switzerland are notable exceptions.) Even strong unitary states like the United Kingdom, Spain, France, and China are roiled by militant demands for devolution or even full independence for some minorities or regions. In such a world, the ability of the United States to achieve political stability and unity while preserving and even enhancing its economic, social, religious, and cultural vitality strikes many of us as a great puzzle. One might even call it a kind of miracle.

Still, explanation is possible. Conceding the elusiveness of causality in such matters, we can identify certain institutional, cultural, and legal factors that help to account for this singular achievement. In a recent book, *Diversity in America*, I closely analyzed the "diversity of diversity" in America, exploring its many meanings, its recent prominence not just as an observable social fact but also as an affirmative social ideal, the normative conflicts it generates, and the social consequences of trying to deal with it through different formal and informal techniques.[4] In various ways and in many policy contexts, government has attempted to import, assimilate, define, certify, subsidize, mandate, protect, or exploit—in a word, *manage*—diversity. "Manage" is a serviceable term for this self-conscious policy approach to diversity, so long as we understand that manage includes not only decisions to subject diversity to active legal intervention, but also decisions to leave diversity to the informal governance of unregulated choices by individuals and groups.

This last observation is especially important because although government has developed a repertoire of legal and policy techniques, most diversity management in the United States is not conducted by government. Compared to other nations, we look more to the fragmented, integrative processes of civil society than to programmatic initiatives launched from the center. These low-level, informal processes are easy to miss, however, unless one looks carefully for them (as sociologists do). Consider some ubiquitous examples of these processes. Members of different ethno-racial groups intermarry, blending their traditions. Immigrants learn English, and their children do so rapidly—especially if the schools do not mire them in native language ghettos. Daily interactions in schools, workplaces, churches, and other cultural entrepôts mute ethnic differences. Religious communities energetically recruit new members to share their beliefs and practices. Mass media and commercial advertising disseminate a steady stream of common cultural symbols. Popular sports and music become foci for allegiances and interests that transcend group boundaries. Private institutions, serviced by a growing army of "diversity consultants," engage in self-conscious efforts to understand and mediate cultural conflicts. Neighbors trade experiences and interpretations of events. People form nonprofit organizations to pursue a breathtaking variety of communal goals.

America's largely hands-off approach to managing diversity is consistent with its laissez-faire orientation toward numerous other arenas of potential social conflict, arenas that in other societies elicit active governmental intervention. Whereas Israel, for example, manages almost every aspect of immigrants' integration (language, housing, job training and placement, income support, social clubs, religious affiliation, and much more), nonrefugee immigrants to the United States are largely on their own except for public schooling. Much the same is true, *mutatis mutandis*, of religious institutions, political parties, mass media, the working poor, the elderly, health care, education, and most other markets for services that are publicly provided or highly regulated elsewhere. In this respect, diversity management, like so much else, is part of an American public philosophy that emphasizes disparate values and private responsibilities.

If diversity were simply an instrumental value, we would be relatively indifferent to its origins. Our interest would only be in how effectively it produces the ultimate end for which we deploy it. But while diversity is instrumental to other ends, it also possesses an independent normative and expressive character that cannot be reduced to its instrumental value. This helps explain why a well-meaning judge who contrives ethno-racial diversity by manipulating jury selection is deemed to have violated the Constitution, and why a housing complex suffers the same fate by engaging in a supposedly diversity-friendly effort to avoid racial tipping by limiting the number of black tenants in the complex. In short, the value to people of any program designed to increase diversity depends on its perceived genuineness and lack of legal contrivance. This in turn depends on where it came from, how it came about, and the process that produced it. One may refer to this as diversity's provenance.

Americans evidently care a great deal about the provenance of their most identity-salient diversities: race, ethnicity, religion, viewpoint, language, and politics. Residential communities, for example, react differently to a legally imposed integration (by race or income level) than to one that is otherwise similar but freely chosen. In the protracted Mount Laurel and Yonkers litigations over the class and racial composition of these communities, much of the opposition occurred because those diversities were mandated and lacked the only provenance—ability to pay—that middle- and upper-class Americans regard as a legitimate basis for admission to their communities.

A similar analysis applies to ethno-racial preferences in higher education, although there the admissions criteria are varied and less clear-cut. Academic achievement or promise (however measured) is the credential that most strongly legitimates admission, but it is not the only one. Many academics, administrators, and members of the public view race, ethnicity, athletics, parentage, and some other nonacademic factors as morally relevant to admission. Many others in the academic community and elsewhere stigmatize members of preferred groups who do not earn admission through academic achievement or promise. Even some beneficiaries of ethno-racial preferences endorse this latter perspective. Again, diversity is not self-authenticating. Its value ultimately depends on its provenance.

CREATING VERSUS PROTECTING DIVERSITY

Because reactions to efforts to manage diversity depend to a considerable extent on their provenance, diversity value is a far more fragile thing than lawmakers often seem to suppose. The crude regulatory resources and techniques at law's disposal are more likely to asphyxiate diversity value than to invigorate it. It matters a great deal, then, precisely how government conceives of and implements diversity management. Some efforts meant to increase diversity value may succeed; others may debase or even destroy it. Whether a particular public law will increase or reduce diversity value is always an open question.

Let us distinguish among different ways in which government and the law approach diversity. Immigration law literally imports diversities that persist even as the process of assimilation transforms them in complex ways. The First Amendment protects an extraordinarily diverse mélange of beliefs and activities of religious, political, and other minorities, even including flag burning and hate speech. Sometimes government seeks not simply to protect an existing diversity but also to create or promote a new one. These are two very different enterprises.

If government wishes to promote a particular diversity, it must define, measure, and certify it as one deserving special legal recognition and support, and must make determinations about provenance and authenticity that it is poorly equipped to make. The Bureau of Indian Affairs, for example, decides which groups to recognize as tribes for purposes of various federal benefits, with the most valuable benefit today being tribal eligibility to establish potentially lucrative gambling casinos. These incentives have embroiled the Bureau, tribes, and individuals in high-stakes disputes over who is and is not an Indian and which groups of Indians constitute tribes. These disputes are sometimes resolved in highly politicized, even corrupt ways. The recent decennial census reveals how official definitions, measurements, and certifications of ethno-racial groups can reify and (at least for a time) ossify anachronistic categories, distort behavioral incentives, and politicize identities that should be matters of private, unsubsidized choice. The way the census handled the Indian, black, and Hispanic groupings is particularly problematic. The fact that the census was conducted with great professionalism only confirms that these distortions are systemic, not incompetent.

Having defined, measured, and certified a certain kind of diversity for promotion, government may then either subsidize or mandate it—particularly if it is a kind that the relevant community is otherwise inclined to resist. My detailed analysis of court-ordered integration of residential neighborhoods across class lines, and of mandated bilingual education for cultural maintenance purposes, demonstrates that many of these efforts have not merely been ineffective but have had perverse results.

Although law has many strengths, the power to create the values and experiences we associate with genuine diversity is not one of them. To Americans, law is no longer (if it ever was) a mystical emanation from a majestic sovereign. Instead, we regard it as a technocratic tool of social control to be assessed according to more mundane criteria: consent, efficiency, fairness, and effectiveness. To be sure, law that is democratically legitimated carries moral force, but its ubiquity and instrumentalism have demystified it. Familiarity with certain forms of coercive law has bred disenchantment, if not contempt. We no longer stand in awe of such law; we are disenthralled. Even when wrapping itself in the mantle of constitutional principle, coercive law has failed (though certainly not for want of trying) to legitimate race-based affirmative action, integrate middle-class suburbs, and educate limited-English children. The inability of coercive law to create diversity value—as distinct from its success in protecting existing diversity value from suppression—seems part of a larger, more endemic limitation. Robert Fogel suggests that the law successfully redistributed material gains in the past but has less purchase on the spiritual values that today's Americans increasingly seek. His insight, I think, also applies to diversity value.[5]

These limitations suggest a paradox about diversity and law. The harder the law tries to create or promote diversity, the more law magnifies and highlights its own weaknesses and reveals the diversity that it fashions as inauthentic, illegitimate, and disvalued. When the federal judge increased the legal pressure on Yonkers to place low-income people in middle- and upper-income neighborhoods, he succeeded only in ratcheting up the city's defiance. Like a man caught in quicksand, his remedial flailing simply worsened his predicament. The more he brandished the law to quell the city's defiance, the more he risked discrediting both the law and the diversity it demanded. Resisters in Yonkers sought to personify the law and hence demystify it by depicting the judge's orders as *his* law imposing *his* diversity. The judge, for his part, naturally saw the mandated diversity as nothing more than *the* law's just remedy for past wrongdoing. His claim of authority was perfectly correct as a legal matter, and as a legal matter the city eventually had to capitulate. As a practical matter, however, the city's compliance was—and remains—as slow, grudging, and incomplete as it could manage. Far from vindicating either law or diversity in Yonkers, public esteem for both probably declined.

This paradox about diversity and law is also evident, albeit far less dramatically, in other diversity-mandating efforts. In hopes of rescuing affirmative action from the grim reality of sharp differentials in group academic performance, the University of California has repeatedly resorted to new manipulations and dissimulations that inevitably sow cynicism about law and about the diversity ideal. The same is true, *mutatis mutandis*, when government retards the assimilation and education of immigrants by mandating particular forms of bilingual education. The authenticity and value of the cultural affinity government seeks to enhance, however, require a provenance of unregulated, unmediated, self-motivated efforts by families and communities. Indeed, an earnest government defeating its own best efforts is the cruelest paradox of all.

In truth, government and law are natural enemies of new diversity programs. This has nothing to do with motives or incentives and has everything to do with the nature of law, government, and diversity.

Why is it so much harder for government to promote new diversities than to protect old ones? I have already discussed one largely structural reason: the tight link between diversity's value and its provenance; we care about where the diversity comes from and whether the process that produced it comports with deeply held norms about morally just deserts and instrumental appropriateness. We value diversity that seems to reflect human spontaneity, personality, and achievement (for example, performance-based selection of students and workers, cultural maintenance managed by immigrant families) more highly than diversity that government designs, manufactures, certifies, and mandates (for example, choosing students by skin color, or using public schools to maintain immigrant children's Spanish when their parents want them to learn English quickly). Genuine diversity value is a product of an opaque, complex, dynamic, mysterious realm of human meaning and identity that we call culture. Where generating diversity value is the goal, law is seriously disabled. This disability, moreover, cannot be readily overcome or accommodated. We can only hope to understand its sources and minimize its worst effects.

GOVERNMENT'S LEGITIMATE ROLE

Government, I have argued, should use its bully pulpit to praise diversity in general and even particular diversities, as President Bush did shortly after September 11, when he exhorted Americans to treat Muslims with respect. But it should not try to create or promote any particular kind of diversity. This is not a proper public function in a society committed to liberal and democratic values. Moreover, law is a singularly poor instrument for performing that function.

This does not mean, however, that government has no role to play in protecting diversity or indeed in promoting it as a worthy social ideal; far from it. Government is indispensable to the protection of existing and emerging diversities from suppression, and it can open the channels through which new diversities may be born. Indeed, *only* government can protect groups whose beliefs and practices differ from those of a dominant group that wants to use the law to impose its own cultural norms on others. I do not mean, of course, that all majority actions of this kind are impermissible; most of them are perfectly appropriate in a democracy. Rather, I simply want to underscore the conventional constitutional rule that such impositions must meet a higher-than-usual standard of justification where they are regulating ethno-racial, religious, political, or associational diversities.

Government's management of diversity, then, should take two general forms. First, it should protect existing diversities against invidious discrimination. Second, it should clear a path for the emergence of other, privately generated diversities (most of which it will be unable to predict) by challenging various forms of monopoly power. I shall discuss each of these in turn, highlighting the role of enhanced choice.

Antidiscrimination. The normatively compelling distinction between nondiscrimination and affirmative action is fundamental, even though the two are frequently discussed as if they were the same. In a society strongly dedicated to genuine equal opportunity, the law must assure individuals that they will not be denied it on the basis of attributes used historically to stigmatize, subordinate, or otherwise disadvantage the group. This means creating a system of antidiscrimination remedies such as the Civil Rights Act of 1964 and the Americans with Disabilities Act of 1990, and ensuring their effective enforcement. The goal of antidiscrimination law is justice conceived of as equal opportunity for individuals. Although employers and others who comply with antidiscrimination law may well end up with more demographic diversity than otherwise, this is beside the central point which is justice, not diversity. (By definition, the law often reduces diversity in another sense, as when it prevents employers or others from using certain screening criteria, a reduction that is sometimes necessary to prevent discrimination on the basis of group characteristics.)

In contrast, affirmative action—at least in its more robust, preferential forms—promotes many new injustices in the name of remedying an old one. It does so by favoring one ethno-racial group over others either for historical reasons that may no longer be relevant as applied to most of the potential beneficiaries (that is, immigrants who comprise about 75 percent of the eligibles), or for diversity reasons that government, as I explained above, cannot effectively or legitimately mandate. And it does so at a time when rapid demographic changes in American society make the system of preferences increasingly difficult to administer justly or even rationally. The Supreme Court has acknowledged this fact by permitting trial courts to mandate affirmative action only when they can narrowly tailor it to remedy specific acts of past discrimination, but the Court bars its use as a remedy for past societal discrimination of a more diffuse sort.

If we truly value diversity, however, we must impose some further limits on the scope of the nondiscrimination norm. Antidiscrimination law was originally intended to protect blacks and other minorities who are most vulnerable to majority oppression and who are guaranteed protection against exclusion and subordination on the basis of group membership under the Equal Protection Clause of the Fourteenth Amendment. More recently, antidiscrimination remedies have been extended to many groups, such as parents, that do not and should not receive the same level of constitutional protection. This may be because the group (for example, parents or women) can more adequately protect itself in the political process and in the market, or it may be because forcing others to transact with the group (for example, homosexuals, families with small children, Medicaid recipients, the obese, members of motorcycle gangs) would violate people's principles, identities, or interests in freely choosing their own associations. The nondiscrimination norm is very powerful and widely embraced in American society, as it certainly should be. But so is the norm favoring group autonomy in the enjoyment and promotion of the group's common values, a norm implied by the religious exemption and other statutory limitations on the scope of antidiscrimination laws.

This norm is also explicit in recent Supreme Court decisions recognizing individual and group rights of "expressive association." These rights should be extended, for example, to allow experimentation with single-sex schools, which reflect a plausible educational theory designed to address an urgent social problem and advance equal opportunity. The government's role, however, is not to promote such schools but only to eliminate discriminatory rules that unfairly inhibit them. The Supreme Court has only begun to flesh out the nature and scope of the expressive association right as it probes the constitutional boundaries between a group's power to define and express its members' values through association of like-minded people who choose to exclude others, and an excluded individual's claim under antidiscrimination law to equal treatment.

This task presents a difficult judicial challenge. The contours of a group's expressive association right will likely depend on factors such as the characteristic on which the exclusion is based, the effect of that characteristic on the group's values, coherence, and identity, the clarity and consistency of the group's identity, and the kind of evidence required to establish these facts. Developing distinctive identities in association with others will often require the exclusion of individuals who the group believes, rightly or wrongly, possess different traits, viewpoints, or interests. These exclusions may cause pain to some of the excluded and may also offend many in the general public, as the Boy Scouts' exclusion of avowed homosexuals evidently does. But if valuing diversity in a liberal society means anything, it means assuring people's freedom to form exclusive groups that embrace unpopular beliefs and to act on those beliefs in ways permitted by the Constitution and without undue interference by the law. Within those very broad limits, a diversity-friendly law must protect not only those values that the majority favors, but also those that it abhors.

The law should define rights of expressive association broadly enough to give individuals the breathing space they need to join with others in private groups that they think can affirm and sustain their values, meanings, and solidarities. In a liberal society, these norms will often be different from (though not necessarily inconsistent with) those enforced or proposed by the state. A liberal law must protect people's right to maintain these differences between their own norms and those norms preferred by the majority. Helping them to preserve these normative differences is one way for the law to counter the state's tendency to try to monopolize norms in an increasingly diverse America. I now turn to other ways.

Antimonopoly. The principle that the law should prevent public and private entities from exercising monopoly power over others is not really debatable—although precisely how this should be done certainly is. In the economic domain, this principle motivates antitrust law, which is a charter for economic diversity (or at least for efficient levels of it) in the interest of consumers. The government, of course, is an important enforcer of antitrust law. In the political domain, a similar principle animates the Free Speech Clause of the First Amendment, which bars the state from using public power to impose its views on the citizenry, to prefer some groups over others, or to stifle speech and viewpoint diversity.

Indeed, a robust First Amendment is the most powerful legal instrument for protecting many other kinds of diversity. The government, usually a defendant in First Amendment cases, should do much more than refrain from violating the Amendment. It should also act affirmatively to vindicate the Amendment's antimonopoly principle. For example, government could diversify campaign finance by giving citizens more control over the allocation of campaign dollars. It could ensure that when it speaks, it speaks in diversity-friendly ways—even when the Constitution does not require it to do so, as when it sponsors public art from diverse sources or funds legal services for diverse constituencies. It could begin planning a phase-out—or at least an appropriate disclaimer—of ethno-racial census statistics and categories, whose growing artificiality, crudeness, inaccuracy, and capacity to mislead are already distorting public policy discourse. Government can also nourish institutions and practices in which diverse visions of the good can meet, compete, and interact—sometimes in the "public square," sometimes in private ones—at a subconstitutional level and in ways that the First Amendment permits but does not necessarily require. Perhaps most important, government should indulge a strong, though rebuttable, presumption favoring decentralized decision making in both the polity and the market, and it should support educational systems that prepare young people for the different ways in which they can comprehend and live in a world far more diverse and dynamic than that inhabited by their parents.

Government can use the law to challenge monopoly power—especially its own. It can empower diversity by enhancing choice. Choice can empower diversity, and enhance enforcement of the nondiscrimination principle, by allowing individuals to self-identify as they wish, rather than having government impute to them racial or other identifiers that they may reject. Parents should have more say about the linguistic education of their limited-English children. So-called diversity visas should be auctioned to qualifying worker-bidders. Private expressive associations that seek to restrict their staff or membership in order to strengthen their common identity should be allowed, as religious groups are, to do so without violating antidiscrimination law. Housing integration should be promoted by giving discrimination victims and other target groups vouchers for rent and other mobility services. Religious practices that do not violate a compelling public interest should be accommodated. People who receive social service subsidies should have equal access to faith-based organization providers. Parents of children in failing public schools should receive vouchers that can help them to choose better schools. All of these proposals have a common feature and goal—to increase the meaningful, autonomous choice for people who now enjoy little choice because the government preempts or monopolizes it.

DECENTRALIZING CHOICE

More than members of any other society, Americans recognize that, absent market failure or other overriding reasons for government choice, social welfare is maximized by having resource allocation decisions made by the affected individuals and firms, not by government. In the liberal tradition, moreover, the normative value of choice is even more important than its economic efficiency. Choice is the means to liberalism's ultimate end, autonomous freedom, whose exercise almost inevitably generates diversity.

The fact that Americans venerate individual choice is evident in numerous public debates—over abortion, smoking, gun control, and school vouchers, for example—where competing interests jockey for the political advantage of justifying their causes in choice rhetoric. But an equally important and less obvious point is that a society that relies on decentralized choice gains an incalculable value—political conflict reduction—that goes well beyond the efficiency and autonomy values enjoyed by those who exercise it. This muting of political conflict is essential to the survival of a polity as diverse and competitive as twenty-first-century America.

In the United States, many institutional arrangements are designed for this purpose. Federalism and a decentralized party system manage much political conflict by channeling it to the states and localities rather than elevating it to the federal level where it would be magnified by the higher stakes in a single national solution. Judiciaries at all levels resolve litigation, much of it political in nature, in a fragmented, low-visibility fashion. Juries, used far more widely in the United States than anywhere else, diffuse and conceal—through their local and independent character, notably ad hoc form, Delphic opacity, and the subjective nature of many legal rules they apply—responsibility for what are often political decisions. The separation of powers also distributes responsibility for political decisions, though it does encourage interbranch conflicts. Many activities that in other countries are matters for political decision are privatized in the United States; they are governed more by contract law and markets than by public law and politics. The private sector itself is also relatively decentralized; small firms account for much of our economic activity, nonprofit groups proliferate, religions are organizationally and often liturgically decentralized, and laws mandating information disclosure help to facilitate and educate private choice.

The decentralization of choice to private individuals and groups and to lower-level governments, then, is a vital element of America's approach to conflict reduction. When politicians cannot agree on a uniform decision rule to resolve a controversial issue, they often leave it to be decided by the concerned individuals or groups, using phrases like "freedom of choice" and "local option" to describe and dignify their deference. The growing diversity, complexity, and competitiveness of American society make it more urgent to extend this conflict-reducing technique (as well as to find others).

For this reason, I propose a number of programmatic devices designed to move the loci of choice from politicians, bureaucrats, and judges to individuals and private groups, thereby reducing political conflict and empowering diversity. These include: full First Amendment protection for private expressive groups with exclusionary membership policies; promotion of cultural maintenance by families, not government; means-tested vouchers for housing, schools, bilingual education, and other publicly funded benefits; broader accommodation of deviant religious practices; greater use of the voluntary choice factor in analyzing church–state disputes; and elimination of mandatory affirmative action (except in the narrow remedial usage now authorized by the courts).

Expanded choice can also be used to diffuse other kinds of disputes. Consider the bitter conflicts that rage in numerous communities over school curricula, particularly over whether to teach Darwinism, creationism, "intelligent design," or some other (pseudo-)scientific creed. Like most educational policy issues, this one is resolved by local school boards, which obviates the need for a national consensus, but does engender a large number of local conflicts producing some dubious decisions. The ferocity of these conflicts, in many cases, is due to the monopolistic nature of the existing public school systems in these communities. This monopoly raises the stakes by mandating a single, one-size-fits-all curriculum.

In principle, a public school system does not require this monistic solution. It could allow different schools in the system to teach in different ways. Charter schools sometimes enjoy this freedom. In practice, however, political and bureaucratic factors almost always dictate a uniform, system-wide curriculum. By relaxing its monopoly over the curriculum and giving low-income families financially viable choices among schools offering different curricula, and other controversial features, government could defuse many such conflicts. Subsidized choice could have much the same effect on conflicts over public housing, public transportation, and many other public services that government now provides in relatively monolithic form on a take-it-or-leave-it basis to those whose poverty limits them to the public system.

I am not suggesting that enhanced choice is equally compelling in all policy domains. Officials must always weigh the value of a national, uniform, or mandatory rule against the value of a decentralized, variable, or permissive rule—or of no rule at all, leaving the matter entirely to individual choice. The advantages of diversifying school curricula, for example, must be balanced against the desire to equip all students for a common democratic American citizenship. Spillover effects are common in complex, interdependent societies and often can be regulated effectively only through a mandatory rule preempting local or individual choices.

In contrast, there is little or no social value in uniformity of some public goods and services; indeed, in these cases, diverse responses to the different needs and desires of different individuals and groups are very desirable. Even when government decides to regulate private conduct through a mandatory rule, as it often does, it should authorize exceptions to the rule where such exceptions will not defeat the rule's underlying policy. More generally, government should not demand uniformity and limit choice beyond what a suitably refined, targeted policy requires. This principle is neither anodyne nor tautological. Taken seriously, it would condemn or alter an immense body of public law.

In urging government to facilitate diversity by deferring more to private (and lower-level governmental) choice, I do not mean to fetishize either diversity or choice. Diversity is not always an unalloyed virtue; it also imposes costs that may be severe. Choice, for its part, only merits its elevated normative status in the liberal tradition when it is sufficiently voluntary and informed to vindicate individual dignity and autonomy. (I say "sufficiently" because choices are almost always constrained and based on imperfect knowledge, so voluntariness and information are inevitably matters of degree.) And although more choice is generally desirable, there can be too much of a good thing. (Mae West famously retorted that "too much of a good thing is wonderful.") Too many choices, empirical evidence suggests, may increase anxiety, not just decision costs. Moreover, certain of the choices opened up by new technologies may create grave moral and political dilemmas, as the debates over cloning, late-term abortion, surrogate motherhood, and many other issues suggest. But while we should always bear in mind these "dark sides" of more choice, they have little or no relevance to the kinds of enhanced choice that I have proposed here.

CONCLUSION

The diversity ideal is still in its infancy, and all of us are responsible for guiding it to maturity and beyond. Like all abstract conceptions, the diversity ideal will be rudely buffeted by the brute experiences of actually living with it. Indeed, as *Diversity in America* (2003) shows, particular versions of that ideal have already generated strong resistance that should chasten anyone who embraces those versions and should humble any others who want government to pursue different ones. Yet these failures have not much tarnished the luster of the ideal itself; it retains a powerful, compelling allure.

Much in American culture demands and nourishes diversity, even as we grope to understand what it means, how much it costs, whether law can effectively manage it, and whether and when other social processes, if any, might do it better. We have only begun to ask these immensely difficult questions. We can take some comfort from the conviction that no other society in history has been better equipped to answer them than twenty-first-century America.

NOTES

1. Jon Butler, *Becoming America: The Revolution before 1776* (Cambridge, MA: Harvard University Press, 2000).
2. Jill Lepore, *A Is for American: Letters and Other Characters in the Newly United States* (New York: Alfred A. Knopf, 2002).
3. Rogers M. Smith, *Civic Ideals: Conflicting Visions of Citizenship in U.S. History* (New Haven, CT: Yale University Press, 1997).
4. Peter H. Schuck, *Diversity in America: Keeping Government at a Safe Distance* (Cambridge, MA: Harvard University Press, 2003).
5. Robert W. Fogel, *The Fourth Great Awakening and the Future of Egalitarianism* (Chicago: University of Chicago Press, 2000).

Chapter 7 Immigration and Social Disorder

Peter Skerry

I wish someone would tell us how the hell we're supposed to act here!
—*Immigrant Leader in Addison, Illinois*

If there is one thing that social scientists have learned since the 1960s and then succeeded in passing on to the wider society, it is the importance of the mundane, informal relations of daily life for the healthy functioning of our neighborhoods and institutions. Back in 1961, when urban planners were still buoyed by a professional hubris sustained by the arrogant abstractions of postwar modernism, Jane Jacobs wrote: "The first thing to understand is that the public peace . . . of cities is not kept primarily by the police, necessary as police are. It is kept primarily by an intricate, almost unconscious, network of voluntary controls and standards among the people themselves, and enforced by the people themselves. . . . No amount of police can enforce civilization where the normal, casual enforcement of it has broken down."[1]

Twenty years later James Q. Wilson and George Kelling were teaching the same lesson through the example of "broken windows."

More than thirty years later, Robert Putnam sparked a similar national discussion, this time focused on "social capital." In advanced societies the informal, the nonprofessional, and the unofficial are continually being subverted by our commitments to individual rights and bureaucratic accountability; hence, the apparent need to dedicate and rededicate ourselves to the value of what James C. Scott calls "the microsociology of public order."

In *Seeing Like a State*, Scott reminds us that "the establishment and maintenance of social order in large cities are, as we have increasingly learned, fragile achievements."[2] This fragility is in part traceable to the nonverbal nature of much of the interaction that defines and sustains the social fabric. Close observers of urban neighborhoods, like Gerald Sutttles, certainly make this point. So does criminologist Mark H. Moore: "Producing community security depends on having or creating some combination of *shared understandings* about acceptable behavior [emphasis added]."[3]

Such arrangements—what Jane Jacobs refers to as "eyes on the street"—are also fragile because of their instrumental nature. As sociologist Robert Sampson reminds us, neighborhoods today are not—if they ever were—"urban villages" held together by intense bonds of ethnic solidarity, psychological support, or deep friendship. They are based instead on relationships between neighbors and acquaintances who typically do not know each other well but who rely on one another to sustain norms of civility that result in public goods like trust and safety. In Morris Janowitz's phrase, contemporary neighborhoods are "communities of limited liability."

Sampson also emphasizes that such neighborhoods depend vitally on stability. Political scientist Wesley Skogan makes a similar point in *Disorder and Decline: Crime and the Spiral of Decay in American Neighborhoods*, where he reports that "high turnover," particularly in poor neighborhoods, leads to high levels of disorder that undermine the informal relationships that sustain social order. Such findings led Sampson to call for community development policies "that are sensitive to the potentially disruptive forces of neighborhood instability induced by unchecked development."[4]

IMMIGRATION AND THE SOCIAL FABRIC

Professor Sampson does not elaborate on what he means by "unchecked development." But such language typically refers to real estate development, urban renewal, and the like. Yet there is one source of unchecked development contributing to substantial instability in American cities that is almost never mentioned: immigration. Just ask any public school teacher or principal who must deal with the continual comings and goings of immigrant children, or any priest or church administrator trying to keep track of parishioners who pledge to tithe to the congregation. There is certainly reason to believe that the current influx of immigrants is putting serious strains on the social fabric of our cities.

Yet these social-order effects of immigration have been widely overlooked. There are several reasons why. The countless casual interactions between neighbors and acquaintances that occur on sidewalks and other public places are, according to Jane Jacobs, "ostensibly utterly trivial"—though she immediately adds that "the sum is not trivial at all." Such impacts are also difficult to quantify, which has been particularly relevant in a policy area so dominated by economists. And as John Higham, dean of American immigration historians, has emphasized about his own work on nativism, there is a tendency for analysts to focus on the economic sources of opposition to immigration.

Then, too, the debate over immigration has been locked into a compelling, but misleading framework that distinguishes sharply between legal and illegal immigration. Immigrant advocates have resisted this dichotomy and rejected the stigmatization of what they refer to as "undocumented immigrants." But since the undeniable public anxiety voiced by passage of California's Proposition 187 in 1994, it has been all but impossible to resist the prevailing paradigm—which assigns all negative outcomes associated with immigration to illegal immigrants, and all benign or positive outcomes to legal immigrants. This formulation may provide cover to politicians and policymakers, but it drastically distorts reality. Certainly, the social-order effects of immigration do not easily fit into this neat legal-illegal dichotomy.

Finally, there is one other reason why these effects have been overlooked and ignored. And this brings us back to "broken windows" and the issue of crime. During the 1960s and 1970s, many analysts and commentators avoided addressing rising crime rates and fears about crime expressed by large numbers of ordinary Americans. At the time it was felt that acknowledging such complaints would be pandering to bigotry and racism and fuel dangerous reaction.

So, too, today many are reluctant to acknowledge any negative effects of immigration. Among the most reluctant are our elites, who happen to benefit from this huge influx of unskilled labor and are at the same time able to insulate themselves from many of its burdens. As one recently minted Berkeley Ph.D. once challenged me, "How can you talk about the social strains associated with immigration without playing into the hands of right-wing conservatives?" However well-meaning or appealing, such thinking has resulted in policies that ignore the fears and anxieties of millions of Americans about the largest wave of immigration in our history. Unacknowledged and dismissed, such sentiments fester and develop into disaffection, even rage. This is—or at least should be—the lesson of Proposition 187, which sought to deny virtually all public services to illegal immigrants in California. A bad idea whose time had come, Prop 187 was approved by an overwhelming majority in 1994, but was eventually gutted by the federal courts. It appealed to so many Californians because up to that point, no public official would address the growing concerns of ordinary citizens about immigration.

Today, our policymakers and politicians have yet to apply to immigration what we have as a society learned about crime—that the fears and anxieties of ordinary Americans, however poorly expressed or not readily confirmed by available statistics, are not prudently ignored or rejected as irrational paranoia or bigotry. More precisely, we have learned that fears about social disorder are just as important, if not more so, than fears about officially designated crime. Similarly, we must now be attentive to popular fears and anxieties about immigration—legal as well as illegal.

The alternative is more contentious, polarizing battles like that over Proposition 187, or Proposition 227 (curtailing bilingual education in California). Such outbursts help advocacy groups—on all sides of the issue—fill their coffers. But permitting things to reach the boiling point hardly fosters an environment conducive to the making of policies beneficial to immigrants, or to Americans generally. And the fact is that the social-order effects of immigration that concern Americans—whether overcrowded housing, gang-ridden neighborhoods, or unsafe working conditions—are harmful to immigrants as well.

Now, the challenges of refocusing the immigration debate on such quality of life issues should not be underestimated. Not all social disorder among immigrants is attributable directly to them; much is the result of public policy. Nor should disorder be equated with crime; or immigrants stigmatized as criminals. Finally, focusing on the mundane social-order effects of immigration will be especially difficult in this post–September 11 period, in which immigration has been fatefully reframed through the lens of homeland security and terrorism.

IMMIGRATION, CRIME, AND DISORDER

To get behind official crime statistics and explore the differences between common crime and neighborhood disorder, Wesley Skogan and his associates surveyed almost 13,000 adults in forty urban residential neighborhoods across the United States. In ten of these neighborhoods they did field research and interviewed hundreds of residents, organization leaders, merchants, police officers, and local officials. The results were highly suggestive for anyone trying to understand contemporary sources of anxiety about immigration.

Asked to identify social as well as physical sources of disorder, urban residents mentioned, in rough order of frequency: public drinking, corner gangs, street harassment—especially of women and the elderly—drug use and sale, noisy neighbors, commercialized sex, vandalism, dilapidated and abandoned buildings, and trash. Skogan confirms that such signs of disorder are clearly associated with residents' anger, demoralization, and fear. He then emphasizes that "even though disorders are not in themselves life-threatening, fear may be a rational reaction to them."[5]

Strikingly, these and related signs of disorder are highly visible in immigrant neighborhoods and have surfaced as the focus of disputes and controversies between immigrants and nonimmigrants across the United States. In San Bernardino and Riverside counties in Southern California, problems associated with Mexican residents have included crowing roosters that wake up the neighbors. In Waukegan, Illinois, north of Chicago, city officials concerned about overcrowded housing in Mexican immigrant neighborhoods pleased some residents but angered others when fire code enforcement was beefed up. Other Chicago-area municipalities have had difficulties addressing parking problems in overcrowded immigrant neighborhoods. In Los Angeles there has been controversy over trash and health issues involving itinerant immigrant food vendors. In Santa Ana, California, the very urban county seat of very suburban Orange County, police have had to move decisively against enclaves of homeless immigrants living under freeway bridges and near heavily used bicycle paths. Throughout Southern California there have been acrimonious disputes over the noise and exhaust fumes from gasoline-powered leaf blowers used by Mexican immigrant gardeners.

The list could go on, and might also include concerns about high rates of pedestrian accidents in the immigrant neighborhoods of Santa Ana, or high accident rates for Hispanics working in construction in northern Carolina. And while there are multiple factors involved in each of these issues, none of these are serious crimes, but rather sources of disorder that never-theless prove bothersome or at times threatening to immigrant and non-immigrant residents.

While these issues often have an ethnic or even racial edge, they don't always. Graciela Diaz is a waitress at a Mexican restaurant in a giant Las Vegas hotel casino. A native of Jalisco, Mexico, who came to the United States illegally, she met her husband, Manuel, when they were both working in a Los Angeles sweatshop. Two years ago the Diazes bought a $125,000 house in a gated community ten miles north of downtown Las Vegas. Ex-plaining why they left their old neighborhood, Mr. Diaz recently told the *New York Times*: "People from Mexico—I call them *paesanos*—were burning tires. They played radios real loud. I was afraid of Cecilia (their daughter) playing outside, that someone would run her over. Here it's quiet and safe for her."

One issue that involves many of these concerns is day-laborer hiring sites. Go to a Home Depot some morning in almost any part of the United States, and you will find individuals congregating at the edge of the parking lot, waiting to sell their labor to passing homeowners and subcontractors. These *jornaleros* are almost always foreign-born males, overwhelmingly Latino, and usually undocumented. While their services are obviously in demand by some, their very presence frustrates and even frightens many others. While waiting to be hired, these men may drink, urinate in public, or make noises and gestures to women passing by. Sidewalks get littered. Fights and petty crime are often problems. Traffic is tied up, sometimes causing accidents. For their part, workers complain frequently of being cheated out of their wages. And police report that criminals, particularly drug dealers, lurk among day-laborers and ply their trade.

The real challenges arise when local authorities attempt to regulate these sites. The efforts of some municipalities to ban them outright have been successfully challenged in the courts by immigrant advocates. Other juris-dictions have sought to impose order on the incipient chaos by providing services to *jornaleros* and certifying their bona fides and skills to prospective employers. But such efforts are usually not successful, either because the workers are sufficiently independent and entrepreneurial that they are not interested, or because some residents regard such programs as condoning illegal immigration. Caught in these cross-currents, most public officials eventually back off.

THE CASE OF ADDISON

Another drama raising these issues has been developing for some years in the village of Addison, a suburb of Chicago, that came to a head in late 1990s. Addison is a blue-collar community about twenty-five miles west of downtown Chicago, not far from O'Hare Airport. In August 1997, the village found itself on the front page of the *New York Times*, where it was announced that this municipality of 32,000 residents was agreeing to one of the largest financial settlements in a federal housing discrimination suit, in which the Justice Department had charged village officials with bias against Latino immigrants.

Until after World War II, Addison was mostly farmland. But soon the village experienced an influx of the adult children of Italian, Polish, and Greek immigrants who had grown up in Chicago's urban neighborhoods and who were buying their first homes. The single-family houses in Addison, especially those involved in this controversy, were built in the 1950s and 1960s. They are typically small but solid structures, one-story brick houses capable of withstanding the harsh midwestern winters. Not coincidentally, many of Addison's homeowners work in the construction trades.

But not all of Addison's dwellings are single-family houses. Many are also small, square apartment buildings of the sort found throughout Chicago and its suburbs: two- and three-storey structures with a central entry and stairwell accommodating two to four apartments per floor. In Addison many such buildings were constructed during the 1960s in clusters near the village's main thoroughfare and its civic center. For ambiguous if not downright shady reasons, these apartments were afforded zoning waivers that allowed them to be built close together, with minimal off-street parking.

At first there were no particular problems, especially since the landlords screened prospective tenants, who were typically flight attendants working out of nearby O'Hare. But things soon began to deteriorate. Tenant screening grew lax or nonexistent. Poor whites took up residence, and by the early 1980s, Mexicans, mostly from the barrios of Chicago but soon also directly from Mexico, were moving in. They were—and continue to be—drawn to the area by abundant employment opportunities in nearby warehouses and light industries. As with most such migrations, the influx was at first mostly young, unattached men, intent on working long hours and amassing money to send home, where most planned to return. These "target earners" crowded into these one- and two-bedroom apartments to maximize their savings, sometimes sleeping in shifts.

But such commendable striving resulted not only in overcrowding, but in wear and tear on buildings, which absentee landlords never maintained very well—even when municipal authorities began serious enforcement of housing and sanitation codes. Even by the late 1990s, when the worst conditions had been addressed, these buildings were dilapidated, with tattered screens and shabby curtains billowing in the wind. A few windows were boarded up with plywood, while in some buildings the main entrance doors had been removed from their hinges.

Parking was an issue from the outset. Although Addison has long prohibited on-street overnight parking, an exception had been granted to these apartment buildings—allowing for higher-density occupancy. But immigrant overcrowding meant that cars were overwhelming the streets and whatever off-street parking that was available. Residents serviced their cars in the street, sometimes leaving old parts on the sidewalks or in the gutters. Abandoned cars were not uncommon. Safety issues arose about children playing around all those cars, hidden from passing drivers. Other concerns were raised about fire safety, especially in winter, when snowed-in cars hindered fire department access to the buildings.

Parking lots were soon covered with broken glass and litter. Shopping carts that had been used to transport groceries home from nearby supermarkets were strewn about, left to rust. Small plots that were once planted with grass became muddy rectangles, long since trampled by residents who would seek relief from the summer heat in overcrowded apartments by congregating outside—sitting in lawn chairs, barbecuing, drinking beer, and partying, often late into the evening. There were comings and goings around the clock, with cars announcing their arrival with honking horns.

Residents of nearby single-family homes were understandably unhappy— even more so when such socializing degenerated into public urination and drag races in the streets. Groups of young Mexicans hanging out at all hours of the day and night harassed neighborhood women who had long been used to walking by the apartments on their way to nearby shopping centers. Fruits and vegetables began disappearing from homeowners' gardens. And graffiti occasionally appeared on the brick facades of their neat houses.

Youth gangs and drug dealing were soon evident. There was violence and at least one shooting death—along with occasional bursts of gunfire, celebrating July 4, for example. As one longtime Addison homeowner, who lived a block from one group of apartments, observed: "It's like the housing projects"—which he and his wife had fled forty years before when they left the Chicago neighborhoods where their immigrant parents had raised them.

The response of Addison officials was not surprising. Police presence in and around the apartments was increased. There were also some initiatives with social programs for neighborhood youths. The police even organized soccer matches between the immigrants and themselves, and according to the chief, his men's defeat was the basis of renewed mutual respect between officers and the Mexicans. An on-street parking ban, consistent with the rest of Addison, was implemented despite criticism that it discriminated against immigrants.

But the most controversial measures were those intended to reduce population density by condemning and then razing several of the apartment buildings. Addison officials then proposed a business redevelopment plan that would have resulted in the rezoning and demolition of several more buildings—and of course, the relocation of many immigrants.

It was around this time, in the mid-1990s, that immigrant advocates joined forces with Chicago-area housing advocates—veterans of the open-housing battles of the civil rights era in what has been widely and correctly regarded as one of the most segregated metropolitan regions in the nation. Objections to Addison's policies became the basis of the federal housing discrimination suit mentioned above. That litigation resulted in the 1997 settlement committing the village of Addison to cease further demolition of apartments and to pull back on its redevelopment initiative. Addison officials also agreed to provide relocation expenses to displaced immigrant tenants and to establish social service programs and a community center for remaining immigrants.

Housing and immigration advocates charged that Addison officials and homeowners were motivated by bigotry. But alternative explanations are more plausible and fair-minded to all parties involved—though undoubtedly less likely to prevail in housing discrimination suits. My own field work and interviews in Addison indicate that prejudice or racism have little to do with what has been going on there. To be sure, there have been heated exchanges in which residents expressed exasperation with "not hearing English on the street." And it would be foolhardy to insist that there is no racism lurking among the working- and lower-middle-class homeowners of Addison. But it is worth pointing out that Latino homeowners and business operators in

Addison (of which there are a few) were among those concerned about the disorder at the apartments—though these Latino residents have felt cross-pressured and have been reluctant to express their concerns publicly.

More to the point, there were few, if any, incidents of hate speech or xenophobia throughout the controversy. The genuine anger expressed was directed—by homeowners and municipal officials alike—at the apartments' absentee landlords. There was little or no animosity toward immigrants generally, or Latinos or Mexicans specifically—though illegal immigrants were frequently denounced. I have examined controversies involving immigrants in communities across the nation and interviewed native-born "Anglo" Americans who *do* harbor negative and hostile sentiments toward newcomers. But I found none in Addison. Perhaps they were in evidence when tensions were at their peak in the mid-1990s, but I found no record of them. By the time I got there in 1998 and on subsequent visits, I certainly encountered nothing of the kind.

One possible explanation is that Addison's homeowners are themselves typically the sons and daughters of immigrants. To be sure, this might render them overly sensitive to the urban disorder many of them fled. But their immigrant origins might also afford Addison residents certain sympathies for the new Mexican immigrants. Such sentiments were certainly expressed both by homeowners and even municipal officials there—at least one of whom was an immigrant from India. As one homeowner, expressing his exasperation with accusations of racial discrimination, put it: "I'm not white. I'm Italian!" Finally, it is worth emphasizing that Addison is a blue-collar suburb whose residents have dealt with other forms of urban disorder and who are hardly preoccupied with maintaining some pristine, privileged suburban enclave.

Another dynamic—worries about job competition from immigrants—was not evident among the homeowners of Addison. Such reactions would confirm the expectations of many observers. Nevertheless, employment concerns have not surfaced in Addison. If anything, as small businessmen have engaged in the construction trades, many Addison residents are prone to regarding these immigrants as potential employees.

Nor for that matter have Addison homeowners been riled up primarily by declining property values. To be sure, housing prices have apparently been affected by these events. For families such as these, whose life savings are tied up in their homes, property values have always been an issue. But when longtime residents emphasize that young families with children are not moving in because the local schools have been overwhelmed by non-English-speaking children, their comments seem driven neither by racism nor pocketbook calculations. They are expressing anxieties about how the community where they raised their families is threatened.

Still another factor not relevant to events in Addison is the presence of illegal immigrants. To be sure, a good number of the immigrants drawn there and to metropolitan Chicago generally are illegals. And these disgruntled homeowners are, like most Americans, quick to disparage them. Yet the problems in Addison have had little to do with these immigrants being undocumented and more to do with being "target earners" focused on returning home with as much savings as possible, or with the disruptions to family life that immigrants have always had to cope with.

Finally, the problems in this and other such communities are rooted not so much in crime as in disorder. This is not exactly news to Addison homeowners. As one housewife who had raised two boys down the street from the apartments noted, "All we need here is some control." She then contrasted the situation in Addison with her own experience, raised by Polish immigrant parents in an apartment building near what later became the Cabrini-Green housing project. She noted how she and her friends would seldom risk stepping on the grassy plot in front of their building—not out of any deep sense of propriety, but out of fear that the resident janitor would scold them or perhaps speak to their parents.

This insight was echoed not only by municipal officials in Addison, but also by one of the Mexican immigrant leaders. Emphasizing how little his countrymen understand about American practices and expectations, this leader pointed out that many of them come from rural areas of Mexico and lack familiarity even with calling 911 in an emergency. Nor, at first, do they understand the seriousness of driving without a license, auto registration, or insurance—until they get caught. At one point acknowledging the validity of some of the complaints about the influx of immigrants into Addison, this person voiced the frustration expressed by other immigrants as well as those providing them services: "I wish someone would tell us how the hell we're supposed to act here!"

IMMIGRATION AND COMMUNITY POLICING

Wesley Skogan has written: "Insecurity is . . . generated by visible signs that no one is in charge or cares about what happens to the area." Skogan is commenting on neighborhood disorder and crime, but he might just as well be writing about immigration. His insight certainly helps explain why Americans are so uneasy with an immigration policy that allows unprecedented numbers of newcomers, illegal and legal, but does little to help orient or integrate them into our culture or institutions. The irony of course is that Addison and communities like it have stepped into this vacuum and attempted to take charge. They may or may not be up to the job. But they deserve better than simply being dismissed as racists.

Insights about the significance of apparently minor neighborhood disorders have of course led to innovative programs like community policing. It is then all the more relevant that research on the implementation of such programs consistently finds that they are not very successful in poor, minority neighborhoods, especially immigrant neighborhoods.

A young officer with the Santa Ana (California) police who patrols his territory on bicycle pointed out one problem. Because immigrants, especially illegal immigrants, typically carry no or false ID, it is difficult to issue them meaningful citations and summonses for minor, quality-of-life infractions like drinking in the park. After all, to do broken-windows-oriented policing you need to know the identity of the individuals you're dealing with.

But the more fundamental problem involves community policing's dependence on cooperative, proactive clients. Race and class immediately complicate this picture. So does diversity, which research reveals weakens the informal relationships and understandings on which community policing relies. All these factors of course come into play with immigrants. But so do others. Illegal immigrants are less likely to cooperate with public officials out of fear of detection and eventual deportation. Other problems arise even with legal immigrants, not the least of which are language barriers between them and the police. Many immigrants arrive with ingrained distrust of police and government authorities. Then, too, immigrants here as target earners are hardly preoccupied with putting down roots and developing community ties.

Let's look again at Santa Ana. It has a longtime commitment to community policing, and has been described by Jerome Skolnick and David Bayley as "the most innovative police organization in the U.S." Santa Ana also has a population that is about 80 percent Hispanic, most of whom are foreign-born. It is then worth listening when a veteran officer there, speaking bluntly but without malice, sums up the dilemma facing him and his colleagues: "How do you do community policing when there is no community?"

Indeed, Wesley Skogan's findings from Houston reveal that Latinos there were strikingly less involved with community policing programs than African Americans and whites. And in his evaluation of Chicago's community policing initiative, Skogan writes that despite some success with whites and blacks, "Hispanics did not benefit, though, and it appears that they did not even get the message." At the end of his exhaustive study, Skogan concludes: "One of the biggest challenges to community policing in Chicago will be to find ways to involve the Hispanic community in it . . . at almost every point, we found that Hispanics were left out of CAPS [the Chicago program]."[6]

Such findings are particularly sobering in light of what we have seen in Addison, for they suggest that one of law enforcement's most promising tools to address urban disorder—community policing—will have limited applicability precisely where disorder is particularly troublesome. And this means that the disorder in immigrant-impacted communities like Addison may well get worse before it gets better.

To be fair, not all disorder in immigrant neighborhoods originates from within. Some comes from outside. As Addison underscores, public policies like urban renewal and business improvement districts displace people. The immigrants living in the buildings demolished in Addison certainly had to go somewhere and probably moved in with friends and relatives, thereby resulting in overcrowding somewhere else.

Another example are the neighborhood sweeps that federal immigration officials have long relied on (though less so in recent years) to apprehend large numbers of illegal aliens. However efficient such methods may be, they are highly disruptive, if not terrifying, undertakings that engender distrust and paranoia among immigrants. In other words, they undermine the social order and communal norms that do exist in these neighborhoods.

To note this is not necessarily to argue against such policies. It is, however, to highlight one of their consequences. But neither is it meant to assign blame to immigrants. The fact is that immigrants, especially poor, uneducated immigrants with limited English, are highly vulnerable, particularly in this tough, competitive society. We Americans, waxing poetic about our immigrant history, are prone to forget this. In this, we are like a football coach who is suddenly horrified when the rookie quarterback he sent into the game without adequate training comes out injured. In any event, their obvious vulnerabilities are one reason why immigrants are invariably—and not unfairly—associated by many Americans with social disorder.

MOVING AWAY FROM DISORDER

So many Americans can and do vote with their feet and flee heavily immigrant-impacted communities. This has certainly occurred in California. And it has happened in Addison, where disgruntled homeowners have picked up and moved away—evidently farther out from the city. The non-Hispanic population of Addison—both as an absolute number and as a percentage—certainly declined between 1990 and 2000, while the Hispanic population mushroomed.

Now, this is a familiar pattern. Geographic mobility coupled with high levels of economic growth has long distinguished us from the nations of Europe and undoubtedly helps explain our relative success in dealing with the strains of mass immigration. As historian Robert Wiebe has put it: "What held Americans together was their ability to live apart."[7]

Yet in the contemporary context, this geographic mobility translates into urban sprawl, one of the costs of victories such as that in Addison that open-housing advocates rarely acknowledge. And like any safety valve, this delays the reckoning that must eventually take place. Without gainsaying the value of "exit" in defusing tensions, this is one reason politicians are able to avoid dealing with immigration. This in turn results in a boom-and-bust policy cycle whose polarizing swings have not led to sound decisions.

Many of the signs of disorder examined here can easily be dismissed as minor—as "nothing serious," as one Chicago resident characterized the nightly gauntlet of comments that she and other women put up with from drunks hanging out at the subway stop near their home. But such incidents have cumulative effects that result in anxiety, anger, avoidance, and eventually exit. Policymakers, elected officials, and ordinary citizens ignore such behaviors at their peril.

Yet the terrorist attacks of September 11, 2001, have clearly made it more difficult for officials to focus on reducing such relatively minor incivilities. The urgency of fighting terrorism has crowded local crime off the policy agenda. With serious crime rates rising but still low in terms of our recent history, the necessary political pressure to put crime back on the agenda may not be there. The social strains and disorder examined here are likely to fare even less well. Indeed, the Bush administration has already made deep cuts in federal programs for local law enforcement, and now federal funds for community policing initiatives are on the block.

But there may be an even more fundamental divide here. Since September

11, there have been enormous efforts among political and policy elites to draw a sharp line between immigrants and terrorists. We have been reminded over and over that "most immigrants are not terrorists." The logic of this perspective was carried to its extreme, not surprisingly, by the *Wall Street Journal* editorial page, commenting on the federal government's failed suit against Tyson Foods for procuring illegal immigrant workers: "We are consoled that Justice lost this case, which should never have been pursued. The government's resources are limited. Time and money spent chasing Mexicans out of chicken plants is better spent tracking people who enter the country to do us harm." Meanwhile, from within the mammoth new department of homeland security, concerns are voiced that immigration enforcement is getting neglected.

If these indeed are the choices facing us, then clearly we must focus on terrorism. But immigration and the social-order effects examined here will not disappear. When these strains resurface, elected officials and policymakers will almost certainly try to avoid dealing with them. But sooner or later we will as a society have to confront this intractable issue.

NOTES

1. Jane Jacobs, *The Death and Life of Great American Cities* (New York: Vintage, 1961): 31–32.
2. James C. Scott, *Seeing Like a State* (New Haven, CT: Yale University Press, 1998): 134.
3. Mark H. Moore, "Security and Economic Development," in Ronald F. Ferguson and William T. Dickens, eds., *Urban Problems and Community Development* (Washington, DC: The Brookings Institution, 1999): 306.
4. Robert J. Sampson, "What 'Community' Supplies," in Ferguson and Dickens, *Urban Problems and Community Development*, 271.
5. Wesley G. Skogan, *Disorder and Decline: Crime and the Spiral of Decay in American Neighborhoods* (Berkeley: University of California Press, 1990): 49.
6. Wesley G. Skogan and Susan M. Hartnett, *Community Policing, Chicago Style* (Chicago: University of Chicago Press, 1997): 245.
7. Robert H. Wiebe, *The Segmented Society: An Introduction to the Meaning of America* (New York: Oxford, 1975): 46.

Part Four **Security and Liberty**

Chapter 8 Fighting the War on Terrorism

Francis Fukuyama

In the wake of the September 11 terrorist attacks, the United States embarked on a "war on terrorism" that within eighteen months unseated two regimes halfway across the world. The war to remove the Taliban regime and oust Al Qaeda from Afghanistan was broadly supported around the world, but the war to topple Saddam Hussein in Iraq was highly controversial and made America's role in the world one of the chief issues in global politics. The unilateral manner in which the latter intervention was undertaken set off a huge backlash, particularly in the Middle East and among America's European allies. Some contested the legitimacy of the U.S. action, others the judgment of American officials.

The underlying terrorist problem will now have to be dealt with in the broader context of an effort to rebuild relationships that were fractured by the Iraq war. America's hard power is unquestioned, but much of the world questions the legitimacy of the use of that power. Recalibrating the balance between power and legitimacy will be an important task for the United States in the second term of the Bush administration. It is clear that neither the existing structure of international institutions nor the unilateral exercise of U.S. power will be adequate to deal effectively and legitimately with the kinds of security threats that now exist. Global order requires a different approach to the exercise of American power, as well as new institutions. But the architecture of these institutions will be complex and their possibility dependent on active sponsorship by the existing large players in the international system.

THE NATURE OF THE THREAT

The "war on terrorism" was from the start a misnomer, and it has proven to be a misleading way of characterizing the problem facing the United States in the wake of the September 11 attacks. As Daniel Pipes, among others, has pointed out, terrorism is simply a means to an end; declaring a war on terrorism makes no more sense than declaring a war on submarines. The United States was led to this curious way of defining its national project out of a certain kind of political correctness.

The real threat that the United States faces is not from terrorism generically, but from radical Islamism and the rapidly morphing Al Qaeda organization—a phenomenon that mixes political extremism with religious themes and has been variously labeled Islamic fundamentalism, Islamo-fascism, and the like. America's problem was that it could not publicly label the enemy with any phrase that contained the word "Islam" without this being misinterpreted in the Muslim world as being anti-Islamic. "Terrorism" thus became a circumlocution that was meant to stand for radical Islamism. But the use of this term muddied U.S. strategic thinking about who America's real friends and enemies were, leading the Bush administration to argue that it had common cause with other regimes facing terrorist threats, like Russia (fighting Chechen separatists) and China (fighting Uighur nationalists in Xinjiang). The United States in fact faces little threat from most terrorist organizations, whether the Irish Republican Army or the Tamil Tigers in Sri Lanka or Hizbollah and Hamas in Gaza and the West Bank.

Neither terrorism, radical Islamism, nor weapons of mass destruction are new phenomena; all had existed as significant international issues from well before the end of the Cold War. What was genuinely new after September 11 was the perception, particularly in the United States, that all three were likely to be combined into a single deadly package that could inflict massive damage on otherwise powerful and wealthy nation-states that had previously been immune to large-scale homeland attack. Although the possibility of terrorism using weapons of mass destruction (WMD) had been much speculated on by security specialists in prior decades, most criminal and terrorist organizations of prior decades would not have had the motivation to use WMD to inflict mass casualties in the nihilistic manner of the World Trade Center attacks. This perception changed dramatically after September 11. The fact that Islamist suicide bombers could deliberately kill nearly 3,000 Americans and bring down a major landmark convinced people, not unreasonably, that if these groups had had access to biological or nuclear weapons, they would not have hesitated to use them.

The possibility that a relatively small and weak nonstate organization could inflict catastrophic damage is something new in international relations and poses an unprecedented security challenge. In all prior historical periods the ability to inflict serious damage to a society lay only within the purview of states. The entire edifice of international relations theory is built around the presumption that nation-states are the only significant players in world politics. If catastrophic destruction can be inflicted by nonstate actors, then many of the concepts that have informed security policy over the past two centuries—balance of power, deterrence, containment, and the like—have lost their relevance. Deterrence theory in particular depends on the deployer of any form of WMD having a return address, and with it equities that could be threatened in retaliation.

The degree to which the world in fact faces a real and ongoing threat of Islamist terrorists using WMD is subject to debate. Indeed, following the 2001 attacks a large gulf in perceptions between Americans and Europeans arose over this issue. Many Americans were convinced that such catastrophic terrorism was both imminent and likely, and that September 11 marked just the beginning of an upward trend in violence. Europeans more often tended to assimilate the September 11 attacks to their own experience with terrorism from groups like the Irish Republican Army or the Basque ETA, regarding it as a lucky, one-off event, an outlier in a phenomenon more commonly marked by car bombs or assassinations. It is not possible to know which of these two views is correct at this point.

THE NATIONAL SECURITY STRATEGY OF THE UNITED STATES

The United States responded to this new security environment through a doctrinal adjustment that was then implemented in its invasion of Saddam

Hussein's Iraq. The doctrine was laid out in *The National Security Strategy of the United States* promulgated in September 2002.[1] All administrations are required to produce doctrinal statements of this sort; most are routine, tedious, and pass into history largely unnoticed. This was not the case with the Bush administration's text.[2]

The National Security Strategy document is, on the surface, unexceptional. It repeats many of the standard goals of American foreign policy such as the promotion of free democratic governments around the world and a global system of free trade. Its most notable innovation was to take note of the simple fact outlined above, namely, that nonstate terrorists armed with weapons of mass destruction could not be dealt with through the usual tools of containment and deterrence. The strategy asserts, quite correctly, that in the face of this kind of threat, it will be at times necessary to act preemptively to break up an attack before it is launched. It goes on to say that the United States prefers to work with allies and international institutions to meet these kinds of challenges, but that at times America would find it necessary to resort to "coalitions of the willing" to deal with certain threats.

As a theory, there is absolutely nothing objectionable to anything stated in the new document. If a country is faced with a catastrophic threat from a nonstate actor, and if it is unable to get help from existing international institutions to meet that threat, it is hard to challenge the view that it can legitimately take matters into its own hands and move preemptively to break up that threat. Preemption has always been an option available not just to the United States but to all countries; it was in effect the justification for the overturning of the Taliban regime in Afghanistan, to which few in the international community objected.

Publication of the strategy document created an enormous uproar outside the United States, however, and did much to cement the view in many quarters that it was not Islamist terrorists but the United States that had become the chief source of global instability. There were a number of reasons for this.

The first problem with the doctrine concerned not so much what it said but what it failed to say and how it was thus interpreted. It did not lay out any criteria or suggest that there were any limits to the United States' use of preemptive/preventive military force. Indeed, the doctrine was promulgated in the context of President Bush's "axis of evil" line in his January 2002 State of the Union address, which naturally led many people to think that the United States was planning preventive wars not just against Iraq but against North Korea and Iran as well. While there may have been individual members of the Bush administration who foresaw repeated application of the new doctrine against rogue states, it is doubtful that there was anything like a consensus on this score. The United States had realistic plans to engage in only one such intervention, in Iraq. But the administration made no effort to clarify its intentions on this score, so it is not surprising that many people simply assumed Iraq was only the beginning of a U.S. effort to use military power to remake the world in its own interests.

The second problem with the doctrine was its broad endorsement of both preemptive and preventive war. A doctrine of preemption against imminent attack is relatively uncontroversial, even if most countries choose not to place a strong rhetorical emphasis on it. A doctrine of preventive war against a threat that may emerge several years down the road is much less so. There are both normative and pragmatic reasons for this. Normatively, virtually any just war theory holds that war is a last resort to which a country resorts only after all possible alternative nonmilitary approaches have been exhausted. In most cases of preventive (as opposed to preemptive) war, it is very hard to show that such alternatives have been exhausted against long-term threats. Prudentially, the record of states waging preventive wars—what Bismarck called committing suicide for fear of death—is not a happy one.[3] States can seldom make accurate judgments about the consequences of political events that lie several years in the future.

A third problem with the new strategy was its implicit delegation of the right to intervene and on occasion to wage preventive war to the United States and not to other countries. The United States was arguing, in effect, that as the world's sole global superpower, it had not just the right but the duty to provide global public goods like security against terrorists and rogue states. The United States was not arguing that this duty devolved on any country that happened to have this dominance in power; had Russia, China, or India been in such a position or promulgated a similar doctrine of preventive war as a means of dealing with their respective terrorist problems, one imagines that the Bush administration—indeed, any American administration—would have objected vociferously. The preventive war doctrine was not one that could be safely generalized throughout the international system. There was thus an implicit assertion of American exceptionalism in the strategy document: by virtue of the constitutional and democratic nature of American values and institutions, such responsibility for providing global public goods could be safely delegated to the United States.[4]

It is not hard to see why other countries, including other liberal democracies, objected to the implicit delegation of responsibility in the new strategy. Some, of course, objected as a matter of principle that any country could arrogate this right to itself and bypass international institutions. This argument, as we will see below, is not a strong one in view of the weaknesses of existing international institutions to provide security. But others objected on purely prudential grounds: they did not trust American judgment in using this power wisely, and did not believe the particular case that the Bush administration was making in favor of immediate war with Iraq.

The final gap in the doctrine concerned the American approach toward allies. The strategy document asserted the need and desirability of working with allies and traditional alliances, but also talked about the need to periodically resort to "coalitions of the willing." The latter phrase is basically a euphemism for American unilateralism. That is, a coalition of the willing arises when it is impossible to get agreement from an existing, well-institutionalized multilateral organization like the UN Security Council or NATO to support American purposes.[5]

Again, as in the case of preemption, there can be no principled objection to a nation acting unilaterally in defense of its own security. Given the weaknesses of existing multilateral security organizations (more about this later), a country would be foolish to trust in the Security Council, NATO, ASEAN, the EU, or any other regional organization if it came under severe threat.

On the other hand, what well-institutionalized, multilateral organizations provide is international legitimacy, which then permits broader international support. This support was not necessary for the high-intensity combat operations in Iraq, but it has certainly become important during the nation-building phase of operations. A year into the American occupation of Iraq, Washington found itself dependent on the United Nations to help negotiate the transfer of sovereignty to an Iraqi provisional government and to help facilitate democratic elections. Hence the real question for U.S. strategy that the document failed to address is how much emphasis the United States will place on the attempt to seek the sanction of multilateral institutions, and whether it would be willing to modify its own goals in any serious way in deference to the views of close allies. It is fair, then, to interpret the strategy document as saying that the United States would work through existing alliances when they are supportive of American purposes, but would otherwise show limited deference to allied views.

The failure to find any weapons of mass destruction in Iraq after the war underlines the problem that many American allies had with the new strategic doctrine. In the wake of the failure to find actual weapons, President Bush remarked that it didn't matter whether they had weapons or merely intentions to acquire weapons. But in fact, when a country is making a case for a voluntary preventive war, it makes a great deal of difference whether the threat actually exists today, or whether it could exist some years down the road. Weapons inspector David Kay, after resigning from the Iraq Survey Group, stated that the Iraqi nuclear program was dormant and that the country was not a year or two from acquiring a nuclear weapon but probably more like seven to eight years away from this capability. The fact that the Bush administration got this wrong has done enormous damage to American credibility and does not increase global confidence that nations can safely delegate judgment in these matters to Washington.

LIMITATIONS OF EXISTING INSTITUTIONS

A coalition of the willing is seen, for better or worse, by many countries around the world as a euphemism for American unilateralism, and as such fails to attract much enthusiasm as a long-term basis for world order. On the other hand, the alternative approach to dealing with serious security issues through international institutions like the United Nations, which many European countries claim to favor, also has a number of serious weaknesses. The UN specifically is deficient with regard to both legitimacy and effectiveness, and it is unlikely that any politically possible reform will fully fix either of these problems.

The concept of legitimacy is related to the concept of justice, but not equivalent to it. People believe that a certain set of institutional arrangements are legitimate because they are just, but legitimacy exists only in the eyes of the beholder. That is, an institution may be considered unjust by some philosophical or absolute principle of justice, and yet still be regarded as legitimate by a given group of people. What matters from the standpoint of an institution's long-term survival and effectiveness is not how it measures up to an absolute standard of justice, but whether the people affected by it regard it as legitimate.

The UN's problem with legitimacy has to do with the fact that membership in the organization is based on formal sovereignty rather than any substantive definition of legitimacy—in particular, it makes no demands on its members to be democratic.[6] This accommodation to the reality of world politics as it existed at the time of the UN's founding has in many ways tainted the subsequent activities of that body.

Since membership in the United Nations is based only on the de facto possession of sovereignty, the organization from the beginning has been populated by states of dubious legitimacy. One does not have to believe that liberal democracy is the only form of legitimacy to see why this is a problem: while there may be other potential nondemocratic grounds for legitimacy, there are clearly regimes that are illegitimate by any standard because of their gross violations of the most basic rights of their citizens.

The ideological conflicts of the Cold War were of course in the end divisions over basic principles of legitimacy, so it is no surprise that the organization was frequently deadlocked and impotent in dealing with security problems. The end of the Cold War aroused hopes that the organization would gain new effectiveness because there would henceforth be greater consensus around broad principles of human rights and democracy. But while most UN members gave lip service to these principles, many of them did not remotely live up to them and yet continued to be treated as members in good standing. Thus could the United States be displaced by Syria on the UN Human Rights Commission in 2001 and Libya become its chair in 2003.

Americans are much more likely to point to the UN's deficit of democratic legitimacy than are Europeans, which explains the substantially higher degree of distrust among Americans for the institution and reluctance to abide by its many pronouncements. Part of this distrust has to do with differences between the United States and Europeans over the meaning of democratic sovereignty. The United States has an abiding belief in constitutional democracy as the source of all legitimacy, and in the legitimacy of its own democratic institutions. Many Europeans, by contrast, have a distrust of sovereignty per se as a source of conflict and war, based on their experiences during two world wars in the first half of the twentieth century. Most European countries have sought to encase their sovereignties in a series of overlapping institutions including both the United Nations and the European Union. It is not surprising, then, that Europeans on the whole regard the UN as more legitimate than do Americans.

A further source of American distrust of the United Nations is a byproduct of its special relationship with Israel and its experience of how the UN has dealt with the Arab–Israeli dispute over the years. The General

Assembly has passed any number of resolutions regarded by both Israel and the United States as unbalanced or lopsidedly pro-Arab, the most infamous of which was the 1975 "Zionism is racism" resolution. Europeans by contrast tend to place greater blame on Israel for these outcomes. In subsequent years the United States has found itself frequently vetoing Security Council resolutions regarded as biased against Israel, thus habituating itself to standing against majority opinion in that organization.

The second problem with the UN has to do with its efficacy as an institution meant to deal with serious security threats. Article 51 authorizations for the use of force must go through the Security Council. But the Security Council, whose membership reflects the winning coalition in World War II, was deliberately designed to be a weak institution: the veto power enjoyed by the five permanent members guaranteed that the Security Council would never act contrary to their interests. The wartime coalition fell apart, of course, in the Cold War, and the Security Council was thereafter never able to agree on responses to serious security threats requiring the use of force, with the exception of Korea, when the Soviet Union mistakenly walked out of the Security Council. With the end of the Cold War, the Security Council came together in authorizing UN action against Iraq after the latter's 1990 invasion of Kuwait. But the organization failed to follow through in enforcing its own disarmament resolutions on Baghdad in the decade following, laying the ground for the American intervention in 2003.

Deficiencies in the UN's ability to authorize force to deal with major security issues does not mean that the organization cannot play an important role in post-conflict reconstruction and other nation-building activities. This has indeed happened in Cambodia, Somalia, Bosnia, Kosovo, and many other places.[7] But while the UN provides legitimacy and a useful umbrella for organizing international peacekeeping and stabilization operations, even here its limitations are evident. The United Nations is not a hierarchical organization that is capable of taking decisive action. It necessarily moves by consensus, and is particularly dependent on its major donors—which in practice means the United States, the Europeans, and Japan—for money, troops, and technical assistance.

Over the years there have been any number of proposals to alter the membership of the Security Council to reflect changes in the distribution of power around the world and to thereby improve the Council's perceived legitimacy. It is very doubtful that any of these reform schemes will work, short of a major crisis. Existing members will veto any proposal that will deprive them of their current influence, while new members will inevitably be opposed by other countries that believe themselves equally deserving of a seat.

Even if the membership of the Security Council could be expanded or changed, the collective action problem will remain. A larger Security Council with veto-bearing members will suffer from even greater paralysis than at present. But to change the voting rules from consensus to some form of majority rule risks making the Security Council more active than any of its members would like. The United States in particular, which has found itself isolated in many Security Council votes, is not realistically ever going to approve a change from the unanimity rule. There is a real question, indeed, whether the world would benefit from a supercharged United Nations that could authorize a major use of force under conditions where its constituent members were sharply divided on its wisdom or legitimacy.

SAME PRINCIPLES, DIFFERENT MEANS

Much of the Bush administration's analysis of the terrorist problem was correct and more clear-eyed than that of its critics; the problem with U.S. foreign policy at this junction concerns rather the means that should be used to pursue its goals.

Radical Islamism is a political movement comparable to European fascism. It is not the inevitable offspring of the religion of Islam, but rather an ideology that feeds off the alienation of deracinated populations and social strata (usually middle-class) in a part of the world that has undergone considerable social change in recent decades. The Bush administration is correct in saying that this alienation feeds off the lack of democracy and pluralism in the political systems of most Arab countries, as well as the region's lack of economic opportunity. It is also correct that an ultimate solution to the problem must in the long term address these underlying causes.

The real question concerns the kinds of tools available to deal with this problem. Invasion and military occupation are crude instruments. Thomas Friedman and other supporters of the Iraq war argued that the shock of the U.S. action would wake local elites out of their torpor and get them to address the democracy deficit more forthrightly. He may still be right, but the impact of the war depended very much on its perceived legitimacy and the successful emergence of a stable, democratic Iraq. The obvious inability of the United States to control events there after the end of combat operations contributed to a sense of malaise and anger throughout the region, and the Bush administration's Broader Middle East Initiative has been poorly conceived and weakly implemented.

On the other hand, events in early 2005, including the election in Iraq on January 30, the anti-Syrian demonstrations in Lebanon following the assassination of Rafiq Hariri and the subsequent withdrawal of Syrian troops, and Hosni Mubarak's announcement that he will permit genuine contestation of the next presidential election, suggest a brighter future for democracy. This being the Middle East, however, the future course of events will be very difficult to predict.

Realistic institutions to pursue the war on terrorism in the post–September 11 period require two things that are often mutually inconsistent: power and legitimacy. Power is needed to deal with threats not just from rogue states but from the new nonstate actors that may in the future employ weapons of mass destruction. It must be capable of being deployed quickly and decisively; its use will in some cases require the violation of national sovereignty and may in some cases require preemption.

International legitimacy, on the other hand, requires working through international institutions that are inherently slow-moving, rigid, and hobbled by cumbersome procedures and methods. Legitimacy is ultimately based on consent, which is in turn a by-product of a slow process of diplomacy and persuasion. International institutions exist in part to reduce the transaction costs of achieving consent, but under the best of circumstances they necessarily move less quickly than security requires.

The power side of the equation will have to be supplied, for the foreseeable future, largely by the United States. The United States spends as much on defense as the next sixteen or so largest military powers combined; its forces have a reach and technological sophistication that will not be challenged for the foreseeable future. While the Europeans, Russians, and Chinese could in principle sharply upgrade their capabilities and spending, they show little inclination to do so in the near term. The Europeans are correct when they say that there are other forms of soft power, like the ability to manage nation-building projects, that they can deploy more readily than the United States. But ultimately, hard power is necessary to meet an important range of security challenges in the current environment.

The real issue for the future is how best to prudently apply American power. The Bush administration's approach to Iraq was wrong less in principle than in the way that it was applied to this specific case. The administration argued that by disarming Iraq it was performing, in effect, an international public service, enforcing a series of UN Security Council resolutions in a situation where the global community was too timid and divided to act. It was expending its own blood and treasure not just to eliminate a serious security threat, but to bring down a tyranny and build a new, democratic society in its place.

There have been many other cases in the past where existing international institutions clearly failed, and where strong U.S. leadership was needed to break the logjam. This happened repeatedly during the Cold War, from the deployment of intermediate-range nuclear weapons in the early 1980s through the negotiations for their elimination in a "double-zero" agreement, to the incorporation of a unified Germany into NATO after the collapse of Soviet power in Eastern Europe. In each of these instances, the United States took an action that was at times strongly opposed by its European allies, and created a fait accompli that they accepted after the fact. Something similar happened in the Balkans during the 1990s, when the Europeans on their own could not agree on a decisive military solution to the underlying problem of Serbian nationalism. This had to be supplied in the end by U.S. airpower (together with the Croatian army) and American leadership.

This means that the United States must not abjure, in principle, unilateralism, preemption, or coalitions of the willing. There will be times when this kind of action is critical, not just for U.S. interests, but for global security more broadly. What is needed is better judgment in the actual application of such power, and a very different rhetorical posture. Instead of beating its chest about its determination to use its power on the world's behalf, it ought to deliberately downplay American hegemony and seek to meet friends and allies more than halfway on the terrain of their concerns. Everybody knows that the United States is very powerful; what is critical is to prevent the formation of hostile coalitions in reaction to the reality of U.S. power.

Besides the more prudent application of U.S. power, there is the question of international institutions. If the United Nations is not ultimately reformable, what can take its place? The answer is likely to be not a single global institution, but rather a multiplicity of international organizations that can provide both power and legitimacy for different types of challenges to world order. A multiplicity of geographically and functionally overlapping institutions will permit the United States and other powers to "forum shop" for an appropriate instrument to facilitate international cooperation. This happened during the Kosovo conflict: when a Russian veto in the Security Council made it impossible for the UN to act, the United States and its European allies shifted the venue to NATO, where the Russians weren't members. The NATO alliance, while operationally cumbersome, provided legitimacy for the military intervention in a way that the UN could not.

Some creativity and institution-building could be useful at this juncture. The Community of Democracies, for example, was founded in 2000 with strong support from Madeline Albright and the Clinton administration, as a club of like-minded democracies that would not suffer from the kinds of legitimacy problems that plague the UN. This organization does not have a security function at present—in fact, few people are even aware of its existence—but with strong backing from the United States it could in time grow into a much more widely accepted international player. Such an organization, led by new democracies in Latin America and Eastern Europe, could play an enormously helpful role in promoting democratic reform in the Arab world. Similarly, the Six-Power framework that has been used to deal with the North Korean nuclear problem could be turned into a permanent five-power consultative group for handling security issues in Northeast Asia.

More prudent use of American power can be coupled directly to a new institutional framework for dealing with security problems. The United States does not have to commit itself to multilateralism on principle; international organizations are simply useful tools for legitimizing cooperative action and serving national objectives. The fear that participation in such organizations will dilute the principle of sovereignty and a world order based on nation-states would seem to be overdrawn, since nation-states remain the only entities capable of deploying hard power for the foreseeable future.

The United States is in effect fighting a global counterinsurgency war, not different in principle from those it fought in Vietnam or in Central America. The problem with all counterinsurgency wars is that the hard-core fighters who must be killed, captured, or neutralized swim in a much larger sea of potential sympathizers—in the case of the radical Islamists, the roughly 1.3 billion Muslims in the world. Counterinsurgency is a highly political form of warfare, in which military power must be employed with great precision and care so as to avoid alienating the terrorists' potential supporters. A hearts-and-minds strategy to divide potential adversaries is critical to success. It seems reasonably clear that neither reliance on existing international institutions nor American unilateralism will be adequate to meet the nexus of problems involving terrorism, weapons of mass destruction, failed states, and weak governance in unstable parts of the world. None of the suggestions laid out here will solve these problems either, but will, in at least some subset of cases, provide a better mix of useable power and international legitimacy than we have seen to date.

NOTES

1. *The National Security Strategy of the United States* (Washington, DC: GPO, 2002).
2. See John Lewis Gaddis, *Surprise, Security, and the American Experience* (Cambridge, MA: Harvard University Press, 2004).
3. Richard K. Betts, "Suicide from Fear of Death?" *Foreign Affairs* 82, no. 1 (2003): 34–43.
4. Pierre Hassner points out that the American constitutional system of checks and balances is designed to limit the delegation of authority to the government, even when that government is democratically elected, and that it is strange that Americans accept the need for checks in their domestic political life but not internationally. See Pierre Hassner, "Definitions, Doctrines, and Divergences," *National Interest* no. 69 (2002): 30–34.
5. President Bush and other members of his administration asserted on a number of occasions that the coalition assembled for the 2003 Iraq war was as large as, or even larger than, the one assembled for his father's 1991 Gulf War. This abstracts completely from the quality of that support. The real test of an alliance is the willingness to put forces at risk in support of military operations, and in that respect, only Britain and, to a lesser extent, Australia were willing to do this in 2003, compared to the significantly larger military coalition in 1991.
6. For a comprehensive discussion of the legitimacy of UN action, see the new foreword to the paperback edition of Robert Kagan, *Of Paradise and Power: America vs. Europe in the New World Order* (New York: Knopf, 2004); and Robert Kagan, "America's Crisis of Legitimacy," *Foreign Affairs* 83, no. 2 (2004): 65–87.
7. See James Dobbins et al., *The UN's Role in Nation-Building: From the Congo to Iraq*, MG-304-RC (Santa Monica: Rand Corporation, 2005).

Chapter 9 Constitutional Responsibility in the War on Terrorism

Michael Vatis

The first three years of the war on terrorism were characterized largely by congressional silence on some of the key issues involved in that war. This allowed the Bush administration to assert nearly exclusive executive authority to fight the war on its own terms. It also led, not surprisingly, to instances of executive encroachment on individual liberties that ultimately caused the judiciary to step in. The most conspicuous example of this pattern concerns the detention and interrogation of individuals deemed by the president to be "enemy combatants."

What accounts for Congress's abdication of its responsibility during the war on terrorism? After all, Congress at other times in our history has mustered the political will to suspend the writ of habeas corpus or otherwise expressly authorize extraordinary executive powers to deal with serious threats to national security.[1] Why, then, has it not done so during the war on terrorism?

A significant reason is the control of both political branches by one party, and the predominance of party loyalty over institutional loyalty among members of Congress. When the president's party

controls Congress, and the majority members of Congress are more interested in advancing the positions of their de facto party leader than in protecting the institutional prerogatives of the legislature, then Congress cannot
play the crucial checking and balancing role envisioned by the Constitution.[2]

The traditional notion of separation of powers assumes that each branch
of government—and especially the two political branches—will constantly
struggle with each other for power, and that this competition will constrain
overreaching by any one branch, thereby protecting individual liberties from
encroachment. As *Federalist* 51 put it:

> The great security against a gradual concentration of the several powers in the
> same department, consists in giving to those who administer each department the
> necessary constitutional means and personal motives to resist encroachments of
> the others. . . . Ambition must be made to counteract ambition. The interest of
> the man must be connected with the constitutional rights of the place. And if
> one branch still went too far, the Supreme Court would act as the ultimate
> guarantor of liberty, overturning an action by one of the political branches that
> exceeded its constitutional powers.[3]

But this traditional view failed to anticipate the situation we commonly
find today in national security matters and especially in wartime: an assertive
executive, a passive or even supine legislature, and an activist judiciary.[4] In
this situation, the legislature fails to check and balance the executive, leaving
the judiciary as the only effective protector of liberty against executive overreaching. But an activist judiciary does not stop at simply deciding that an
executive action is unconstitutional; it goes on to prescribe its own remedy
for whatever ill the executive was attempting to cure.

This situation is troubling, for it means that the most difficult decisions
on issues affecting liberty and security are made by the two least representative branches of government, the executive and the judiciary. Moreover,
this result disserves both liberty and security. When the executive acts on its
own, it will typically err on the side of security at the expense of individual
liberty. And if overweening executive actions lead the judiciary to intercede,
courts will devise solutions in an area in which they have the least institutional competence—war-fighting—with potentially adverse effects for security. Moreover, when Congress is quiescent, necessary but controversial
executive actions will have little staying power when the going gets tough.
For all these reasons, then, meaningful congressional involvement in addressing matters of national security is imperative.

This is particularly true for the war on terrorism. For unlike a traditional war against a foreign nation, where the principal actions to defend our security take place abroad, with little direct impact on the citizenry, the war on terrorism entails significant actions within the United States. The government must detect and interdict activity within our borders by terrorists who seek to mingle with the general population unnoticed until it is time for them to strike. This war thus blurs the traditional boundaries between military activity and law enforcement, between law enforcement and intelligence, between alien enemies and citizens, and between foreign and domestic threats—meaning that actions by the government will necessarily have significant impacts on citizens' liberty. It is therefore especially important that the people's representatives have a significant voice in determining how our government balances security and liberty interests.

How do we address this breakdown in the system of checks and balances? Ultimately, the only real solution is the ballot box—only voters can hold individual legislators accountable for congressional inaction or mandate divided government at the ballot box. But in a collective body, accountability for inaction becomes diffused, making it difficult for voters to determine which members of Congress should be held responsible for collective inaction. Punishing Congress for its institutional failures would require the separate constituencies of a majority of the members of Congress to vote out their representatives. Elections thus offer, at best, a slow and difficult solution to the problem of congressional passivity.

The judiciary, however, can play an important role in redressing this problem by developing a jurisprudence of constitutional responsibility to supplement the traditional notion of the separation of powers. Such a jurisprudence would be founded on the idea that just as individuals have both rights and responsibilities, so the branches of government have both powers and responsibilities. Under this jurisprudence, courts would ask not only whether the executive has the constitutional power to perform a certain action without congressional authorization, but also whether Congress has a constitutional responsibility to address that same matter. And courts would consider the effect of their decisions on the political dynamics affecting Congress and seek to encourage, rather than further dilute, political accountability for legislative inaction.

Although at first glance a jurisprudence of constitutional responsibility might seem to suggest a more expansive role for the courts, in fact it requires a more restrained role. For the courts ultimately would simply assess whether a particular governmental action was constitutional, but would not remedy any deficiencies left by Congress or the president by reading terms into statutes or supplying missing procedural protections. This would put the onus back on Congress to supply the necessary solutions, and draw public attention to the need for corrective action from the legislature. In this way, courts could create the necessary incentives for Congress to perform its responsibilities.

CONGRESSIONAL PASSIVITY IN THE
WAR ON TERRORISM

Throughout the first three years of the war on terrorism, the majority in Congress overwhelmingly chose party loyalty over protecting congressional prerogatives, and largely ceded responsibility for fighting the war on terrorism to the executive branch.

The first major policy initiative undertaken in the wake of the terrorist attacks on September 11, 2001, was the passage of the USA Patriot Act.[5] This legislation was a compendium of provisions that, among other things, expanded government investigative authorities and removed impediments to the sharing of information between law enforcement and intelligence agencies. The legislation was introduced less than a week after September 11, and signed into law a mere five weeks later, after precious little debate and deliberation over the need for the enhanced authorities, their likely efficacy, or their effect on liberty.

Yet as it happens, this cursory treatment by Congress of the issues in the Patriot Act actually represents the apogee of congressional involvement in the war on terrorism, at least for the first three years of that war. For whatever one thinks of the Act's provisions or the lack of meaningful debate over them, at least Congress gave the legislation *some* consideration, and did *something*. Moreover, in a novel experiment, Congress enacted a sunset provision that calls for some of the most controversial provisions of the Act to expire in 2005 unless Congress were to vote to extend them or make them permanent, thereby ensuring at least eventual consideration of the issues. The Patriot Act thus at least represents some expression of the will of the community on difficult issues, however flawed the process and the end result may be.

The other major action by Congress, just a week after September 11, was passage of a joint resolution authorizing the president to "use all necessary and appropriate force against those nations, organizations, or persons he determines planned, authorized, committed, or aided the terrorist attacks" or "harbored such organizations or persons, in order to prevent any future acts of international terrorism against the United States by such nations, organizations or persons." The Authorization of Use of Military Force (AUMF),[6] however, amounts to giving the president carte blanche to do what he sees fit, without any delineation of the limits on executive action by Congress.

Aside from these two pieces of hastily passed legislation, Congress has been essentially silent, letting the executive branch determine on its own how to fight the war on terrorism, and largely failing to exercise meaningful oversight. The most glaring example of this congressional passivity concerns the government's detention of suspected terrorists and other "enemy combatants" within the United States and abroad, and its use of coercive interrogation techniques against detainees. In both areas, the executive branch has made astonishing claims of exclusive executive authority to do what it deems necessary. And, in the face of such claims, Congress has essentially acquiesced, without passing legislation that might either support or limit executive action, and without even holding meaningful oversight hearings. This silence on the part of the most representative branch of government constitutes a significant failure.

Shortly after September 11, government agents seized and detained dozens of immigrants in the United States as "material witnesses" to a crime. The material witness statute allows individuals to be arrested and detained when the government believes they could offer testimony that would be material to a criminal proceeding but it would be "impracticable" to secure their appearance by subpoena. It was never intended as an omnibus detention provision allowing the government to detain people indefinitely for security reasons where it did not have sufficient evidence to charge them with a crime.[7] Yet that was exactly how the executive branch used the statute, and Congress acquiesced without a word—neither prohibiting such security detentions nor providing clear authority, and limits, for them.

Yet at least with the material witness statute, the detention takes place within an established criminal justice system that accords some rights to the detainee and provides some judicial supervision. But the Bush administration went much further than its broad use of that statute. It asserted that the president, as commander-in-chief of the armed forces, has virtually unreviewable authority to use the military to detain anyone he deems to be an "enemy combatant." And it asserted this authority not just with respect to combatants detained on a battlefield abroad, but also to U.S. citizens detained within the United States. Thus, in addition to detaining hundreds of suspected Al Qaeda or Taliban members at the U.S. Naval Base in Guantanamo Bay, Cuba, the government also detained two American citizens in the United States: one, Yaser Esam Hamdi, captured in Afghanistan, and one, Jose Padilla, seized in Chicago, Illinois.[8]

The government argued that the detention of alien combatants in Guantanamo could not be reviewed by the courts *at all* because Guantanamo was not a territory of the United States. In the cases of Hamdi and Padilla, the government conceded that courts could review the detention of citizens in the United States. But its concession was, in reality, a small one. It asserted that any factual inquiry by a court into the detainee's status—that is, whether he was truly an enemy combatant—or the circumstances of his detention would be inappropriate as a constitutional matter. It argued that " 'respect for separation of powers and the limited institutional capabilities of courts in matters of military decision-making in connection with an ongoing conflict' ought to eliminate entirely any individual process, restricting the courts to investigating only whether legal authorization exists for the broader detention scheme." "At most," the government argued, "courts should review [the executive branch's] determination that a citizen is an enemy combatant under a very deferential 'some evidence' standard," under which "a court would assume the accuracy of the Government's articulated basis for [the] detention . . . and assess only whether that articulated basis was a legitimate one." As Justice Souter noted, "The Government's concession of jurisdiction to hear [a detainee's] habeas claim is more theoretical than practical, leaving the assertion of executive authority close to unconditional."[9]

When it came to the treatment of its detainees, the Bush administration went even further. In an August 2002, memorandum, the Justice Department's Office of Legal Counsel—which is responsible for determining the executive branch's official view of what the law is on a given subject— provided a lengthy discourse on why various coercive interrogation techniques did not constitute "torture" under U.S. or international law, and why even if they did, government agents responsible for the abuse might still have a valid legal defense against prosecution. But the most remarkable part of the memorandum, from the perspective of legal scholars, was the assertion that the executive branch could engage in any conduct toward detainees that it saw fit, even in the face of an explicit U.S. law forbidding that conduct.[10]

The Justice Department opined that a federal statute that makes it a criminal offense for any person "outside the United States [to] commit[,] or attempt[,] to commit torture,"[11] would be unconstitutional if applied to interrogation techniques undertaken by executive branch personnel pursuant to the president's commander-in-chief authority. It asserted that the "president enjoys complete discretion in the exercise of his Commander-in-Chief authority" and that "Congress lacks authority under Article I to set the terms and conditions under which the president may exercise [that] authority . . . to control the conduct of operations during a war." It concluded that "[a]ny effort by Congress to regulate the interrogation of battlefield combatants would violate the Constitution's sole vesting of Commander-in-Chief authority in the president."[12]

Yet, astonishingly, the memorandum failed even to mention that the Constitution grants specific powers to Congress that apply directly to the issue at hand—the conduct of our armed forces toward detainees during military conflict—including the power to "make rules concerning captures on land and water," and "make rules for the government and regulation of land and naval forces." Nor does it mention Congress's more general "war powers," including the power to "provide for the common defense," "declare war," "raise and support armies," and "provide and maintain a navy," or its power to "define and punish . . . offences against the law of nations."[13] Only by utterly ignoring the Constitution's grant of such powers to Congress could the Justice Department claim that Congress lacks the authority to make rules governing the military's treatment of enemy combatants.[14]

In the wake of the public uproar following revelation of the abuse of prisoners held by the United States in Iraq and of a secret CIA practice of detaining and coercively interrogating prisoners around the world, the White House eventually disavowed the Justice Department memorandum, and the Justice Department issued a new memorandum containing a different interpretation of the law governing torture. But in fact the original memorandum's assertion of executive authority (which was not addressed in the later memorandum) was entirely consistent with the Bush administration's approach to the war on terrorism, which rested on the belief that the president had virtually unlimited authority to do what he believed necessary to defend the nation's security, without regard to the other branches of government or to international treaties ratified by the United States.[15]

One might have expected that the revelation of the prisoner abuses (and, later, of an apparent CIA practice of sending detainees to other countries such as Syria and Egypt where some detainees were allegedly tortured) might have prompted extensive congressional oversight hearings, and that the Justice Department's explicit assault on Congress's constitutional prerogatives might have caused Congress to assert itself by passing legislation governing the detention of enemy combatants in wartime. But in fact, other than a few sporadic hearings, all one heard from Congress was resounding silence.

THE SUPREME COURT STEPS IN

While Congress was willing to lie supine in the face of the executive's sweeping assertions of authority, the Supreme Court was not. In *Rasul v. Bush* and *Hamdi v. Rumsfeld*, the Court rejected the administration's arguments that it could detain enemy combatants at Guantanamo or within the United States without any meaningful judicial review.[16] Although the Court's actions were certainly a positive development in terms of checking executive encroachments on individual liberty, its decisions also created new problems, with adverse effects for both liberty and security. In some of the justices' opinions, however, we can see traces of an implicit jurisprudence of constitutional responsibility that offers a potential way out of the dilemma created by Congress's inaction.

Rasul v. Bush

In *Rasul*, the Supreme Court ruled 6–3 that federal courts have jurisdiction to hear challenges to the detention of foreign nationals at Guantanamo under the habeas corpus statute.[17] The Court was animated in part by the deep historical roots of the writ of habeas corpus, by which courts have reviewed the legality of an individual's detention by the executive:

> Executive imprisonment has been considered oppressive and lawless since John, at Runnymede, pledged that no free man should be imprisoned, dispossessed, outlawed, or exiled save by the judgment of his peers or by the law of the land. The judges of England developed the writ of habeas corpus largely to preserve these immunities from executive restraint.[18]

But the legal rationale for the decision, and its ultimate scope, were far from clear. In the main, the Court simply distinguished an earlier decision that had denied habeas jurisdiction to alien combatants captured in wartime.[19] The Guantanamo detainees, the Court reasoned, "are not nationals of countries at war with the United States, and they deny that they have engaged in or plotted acts of aggression against the United States; they have never been afforded access to any tribunal, much less charged with and convicted of wrongdoing; and for more than two years they have been imprisoned in territory over which the United States exercises exclusive jurisdiction and control."[20] But it is not clear which of these factors were determinative in the Court's analysis, and what combination of them is necessary to find habeas jurisdiction.

While the peculiar legal status of Guantanamo—over which the United States exercises "jurisdiction" under its lease with Cuba, though not ultimate sovereignty—was seemingly an important factor in the decision, parts of the Court's opinion suggest that habeas jurisdiction extends to detainees held by the U.S. government anywhere in the world,[21] as long as it is in a place where the United States exercises some sort of jurisdiction, though that term is undefined, or the detainees' custodian is located within the jurisdiction of a federal court.[22] If the decision is interpreted in that manner by lower courts, the consequences for the war on terrorism could, as Justice Scalia argued in dissent, be "breathtaking":

> [The court's holding] permits an alien captured in a foreign theater of active combat to bring a [habeas] petition against the Secretary of Defense. Over the course of the last century, the United States has held millions of alien prisoners abroad. . . . A great many of these prisoners would no doubt have complained about the circumstances of their capture and the terms of their confinement. . . . From this point forward, federal courts will entertain petitions from these prisoners, and others like them around the world, challenging actions and events far away, and forcing the courts to oversee one aspect of the Executive's conduct of a foreign war.[23]

The lack of clarity in the Court's opinion left the Department of Defense in a state of considerable confusion about what review process it must afford detainees. *Rasul* left unanswered questions such as: Does habeas jurisdiction extend to detainees held in foreign locations other than Guantanamo, where the United States does not have a long-term lease but does have some understanding (formal or informal) with the local government to detain prisoners at a U.S. military base, or at a secret CIA safe-house? If not, the effect of *Rasul* will be rather limited, and the military will simply detain people in other locations. Does habeas extend to U.S. military detainees in Iraq, even after the transfer of sovereignty to an Iraqi government? Does habeas extend to detainees who have been afforded a more rigorous military review of their status than the detainees in *Rasul* received? If habeas still applies in that circumstance, is the scope of judicial review on habeas lessened? What sort of review suffices? Those questions will not be answered until many more habeas challenges are brought in federal courts across the country, on behalf of detainees located around the world, and those challenges then work their way through the appellate process and, ultimately, back to the Supreme Court. In the meantime, many detainees will continue to be held in facilities around the world.[24]

But the Supreme Court bears only so much blame for this result. The Court can only decide the cases presented to it, and what it faced in *Rasul* was a situation in which Congress had not defined the boundaries of habeas jurisdiction as to foreign detainees nor established any sort of military review process, and the executive acted, as it is wont to do, to the outer limits of its perceived authority, providing no meaningful military review of detainees' status and denying the existence of habeas jurisdiction altogether. Had Congress acted to fill that void, it might have averted some of the very real problems caused by the Court's "bringing the cumbersome machinery of our domestic courts into military affairs," and potentially having lower courts conduct deep factual inquiries into detentions of enemy combatants abroad, even to the point of summoning witnesses from around the world, requiring the depositions of military officers, and the like. Similarly, the confusion engendered by *Rasul* can be dispelled most quickly and effectively if Congress were to step in and delineate the terms and conditions for detention of enemy combatants, including a military review process, and define the extent of habeas review.[25]

Hamdi v. Rumsfeld

In the second case, *Hamdi*, the problems caused by Congress's abdication of responsibility are even more apparent. There the Court held that an American citizen captured abroad could be detained by the military as an enemy combatant within the United States, but that he must be afforded a meaningful opportunity to contest the basis for his detention before a neutral arbiter. The Court was deeply fractured, however, issuing four separate opinions, none of which garnered a majority. The Court thus created additional confusion about exactly what the law requires when it comes to wartime detainees.

The end result of *Hamdi* was that a majority of five Justices—Chief Justice Rehnquist and Justices O'Connor, Kennedy, and Breyer, in a plurality

opinion written by Justice O'Connor, along with Justice Thomas, in a separate opinion—held that Congress's Authorization of Use of Military Force
legislation, despite its extremely general terms, provided sufficient statutory
authorization for military detention of a U.S. citizen. Six Justices, though—
the plurality of four, plus Justices Souter and Ginsburg in a separate concurring opinion—held that Hamdi must be given a meaningful chance to
challenge his "enemy combatant" status in a lower court, though the justices'
reasoning differed. Two other justices, Scalia and Stevens, would have required Hamdi's immediate release from detention unless he were promptly
charged with a crime or Congress acted to suspend the writ of habeas corpus
and thereby allow detentions outside the normal criminal justice process.
Finally, Justice Thomas would have upheld Hamdi's detention, finding that
Hamdi was afforded all the process required by the Constitution.

The justices' differing rationales demonstrate how a jurisprudence of constitutional responsibility would differ from the traditional separation-of-
powers analysis in terms of both how the Court assesses the constitutionality
of executive action and how it perceives its own role. And they show how
that jurisprudence would cut across the usual political labels of "liberal" and
"conservative."

The plurality of four justices, including three so-called conservatives who
normally profess belief in a limited judicial function, in this case adopted
an activist view of the Court's role, setting out the procedures that it thought
should be utilized to protect individual rights against executive encroachment. In contrast, Justices Souter, Ginsburg, Stevens, and Scalia—a group
that cuts across the ideological spectrum—assumed a more limited role for
the Court of simply ensuring that the executive not exceed its authority,
while leaving to Congress the responsibility to specify the terms and conditions for detention of enemy combatants. Finally, the conservative Justice
Thomas would have the Court play an extremely limited role, and generally
defer to the president's exercise of his commander-in-chief authority.

The first question addressed by the plurality was whether the AUMF's
general language authorized the military detention of American citizens
within the United States. An earlier statute, the Non-Detention Act, had
provided that "No citizen shall be imprisoned or otherwise detained by the
United States except pursuant to an Act of Congress." The Non-Detention
Act was passed to prevent a reprise of the internment by the government of
Japanese-Americans during World War II. The plurality (joined by Justice
Thomas) found that the AUMF constituted "explicit congressional author-

ization for the detention of individuals" like Hamdi, despite its failure even to mention detention. "Because detention to prevent a combatant's return to the battlefield is a fundamental incident of waging war," the plurality reasoned, "in permitting the use of 'necessary and appropriate force,' Congress has clearly and unmistakably authorized detention in the narrow circumstances considered here."[26]

But just as the plurality so confidently found "detention" to be "explicit[ly]," "clearly," and "unmistakably" present in the words "necessary and appropriate force," it then went on to read limits into the AUMF's purported authorization of detention. It said, for instance, that detention cannot be indefinite, but can last only "for the duration of the relevant conflict." The basis of this conclusion, however, was nothing in the AUMF or its legislative history, but rather "longstanding law-of-war principles" found in international law.[27] Although this limit seems eminently reasonable in substance, the act of reading it into the general terms of a congressional resolution that does not even mention detention suggests, at the least, an expansive view of the role of the Court in setting the terms of the president's execution of his war powers.[28]

The plurality next addressed what process must be afforded a citizen to contest his status as an enemy combatant. On this question, the plurality held that the Due Process Clause of the Constitution requires some meaningful judicial review of the detainee's status.[29] In reaching this conclusion, the plurality "reject[ed] the Government's assertion that separation of powers principles mandate a heavily circumscribed role for the courts in such circumstances . . . as this approach serves only to *condense* power into a single branch of government. . . . Whatever power the United States Constitution envisions for the Executive in its exchanges with other nations or with enemy organizations in times of conflict, it most assuredly envisions a role for all three branches when individual liberties are at stake."[30]

But the plurality did not merely find that judicial review was required. It went further and specified the sort of review procedures it thought necessary. Concluding that neither the minimal review proposed by the government nor the more fulsome evidentiary review required by the district court "strikes the proper constitutional balance," the plurality set forth its own view of how to strike the right balance:

> A citizen-detainee seeking to challenge his classification as an enemy combatant must receive notice of the factual basis for his classification, and a fair opportunity

to rebut the Government's factual assertions before a neutral decisionmaker. . . . At the same time, the exigencies of the circumstances may demand that . . . enemy combatant proceedings may be tailored to alleviate their uncommon potential to burden the Executive at a time of ongoing military conflict. Hearsay, for example, may need to be accepted as the most reliable available evidence from the Government in such a proceeding. Likewise, the Constitution would not be offended by a presumption in favor of the Government's evidence, so long as that presumption remained a rebuttable one and fair opportunity for rebuttal were provided. Thus, once the Government puts forth credible evidence that the habeas petitioner meets the enemy-combatant criteria, the onus could shift to the petitioner to rebut that evidence with more persuasive evidence that he falls outside the criteria.[31]

While most of its opinion was devoted to defending the role of the courts in reviewing military detentions, toward the end the plurality held open "the possibility that the standards we have articulated could be met by an appropriately authorized and properly constituted military tribunal," and suggested that it is only "in the absence of such a process . . . [that] a court that receives a petition for a writ of habeas corpus from an alleged enemy combatant must itself ensure that the minimum requirements of due process are achieved."[32] As the Court did in *Rasul*, then, the plurality left unclear whether a meaningful opportunity for a detainee to challenge his detention in a military tribunal would *preclude* judicial review, or merely reduce the level of scrutiny by a reviewing court and entitle the executive's decision to greater deference.

Thus, while the plurality might have thought it was providing helpful guidance, in the end it left massive confusion in its wake. As with *Rasul*, the ramifications of *Hamdi* are not likely to be ironed out for months, if not years, as the military attempts to fashion an internal review process for detainees, and individual detainees challenge their continued detention in the courts.

The plurality's opinion can thus be seen as an example of the traditional judicial approach to separation of powers, in which the judiciary acts to protect individual liberties by constraining the executive when it exceeds its constitutional authorities. But by reading authorization for detention into such a general statute and then supplying the procedures that should be employed in reviewing detentions, the plurality effectively allowed Congress to evade its responsibility to decide these difficult questions and took on that responsibility for the Court. Yet the confusion created by the plurality's opinion demonstrates why setting the terms of detention and prescribing the scope of judicial review are tasks best left to Congress.

In contrast to the plurality, Justice Souter, joined by Justice Ginsburg, found that the AUMF did not authorize detention of an American citizen. Congress, Souter reasoned, "never so much as uses the word detention, and there is no reason to think Congress might have perceived any need to augment executive power to deal with dangerous citizens within the United States, given the well-stocked statutory arsenal of defined criminal offenses covering the gamut of actions that a citizen sympathetic to terrorists might commit."[33]

Justice Souter rejected the plurality's view that the AUMF should be interpreted broadly, arguing that separation-of-powers principles demanded a clear statement by Congress to justify military detentions.[34] Otherwise, the decision on where to strike the balance between liberty and security would effectively be left to the executive alone, which would inevitably favor security over liberty.

> The defining character of American constitutional government is its constant tension between security and liberty, serving both by partial helpings of each. In a government of separated powers, deciding finally on what is a reasonable degree of guaranteed liberty whether in peace or war (or some condition in between) is not well entrusted to the executive branch of Government, whose particular responsibility is to maintain security. For reasons of inescapable human nature, the branch of the Government asked to counter a serious threat is not the branch on which to rest the Nation's entire reliance in striking the balance between the will to win and the cost in liberty on the way to victory; the responsibility for security will naturally amplify the claim that security legitimately raises. A reasonable balance is more likely to be reached on the judgment of a different branch. . . . Hence the need for an assessment by Congress before citizens are subject to lockup, and likewise the need for a clearly expressed congressional resolution of the competing claims.[35]

In requiring a clear statement by Congress before finding that it had authorized military detentions of American citizens, Justice Souter's opinion reveals traces of a jurisprudence of constitutional responsibility. The central element of that responsibility is the duty of Congress to make difficult choices, and to endure the political consequences of its decisions, and not, through passivity or ambiguity, to transfer its responsibility, and concomitant political accountability, to the president or the Supreme Court. If Congress does not adequately fulfill this responsibility, in this view, the Court should not take up the slack by filling in the blanks or essentially putting words in Congress's mouth.

Perhaps surprisingly, Justice Scalia's opinion, joined by Justice Stevens, goes even further, providing the clearest indications of a jurisprudence of constitutional responsibility. In Scalia's view, the Constitution provides only one alternative to detaining someone pursuant to criminal charges, which is for Congress to exercise its extraordinary constitutional authority to suspend the writ of habeas corpus "when in cases of rebellion or invasion the public safety may require it." Short of an explicit suspension of the writ, even an otherwise specific, but ordinary, statute authorizing military detention of U.S. citizens would not be enough. While an act suspending the writ would be passed in the same way as any other statute, for Scalia it matters that Congress make it clear that it is performing an action that is highly unusual and gives extraordinary authority to the executive.[36] In this way, Congress makes itself most fully accountable for its actions, and most clearly puts the community behind the decision.

Scalia's approach would also keep the judiciary out of the business of setting the rules for how the executive fights a war, leaving that job to Congress: "A suspension of the writ could, of course, lay down conditions for continued detention, similar to those that today's [plurality] opinion prescribes under the Due Process Clause. . . . But there is a world of difference between the people's representatives' determining the need for that suspension (and prescribing the conditions for it), and this Court's doing so."[37]

The problem with the Court's stepping in and making up for Congress's inaction is twofold. First, it actually accrues to the Court the power to make grave decisions about the conduct of war, rather than leaving those decisions to be made first by the people's representatives. This is not only undemocratic, but takes the Court into an area in which its institutional competence is at its lowest ebb.[38]

Second, when the Court steps in as the plurality would have it do, it actually encourages the political branches to shirk their constitutional responsibilities in the future, because they can rest assured that the Court will be there to fill the void. As Scalia wrote:

> There is a certain harmony of approach in the plurality's making up for Congress's failure to invoke the Suspension Clause and its making up for the Executive's failure to apply what it says are needed procedures—an approach that reflects what might be called a Mr. Fix-it Mentality. The plurality seems to view it as its

mission to Make Everything Come Out Right, rather than merely to decree the consequences, as far as individual rights are concerned, of the other two branches' actions and omissions. Has the Legislature failed to suspend the writ in the current dire emergency? Well, we will remedy that failure by prescribing the reasonable conditions that a suspension should have included. And has the Executive failed to live up to those reasonable conditions? Well, we will ourselves make that failure good, so that this dangerous fellow (if he is dangerous) need not be set free. The problem with this approach is not only that it steps out of the courts' modest and limited role in a democratic society; but that by repeatedly doing what it thinks the political branches ought to do it encourages their lassitude and saps the vitality of government by the people.[39]

To remedy this problem, and encourage Congress and the president to perform their constitutional responsibilities, Justice Scalia would have the Court impose real consequences for the political branches' inaction: requiring the executive to lodge criminal charges against Hamdi or else set him free.[40] While this result may appear draconian, the desire to avoid political accountability for setting an enemy combatant free during wartime would presumably provide sufficient incentive for Congress to suspend the writ or the president to muster sufficient evidence to file criminal charges.

TOWARD A JURISPRUDENCE OF
CONSTITUTIONAL RESPONSIBILITY

The Court's detention decisions demonstrate that when Congress abdicates its responsibility to make tough decisions on national security questions, the executive will overreach, infringing on individuals' liberty, and the judiciary will then step in and try to fix things, but with results that may protect neither liberty nor security. Only if Congress fulfills its responsibility to take meaningful action on national security issues can our structure of government work as intended by the framers of the Constitution, and in a way that is adequate to the problems that face us in the war on terrorism.

In the wake of the Court's decisions, public and media attention focused on how the Court had stood up for individual rights and taken the president down a peg. What went largely unnoticed was the role of the missing actor in this scene—Congress.

Yet, in the Court's decisions, particularly the opinions of Justices Souter and Scalia in *Hamdi*, there are traces of an incipient jurisprudence of constitutional responsibility that offers a different way of looking at the separation of powers—and one which cuts across the usual ideological lines. With this approach, courts can play an important role in spurring Congress to act where it is supposed to. This would require courts to consider not just the constitutional powers of each branch but also their responsibilities, and to craft their rulings in a manner that creates political consequences for congressional inaction rather than attempting to do Congress's job. In this way, a jurisprudence of constitutional responsibility can bring a new vitality to the separation of powers, which depends on an active and assertive Congress to prevent executive overreaching and thereby protect individual liberty.

NOTES

1. See, for example, *Hamdi v. Rumsfeld*, No. 03-6696 (U.S. Supreme Court, June 28, 2004), slip opinion at 9-11 (Scalia, J., dissenting). See also *Youngstown Co. v. Sawyer*, 343 U.S. 579, 653 (1952) (Jackson, J., concurring) ("In the practical working of our Government we already have evolved a technique within the framework of the Constitution by which normal executive powers may be considerably expanded to meet an emergency. Congress may and has granted extraordinary authorities which lie dormant in normal times but may be called into play by the executive in war or upon proclamation of a national emergency. . . . Under this procedure we retain Government by law—special, temporary law, perhaps, but law nonetheless. The public may know the extent and limitations of the powers than can be asserted, and persons affected may be informed from the statute of their rights and duties").

2. The predominance of party loyalty over institutional loyalty is as old as the party system. As Justice Jackson wrote in *Youngstown Co. v. Sawyer*: "[The] rise of the party system has made a significant extraconstitutional supplement to real executive power. No appraisal of his necessities is realistic which overlooks that he heads a political system as well as a legal system. Party loyalties and interests, sometimes more binding than law, extend his effective control into branches of government other than his own and he often may win, as a political leader, what he cannot command under the Constitution. . . . But I have no illusion that any decision by this Court can keep power in the hands of Congress if it is not wise and timely in meeting its problems. A crisis that challenges the President equally, or perhaps primarily, challenges Congress. If not good law, there was worldly wisdom in the maxim attributed to Napoleon that 'The tools belong to the man who can use them.' We may say that power to legislate for emergencies belongs in the hands of Congress, but only Congress itself can prevent power from slipping through its fingers" [343 U.S. 579, 654 (1952) (Jackson, J., concurring)].

3. The classic expression of the Supreme Court's traditional separation of powers analysis is found in Justice Jackson's concurrence in *Youngstown Co*. In that case, the Court rejected President Truman's assertion that his constitutional authority as "Commander in Chief" allowed him to seize and operate domestic steel mills to ensure production

needed for the Korean War. In a separate opinion, Justice Jackson described an approach for examining assertions of executive power that is often cited by courts and legal scholars examining the constitutionality of executive action. Jackson divided executive actions into three categories. "1. When the president acts pursuant to an express or implied authorization of Congress, his authority is at its maximum, for it includes all that he possesses in his own right plus all that Congress can delegate. . . . If his act is held unconstitutional under these circumstances, it usually means that the Federal Government as an undivided whole lacks power. A seizure executed by the president pursuant to an Act of Congress would be supported by the strongest of presumptions and the widest latitude of judicial interpretation, and the burden of persuasion would rest heavily upon any who might attack it. 2. When the president acts in absence of either a congressional grant or denial of authority, he can only rely upon his own independent powers, but there is a zone of twilight in which he and Congress may have concurrent authority, or in which its distribution is uncertain. Therefore, congressional inertia, indifference or quiescence may sometimes, at least as a practical matter, enable, if not invite, measures on independent presidential responsibility. In this area, any actual test of power is likely to depend on the imperatives of events and contemporary imponderables rather than on abstract theories of law. 3. When the president takes measures incompatible with the expressed or implied will of Congress, his power is at its lowest ebb, for then he can rely only upon his own constitutional powers minus any constitutional powers of Congress over the matter. Courts can sustain exclusive presidential control in such a case only by disablingthe Congress from acting upon the subject. Presidential claim to a power at once so conclusive and preclusive must be scrutinized with caution, for what is at stake is the equilibrium established by our constitutional system." The second category described by Jackson is the one that concerns us here. But his approach offers little guidance on how the Court should determine whether the president possesses constitutional power in the face of congressional quiescence, since the Constitution's broad grant of unenumerated powers to the president is elastic enough to allow presidents to claim authority to do nearly anything, particularly in wartime. Only by supplementing an examination of executive powers with an analysis of congressional responsibility can we find an adequate way of answering the juridical question posed in cases that fall into Jackson's second category.

4. Ironically, the Framers thought that the legislative branch would "necessarily predominate" and therefore needed to be checked by dividing it into two houses, and that "the weakness of the executive may require . . . that it should be fortified." See *Federalist* 51. In this respect, the Framers failed to anticipate the overreaching executive and the acquiescent Congress we have today. See also *Federalist* 48.

5. The full name of the Act is the *Uniting and Strengthening America by Providing Appropriate Tools Required to Intercept and Obstruct Terrorism Act of 2001*.

6. 115 Stat. 224.

7. Adam Liptak, "For Post-9/11 Material Witness, It Is a Terror of a Different Kind," *New York Times* (August 19, 2004), A1. See 18 U.S.C. § 3144. Steve Fainaru and Margot Williams, "Material Witness Law Has Many in Limbo," *Washington Post*

(November 24, 2002), A1. Even the federal appeals court that upheld the government's use of the statute to detain "material witnesses" in connection with grand jury proceedings, as opposed to criminal trials, noted that "it would be improper for the government to use [the material witness statute] for other ends, such as the detention of persons suspected of criminal activity for which probable cause has not yet been established." *U.S. v. Awadallah* (2d Cir. Nov. 7, 2003), slip opinion at 43. But since the government can always claim that someone who is himself suspected of involvement in terrorism might also have material testimony to offer to a grand jury, the broadly written statute invites exactly the sort of abuse that the court said would be improper.

8. Hamdi was seized by the Northern Alliance (a coalition of groups opposed to the Taliban government) in Afghanistan in 2001 and then handed over to the U.S. military, which eventually moved him to a navy brig in South Carolina. The government alleged that Hamdi was an enemy combatant because he affiliated with a Taliban military unit, received weapons training, and remained with that unit even after September 11 when the Taliban engaged in armed conflict with the United States. *Hamdi* at 5 (Opinion of O'Connor, J.). Hamdi disputed these allegations. The government initially denied Hamdi access to counsel, but then relented and appointed counsel for him after the Supreme Court decided to hear the case. Ibid. at 32. Following the Supreme Court's decision holding that Hamdi must be afforded some access to U.S. courts to challenge his detention (discussed infra), the government released him and sent him to Saudi Arabia. Padilla, was arrested in 2002 at O'Hare airport in Chicago as he stepped off a plane after flying from Pakistan. He was initially detained as a material witness in connection with the September 11 investigation, but was then deemed an enemy combatant and transferred to military custody by order of the president. The government alleged that Padilla was associated with Al Qaeda and had "engaged . . . in hostile and war-like acts, including . . . preparation for acts of international terrorism" against the United States. *Rumsfeld v. Padilla*, No. 03-1027 (U.S. Supreme Court, June 28, 2004), slip opinion at 1–2 & n.2. Padilla disputed these allegations. Following the Supreme Court's decision in *Hamdi*, discussed infra, a federal district court in early 2005 ordered that Padilla be released if the government did not file criminal charges against him. *Padilla v. Hanft*, Civil Action No. 2:04-2221-26AJ (U.S. Dist. Ct. for the Dist. of South Carolina, Feb. 28, 2005).

9. *Hamdi* at 20 (Opinion of O'Connor, J.) (quoting Government's Brief at 26). *Hamdi* at 2 (opinion of Souter, J., concurring in part, dissenting in part, and concurring in the judgment).

10. U.S. Department of Justice, Office of Legal Counsel, Memorandum for Alberto R. Gonzales, Counsel to the president, Re: Standards of Conduct for Interrogation under 18 U.S.C. §§ 2340-2340A (Aug. 1, 2002) ("DoJ Interrogation Memo").

11. 18 U.S.C. §§ 2340A.

12. DoJ Interrogation Memo at 33, 34–35, 39.

13. U.S. Constitution, Art. I, § 8, cls. 11, 14. Ibid., cls. 1, 11, 12, 13. Similarly, the Constitution gives Congress the power "to provide for organizing, arming, and disciplining, the Militia, and for governing such part of them as may be employed in the

Service of the United States. Ibid., cl. 16. Ibid., cl. 11. It also failed to mention Congress's "power . . . to make all laws which shall be necessary and proper for carrying into execution the foregoing powers, and all other powers vested by this Constitution in the government of the United States, or in any department or officer thereof." Ibid., cl. 18.

14. Indeed, as Justice Scalia wrote in his dissent in *Hamdi* (at page 16): "Except for the actual command of military forces, all authorization for their maintenance and all explicit authorization for their use is placed in the control of Congress under Article I, rather than the president under Article II."

Justice Jackson makes the same point in his concurrence in *Youngstown Co.*—an opinion that the OLC memo also glaringly omits in its discussion of the separation of powers: "[The president] has no monopoly of 'war powers.' . . . While Congress cannot deprive the president of the command of the army and navy, only Congress can provide him an army or navy to command. It is also empowered to make rules for the 'Government and Regulation of land and naval Forces,' by which it may to some unknown extent impinge upon even command functions. That military powers of the Commander in Chief were not to supersede representative government of internal affairs seems obvious from the Constitution and from elementary American history. . . . Congress, not the executive, should control utilization of the war power as an instrument of domestic policy. . . . No penance would ever expiate the sin against free government of holding that a president can escape control of executive powers by law through assuming his military role. What the power of command may include I do not try to envision, but I think it is not a military prerogative, without support of law, to seize persons or property because they are important or even essential for the military and naval establishment" [343 U.S. at 644-646].

15. Mike Allen and Susan Schmidt, "Memo on Interrogation Tactics Is Disavowed," *Washington Post* (June 23, 2004), A1. U.S. Department of Justice, Office of Legal Counsel, Memorandum for James B. Comey, Deputy Attorney General, Re: Legal Standards Applicable Under 18 U.S.C. §§ 2340-2340A (December 20, 2004). The second Justice Department memorandum was issued just before the Senate hearings on the nomination of Alberto Gonzales for Attorney General.

16. The Supreme Court decided a third case, *Rumsfeld v. Padilla*, on procedural grounds, holding that Jose Padilla filed his habeas corpus petition in the wrong district court, and so it did not address the constitutional and statutory issues concerning the president's authority to detain U.S. citizens.

17. Justice Kennedy concurred in the court's judgment, but did not sign the majority's opinion.

18. *Rasul v. Bush*, No. 03-334 (U.S. Supreme Court, June 28, 2004), slip opinion at 6 (quoting *Shaughnessy v. United States ex rel. Mezei*, 345 U.S. 206, 218–219 (1953) (Jackson, J., dissenting).

19. In that case, *Johnson v. Eisentrager*, 339 U.S. 763 (1950), the Court denied habeas jurisdiction to German citizens tried for war crimes by a U.S. military commission in China and then incarcerated in a U.S. prison in occupied Germany after World War II.

20. *Rasul* at 7–8.

21. *Rasul* at 11 (Scalia, J., dissenting) ("the Court boldly extends the scope of the habeas statute to the four corners of the earth").

22. The Court states, for instance: "In the end, the answer to the question presented is clear. Petitioners contend that they are being held in federal custody in violation of the laws of the United States. No party questions the District Court's jurisdiction over petitioners' custodians. [The habeas statute], by its terms, requires nothing more." *Rasul* at 15.

23. *Rasul* at 11–12 (Scalia, J., dissenting). Justice Kennedy, like Justice Scalia, appears to think that the majority's reasoning might "creat[e] automatic statutory authority to adjudicate the claims of persons located outside the United States." *Rasul* at 4 (Kennedy, J., concurring in judgment).

    Justice Scalia's concern is probably hyperbolic. In the final analysis, it seems likely that the presence of the secretary of defense or other senior officials within the territorial jurisdiction of a U.S. court would not in itself give rise to habeas jurisdiction. On the same day it decided *Rasul*, the Court held in *Padilla* that a habeas petition must be brought against the detainee's "immediate custodian," such as the commander of the detention facility, and not against that commander's superior, even if the latter maintains ultimate "legal control" over the detainee. *Padilla* at 10–11. Thus, despite the Court's broad language in *Rasul*, it would seem that the presence of the secretary of defense or other senior officials in the jurisdiction of a district court would not be enough to establish habeas jurisdiction, and that some other factors found in *Rasul* would have to be present. But *Rasul* leaves unclear what those factors are. On the other hand, in *Padilla*, it was clear that habeas jurisdiction would exist *somewhere*, since Padilla's immediate custodian, the commander of the navy brig in Charleston, was within the jurisdiction of a federal court in South Carolina. If a detainee is held outside of the United States and the commander of that facility is also outside the United States, the Court might not be as strict in enforcing the "immediate custodian" rule it enunciated in *Padilla*. But one cannot be sure, since the Court's reasoning is so unclear.

24. The Defense Department's initial response to the *Rasul* decision was to provide Combatant Status Review hearings at Guantanamo, in which a detainee could contest his status as an enemy combatant before a panel of three military officers with the assistance of a military representative, but would not be allowed to see all of the government's evidence against him or have the assistance of a lawyer. It is not at all clear whether the Supreme Court would find that such hearings were sufficient to avoid habeas review altogether or to minimize the degree of judicial scrutiny. At least one court, post-*Rasul*, found that these military review hearings did not satisfy the constitutional requirement of due process. *In re Guantanamo Detainee Cases*, Civil Action Nos. 02-CV-0299 et al. (U.S. Dist. Court for D.C. Jan. 31, 2005).

    In fact, the confusion about *Rasul's* meaning could be seen in conflicting judicial interpretations several months after the Supreme Court's decision. Compare *ibid. at 18* ("While th[is] Court would have welcomed a clearer declaration in the *Rasul* opinion regarding the specific constitutional and other substantive rights of the petitioners . . . th[is] Court interprets *Rasul* . . . to require the recognition that the detainees at Guantanamo Bay possess enforceable constitutional rights") with *Khalid v. Bush*, Civil Case No. 1:04-1142 (RJL) at 18–21 (U.S. Dist. Court for D.C., Jan 19, 2005) (interpreting *Rasul* as holding merely that Guantanamo detainees have a right to a judicial hearing, but not that they have any substantive constitutional rights).

25. *Rasul* at 19 (Scalia, J., dissenting). While some judicial process would inevitably follow to evaluate the constitutionality of this regime as applied to individual detainees, the specific rules set by Congress will be clearer than any the courts are likely to provide. Reviewing courts are more likely to defer to a system constructed by both political branches rather than by the executive alone, and the rules will have the imprimatur of the people's representatives. Yet Congress, as of this writing, has still shown no inclination to get involved. As Justice Scalia noted: "Congress is in session. If it wished to change federal judges' habeas jurisdiction.., it could have done so. And it could have done so by intelligent revision of the statute, instead of by today's clumsy, countertextual reinterpretation." *Rasul* at 19–20 (Scalia, J., dissenting).

26. 18 U.S.C. § 4001(a). *Hamdi* at 9 (opinion of O'Connor, J.); *Hamdi* at 4–6 (opinion of Souter, J.). *Hamdi* at 10, 12, 9 (opinion of O'Connor, J.). The plurality therefore did not need to reach the president's argument that "the Executive possesses plenary authority to detain pursuant to Article II of the Constitution" and that therefore "no explicit congressional authorization is required." See also *Hamdi* at 9–10 (Thomas, J., dissenting).

27. *Hamdi* at 13 (opinion of O'Connor, J.). The plurality expressed concern over the idea that a detainee could be held for the duration of the open-ended war on terrorism, a conflict of potentially "perpetual" duration. Ibid. at 12. But because Hamdi was alleged to be a member of the Taliban rather than of Al Qaeda or another terrorist group, the plurality concluded simply that Hamdi could be held only as long the U.S. military was engaged in active combat in Afghanistan, without having to define the permissible duration of detention of an alleged terrorist during the war on terrorism. Ibid. at 13–14.

28. Justice Thomas disagreed that the AUMF limited the duration of detention, stating that international treaties could not limit the government's war powers, that the question of whether the U.S. was still at war was one for the political branches to decide, and that, in any event, detention could last beyond the cessation of formal hostilities. *Hamdi* at 10 (Thomas, J., dissenting).

29. "[A]s critical as the Government's interest may be in detaining those who actually pose an immediate threat to the national security of the United States during ongoing international conflict, history and common sense teach us that an unchecked system of detention carries the potential to become a means for oppression and abuse of others who do not present that sort of threat." *Hamdi* at 23–24 (opinion of O'Connor, J.).

30. Ibid. at 30.

31. The plurality reached this determination by engaging in a traditional judicial balancing test, "weighing 'the private interest that will be affected by the official action' against the Government's asserted interest, 'including the function involved' and the

burdens the Government would face in providing greater process" and analyzing " 'the risk of an erroneous deprivation' of the private interest if the process were reduced and the 'probable value, if any, of additional or substitute safeguards.' " *Hamdi* at 22 (quoting *Mathews v. Eldridge*, 424 U. S. 319, 335 (1976)). The district court had found that the sole evidence offered by the government—an affidavit of a Defense Department official recounting in general terms the circumstances of Hamdi's capture and his detention and interrogation—as falling "far short" of what was necessary to justify Hamdi's detention, and it required the government to turn over numerous documents for the court's review, including copies of Hamdi's own statements, notes of interviews with him, a list of his interrogators, statements by his Northern Alliance captors, a list of the dates and locations of his capture and detentions, and the names and titles of the government officials who determined that he was an enemy combatant. Ibid. at 5–6, 26–27.

32. Ibid. at 51–52.

33. *Hamdi* at 9–10 (opinion of Souter, J.).

34. Justice Souter also argued the Non-Detention Act's specific prohibition on detentions other than "pursuant to an act of Congress" and the fact that that Act was designed to constrain executive confinement of citizens during wartime indicated that "Congress necessarily meant to require a congressional enactment that clearly authorized detention or imprisonment." Ibid. at 5–6. He also cited a principle of statutory interpretation "that subjected enactments limiting liberty in wartime to the requirement of a clear statement." Ibid. at 6. Under that principle, " 'in interpreting a wartime measure we must assume that [its] purpose was to allow for the greatest possible accommodation between . . . liberties and the exigencies of war. We must assume, when asked to find implied powers in a grant of legislative or executive authority, that the law makers intended to place no greater restraint on the citizen than was clearly and unmistakably indicated by the language they used.' " Ibid. (quoting *Ex Parte Endo* 323 U.S. 283, 300 (1944)).

35. Ibid. at 6–7. Justice Souter also noted that in the Patriot Act, passed thirty-eight days after the AUMF, Congress had "authorized the detention of alien terrorists for no more than seven days in the absence of criminal charges or deportation proceeding." He therefore found it "very difficult to believe that the same Congress that carefully circumscribed executive power to detain alien terrorists" would provide much broader authority to detain American citizens. Ibid. at 13–14.

36. Justice Scalia noted, though, that such extraordinary detention authority has usually been unnecessary, as presidents have normally found the criminal justice system adequate to their purposes even during wartime (including the prosecution and conviction of another American captured in Afghanistan, John Walker Lindh). *Hamdi* at 6–8 (Scalia, J., dissenting). U.S. Const., Art I, sec. 9, cl. 2. As Justice Scalia wrote, "The Suspension Clause of the Constitution, which carefully circumscribes the conditions under which the writ can be withheld, would be a sham if it could be evaded by congressional prescription of requirements *other than the common-law requirement of committal for criminal prosecution* that render the writ, though available, unavailing. If the Suspension Clause does not guarantee the citizen that he will either be tried

or released, unless the conditions for suspending the writ exist and the grave action of suspending the writ has been taken; if it merely guarantees the citizen that he will not be detained unless Congress by ordinary legislation says he can be detained; it guarantees him very little indeed." *Hamdi* at 23 (Scalia, J., dissenting) (emphasis in original).

37. Ibid. at 21.
38. As Scalia wrote, "It should not be thought . . . that the plurality's evisceration of the Suspension Clause augments, principally, the power of Congress. As usual, the major effect of its constitutional improvisation is to increase the power of the Court. Having found a congressional authorization for detention of citizens where none clearly exists; and having discarded the categorical procedural protection of the Suspension Clause; the plurality then proceeds, under the guise of the Due Process Clause, to prescribe what procedural protections *it* thinks appropriate." Ibid. at 23. As Scalia argued: "I frankly do not know whether [normal criminal detention authorities] are sufficient to meet the Government's security needs, including the need to obtain intelligence through interrogation. It is far beyond my competence, or the Court's competence, to determine that. But it is not beyond Congress's. If the situation demands it, the Executive can ask Congress to authorize suspension of the writ—which can be made subject to whatever conditions Congress deems appropriate, including even the procedural novelties invented by the plurality today. To be sure, suspension is limited by the Constitution to cases of rebellion or invasion. But whether the attacks of September 11, 2001, constitute an 'invasion,' and whether those attacks still justify suspension several years later, are questions for Congress rather than this Court. If civil rights are to be curtailed during wartime, it must be done openly and democratically, as the Constitution requires, rather than by silent erosion through an opinion of this Court."

Ibid. at 26 (citation omitted). Justice Thomas, in his dissent, agreed with Justice Scalia that courts lack the competence to make decisions about how war should be conducted. But he gave short shrift to the role that Congress must play in making those decisions and to the court's legitimate role as the interpreter of the law and the ultimate enforcer of the structure of separation of powers.

39. Ibid. at 24–25.
40. Justice Scalia wrote: "It is not the habeas court's function to make illegal detention legal by supplying a process that the Government could have provided, but chose not to. If Hamdi is being imprisoned in violation of the Constitution (because without due process of law), then his habeas petition should be granted; the executive may then hand him over to the criminal authorities, whose detention for the purpose of prosecution will be lawful, or else must release him." Ibid. at 24.

It appears likely that Justices Souter and Ginsburg would agree with this outcome in Hamdi's case, given the lack of a clear statute authorizing detention. But recognizing that they lacked the votes to force that disposition, Souter and Ginsburg went along with the plurality's view that Hamdi could continue to be detained by the military, but must be given a meaningful chance to challenge his enemy combatant status in court. See ibid. at 15 (opinion of Souter, J.).

Part Five   **Character, Citizenship, and Values**

Chapter 10 Character Education and the Challenge of Raising a Moral Generation

Chester E. Finn, Jr.

Every society, primitive or sophisticated, has devised mechanisms for teaching its young what they must know to succeed as adult members of that community. This preparation-and-induction process typically inculcates the society's essential skills, rules, and mores, as well as its core values.

In advanced countries, this process engages myriad institutions, including family, neighborhood and church, a host of other civil society organizations, and—our present focus—the system of formal education.

In the United States, just about everyone agrees that we want to raise moral, well-behaved, and civic-minded children, and we look to schools to help accomplish this. Indeed, we typically look to the schools for too much help—and thus slough off a portion of our responsibilities as parents, grandparents, aunts and uncles, neighbors, scoutmasters, employers, and preachers.

Striving to rise to this challenge, American schools have long viewed forging citizens as a core mission, along with imparting basic academic skills and knowledge, preparing young people for further education, and equipping them to earn a living. This sense of civic obligation dates back to the founding of the public school system. Writes one of Horace Mann's biographers, "At the core of Mann's thinking was the conviction that it was possible to define a set of values that were essential to citizenship in a democracy and which while not identified with any particular religious sect, were nonetheless compatible with all." John Dewey's oft-cryptic writings are full of references to the obligation of schools to instill democratic values and personal morality.

That is all well and good. Where but in its public schools ought a free society look to bridge its differences, compromise its rivalries, tame its individual and group interests, and come together in pursuit of so obvious a common good as the preparation of today's children to be tomorrow's citizens?

DESIRE FOR CIVIC FORMATION

That sense of obligation has never vanished. Indeed, when Americans are asked about the desired attributes of a successfully educated person at the conclusion of compulsory schooling, most place citizenship high on the list. Hence, when developing standards and curricula in subjects like social studies, states and communities generally accompany the traditional academic content with attention to citizenship, social norms, and the like. This may include overt "character education" or "moral education" and nearly always incorporates civic values, rights, responsibilities, and participation, at least in its statement of aspirations. Here, for example, is the opening paragraph of New Jersey's description of its "core curriculum content standards for social studies":

> Citizen participation in government is essential in forming this nation's democracy, and is vital in sustaining it. Social studies education promotes loyalty and love of country and it prepares students to participate intelligently in public affairs. Its component disciplines foster in students the knowledge and skills needed to make sense of current political and social issues. By studying history, geography, American government and politics, and other nations, students can learn to contribute to national, state, and local decision-making. They will also develop an understanding of the American constitutional system, an active awareness, and commitment to the rights and responsibilities of citizenship, a tolerance for those with whom they disagree, and an understanding of the world beyond the borders of the United States.[1]

This aspiration has freshened in the aftermath of terrorist attacks, in the face of weakness in other key institutions (such as the family), and in the presence of mounting evidence that some antidote to malignant values transmitted by popular culture and the mass media is needed.

Yet it is easy to exaggerate the school's capacity to attain such lofty goals. Formal schooling occupies a relatively small place in children's lives and depends on other institutions to buttress and amplify its teachings. Moreover, we tend to overstate Americans' consensus on values that everyone wants to see the public schools impart to their own and everyone else's daughters and sons. Although we cherish the image of yesterday's schools transforming young immigrants (and frequently their parents) into stalwart and assimilated Americans, we also do well to recall that, as early as the 1890s, what passed for shared values among many were repugnant to others—in that case Roman Catholics who balked at the pervasive Protestantism of the period's public schools and turned instead to their own new network of parish schools. We are also wise to remember that, in 1922, the Supreme Court ratified the right of parents to send their children to schools other than those operated by the state.

Yet a kernel of expectation remains, and sometimes it is justified. When the citizens of a community are able to embrace a coherent set of civic values, behavioral norms, and morals that represent a reasonable consensus of that community; when the schools' teachings are reinforced by other key institutions, and adults do a decent job of supporting these values and shielding children from harmful influences that push the other way; and when inculcating "citizenship" is widely viewed as a major duty of the schools—under such circumstances, we can reasonably expect much help from schools in socializing the young.

Today, though, those ideal circumstances are lamentably rare. In most parts of contemporary America, the schools' potency in forging citizens is impaired by five tough challenges: (1) crumbling agreement on matters of values, citizenship, and morality; (2) failure of nerve among educators; (3) powerful pressures on the schools to focus on other matters; (4) unprecedented strength of those that send contrary signals to schools and teachers; and (5) the limited leverage of schooling itself, particularly in the face of weakness in many institutions that should backstop the schools and their teachers.

ELUSIVE CONSENSUS

For forty years now, public schools have been caught in the crossfire of the "culture wars," and they're showing plenty of bullet holes. Sure, there is still a narrow band of quintessential American values that just about everyone agrees schools should teach and model: tolerance, freedom, courage, honesty, responsibility, and so forth. One can often see these in elementary or middle schools, perhaps a single word inscribed on a large piece of paper under the heading "value of the month."

That is fine as far as it goes, but it does not go far. Introduce such concepts as "patriotism," "family," or "religion" and you quickly get labeled a "right-winger." Try such propositions as "privacy," "a woman's right to choose," and "gun control" and you will be dubbed a "liberal." So public schools tend simply to steer clear of such "values" and the arguments they engender. It gets worse if the teacher should take up such touchy matters as terrorism, Islam, evolution, immigration, divorce, racism, crime, or the military. Prudent teachers just do not go there. But not going is apt to mean that schools have little opportunity to expose students in any constructive way to many of the debates that (perhaps unfortunately) lie near the heart of our civic and moral consciousness.

Public schools are among today's bloodiest battlefields in these wars. Even as the demand builds for better "civic education" for young Americans, if only to equip them for successful adulthood in a world where democratic values in general and America in particular are under assault, educators are encouraged, first by those who train them and then by their employers and professional peers, to remain agnostic on controversial topics, relativistic about such distinctions as good and evil, nonjudgmental with regard to behavior, and quasi-therapeutic rather than doctrinaire when it comes to student attitudes and character traits. (Recall, for example, the advice that myriad education organizations gave teachers regarding the appropriate classroom response to the September 11 terrorist attacks. It could be summarized as "make sure your students feel safe and quash any hostility toward Muslims.")

At bottom, there is a lot that Americans do not agree about today, and public schools have great difficulty tackling those issues. The core problem is that we are no longer sure we are even supposed to agree—that is, that common values and cultural norms ought to soften and bridge our differences, that the "unum" needs to balance the "pluribus." Having replaced the "melting pot" with a "salad bowl," we are left with a society in which some insist that their kids learn about carrots while others are obsessed with tomatoes or celery.

To an alarming degree, the education profession is awash in relativism, postmodernism, multiculturalism, and child-centeredness, all calculated *not* to produce teachers (or textbooks, lesson plans), who think it is their job to instruct children on the difference between right and wrong, good and bad, beautiful and ugly, democratic and authoritarian. A 1997 survey of education-school professors made clear that their own beliefs about what is important for teachers to know and schools to do are far from the American main-stream.[2] We also know that teachers, like everyone else, live and learn within a broader culture that transmits noisome values (via television, movies, pop-ular music, etc.) while signaling that anything goes, that one's own pleasures and needs deserve top priority, and that self-respecting grown-ups do not render harsh judgments or make invidious comparisons.

No wonder some educators flirt with moral relativism, excessive deference to the "pluribus," and cynicism toward established cultural conventions, civic institutions, and traditional sources of authority. But transmitting such du-bious values to children will gradually weaken the moral foundations of a free society and thus make matters worse than never addressing these topics at all.

Some educators are simply gun-shy—and with reason. There was a time, primarily in the 1980s, when states urged them to poke into students' values and, especially, behavior. Known as "outcomes based" education, this began as a logical response to the era's new focus on schooling's discernible results rather than its inputs and requirements. In some jurisdictions, however, it led to a focus on pupil attitudes and actions, such as "respecting diversity" and "working collaboratively with others." This proved politically untenable, as parents protested against government imposing patterns of behavior or thought on children under the guise of mandatory academic standards. So most states pulled back from behavioral and affective standards and confined their standards to the cognitive domains. The signal this sent to educators was to avoid sensitive topics that might inflame parents or their elected representatives.

There had been an earlier time, mainly during the 1970s flowering of relativism on university campuses, when some prominent educators, most famously Harvard professor Lawrence Kohlberg, urged schools to encourage children to "clarify" their own values. Instead of instructing youngsters on which values they should hold, such educators held that their responsibility was to refrain from being "judgmental" and, instead, to elicit the values that presumably lurk within the bosom of every human being. This produced a backlash among parents who felt that teachers should admonish children as to the difference between right and wrong, not refrain from such distinctions. In this case the message from parents to teachers was to plunge in. These contrary messages left a lasting imprint on the education profession and the training of teachers and principals. No wonder some teachers are confused about their role.

COUNTERVAILING PRESSURES

Schools are expected to do so much. The federal No Child Left Behind (NCLB) act demands that they make every single student "proficient" in reading and math. Many states insist that they also prepare young people to pass "high stakes" tests in various subjects, tests on which hinge their high school graduation and college prospects.

Besides preparing for the tests, all manner of subjects must be taken, according to the dictates of legislators, school boards, and sometimes judges: U.S. history, state history, health, physical education. Then there are the myriad topics and issues—environmentalism, black history, drug education, sex (or abstinence) education—to which schools are asked to introduce their young charges.

It sometimes seems that every adult dispute, every social malady, and every modern plague leads to demands for schools to tackle this problem, to "educate" children about it in the hope that it will ease or go away. Never mind that this impulse to solve problems via education is naïve; never mind that it lightens the burden on those agencies and institutions that might properly be expected to shoulder responsibility for such solutions. Consider, simply, the huge curricular and extracurricular burden that it places on the schools. And ask how, then, can they reasonably be expected also to forge moral citizens with good character and sound values? Such things cannot be consigned to a twenty-minute curricular slot on Tuesdays and Thursdays. If done at all, they must suffuse every aspect of the school. But how can they do that when teachers and principals are consumed by test prep, math drill, pep rallies, in-service days, state day, Valentine's Day, Kwanzaa, and the proper use of condoms?

American youngsters spend relatively little of their lives under the school roof: only 9 percent of their hours on earth between birth and their eighteenth birthdays.[3] This means that more than nine-tenths of their time is spent elsewhere.

Middle-class parents sometimes insist that such statistics cannot be true, that their entire lives revolve around school. And it is true that school may influence a larger fraction of many middle-class days, especially if homework is heavy, if extracurricular activities engage youngsters until late afternoon, if the school sponsors after-school projects and weekend events, and if it is located far enough from home to force much time to be spent commuting. The sense that life is school-centered is keenest in households where parents calibrate family rhythms to school schedules, oversee homework assignments, and limit television and other nonacademic pursuits lest they interfere with schoolwork. The picture is very different, however, for youngsters from disorganized families and heedless parents, whose school attendance may be spotty, whose attention to homework may be patchy, and whose lives from 2:30 P.M. until 8:00 A.M.—and all day on weekends and during summers—are scarcely touched by the demands and expectations of teachers and schools.

From a "values and morals" standpoint, the school's limited leverage can be good or bad. On the plus side, it means that if parents, churches, and other nonschool institutions are purposeful and effective in their nurturing of youthful virtue, they can exert a powerful and positive influence on how children turn out. On the minus side, it means that, for many youngsters, time outside school is spent in the grip not of positive, value-shaping institutions but in the clutch of the popular culture (or, worse, street and gang culture). In that case, even a conscientious effort by teachers and schools to instill sound values during their modest portion of the day is apt to be swamped by the forces at work on youngsters during the other 91 percent.

Schools, fortunately, are not our only sources of socialization and nurturing. Many young Americans have ready access to a still-vibrant civil society. A lot of parents, neighborhoods, and churches take such matters seriously. We have other institutions (for example, the military) that do a pretty good job of civic formation (though Abu Ghraib rattles one's confidence on that front). We have reasonably sturdy political structures, abiding patriotism, and a general awareness that our system is based on ideas and principles that command wide assent among Americans. We also have a lot of other education delivery systems, formal and informal, and a burgeoning school-choice movement that is giving people more options, including some that are energetic on the civic/morals/values front.

But let us not overstate the potential for dramatic gains via other institutions, especially for the young people in greatest need. A troubling fraction of American kids is largely beyond the reach of those positive influences, while firmly in the grip of the culture's ample supply of harmful influences (TV, rap, bloody movies, etc.). And it is a bit ironic to celebrate as transmitters of citizenship institutions whose most notable characteristic is their freedom from public control.

Despite private schooling, home schooling, and virtual schooling, moreover, most young Americans still get most of their formal instruction from government-operated public schools. Yet this heavy reliance on government as the main source of schooling creates its own paradox when it comes to educating American children in values, morals, and citizenship; two paradoxes, actually.

Paradox one: because we cherish freedom as a core value and insist that the state is the creature of its citizens, we are loath to allow state-run institutions to instruct tomorrow's citizens in how to think, how to behave, and what to believe. Because a free society is not self-maintaining, because its citizens must know something about democracy and individual rights and responsibilities, and because they must also learn how to behave in a law-abiding way that conforms to basic societal norms, it is the obligation of all governmental and nongovernmental educational institutions to assist in the transmission of these core ideas, habits, and skills. Indeed, we fret when we learn of schools that neglect this role. A frequent argument against voucher plans, for example, is that "Klan schools," "witchcraft schools," and "madrasas" will qualify for public subsidy. But should government define which values are sound? A paradox indeed. We want good citizens to emerge from all our schools, yet we do not really want agencies of the state to dictate their values and virtues.

Paradox two: classically, one might view government and its classrooms as a democracy's natural mechanism for transmitting consensual values and mainstream morals to the next generation. Public schooling's key role in the forging of American citizens during the first two-thirds of the twentieth century has been widely lauded, not just by that era's immigrants and their heirs but also by analysts of civic education and civil society.

Yet decades of cultural conflict have left us hyper-squeamish about public entities taking sides in matters which have become the stuff of contention more than consensus. Consider, for example, the battles over selecting textbooks in subjects like history, setting state academic standards, and preparing teachers. One might even say that today's government-controlled institutions have become the least trusted and perhaps least effective in our society when it comes to expressing shared values.

NEW RECOMMENDATIONS, NEW BATTLES

How, then, will our children learn what it means to be an American and how to behave as a moral member of adult society? Endless commission reports, foundation-supported projects, federal programs, and solemn jeremiads address the dilemmas of "civic education" in the United States in the early twenty-first century.

This repair project is a sticky topic, however, verging on a culture war of its own. On the one hand are those (such as the Carnegie Corporation, the Carnegie-funded "CIRCLE" project, and the Center for Civic Education) who contend that effective civic education via the public schools is primarily a matter of focus and funding. In other words, it could be done well if we were serious about it.

On the other hand are those who ruefully judge this enterprise to be essentially doomed, at least in the near term, at least as regards the public schools, and who accordingly invest greater hope in alternative providers.

Complicating this discussion is our gradual shifting of essential decisions about schooling farther away from home and community and thus from the most natural source of consensus on values and morals.

This is a relatively recent development in our history. When it comes to the content of education, for more than a century such determinations were made locally—at the town level, the principal's office, even the individual classroom. The state generally discharged its self-imposed education responsibility by furnishing free public schools and enacting "compulsory attendance" laws. Although school resources and operations were governed by many laws and regulations, the distant state said little about what pupils would actually learn.

This variability was a mixed blessing. It meant, on the one hand, that some children could complete their primary-secondary schooling without necessarily having learned much. On the other hand, in well-functioning communities it meant they were apt to imbibe those lessons—in matters civic as well as academic—that their elders deemed most important.

From a child's perspective, such local control amounted to an education crap shoot. In the right school or school system, one might encounter a terrific curriculum, well taught and faithfully grounded in the community's core values, which were in reasonable harmony with broader societal norms. In a bad school or ill-starred system, however, one might never learn more than was needed to, say, mine coal or push a plow like one's father or—worse—one might draw life's main lessons from the culture of the street corner or gang.

Beginning in the mid-twentieth century, states started to intrude into this tradition of local control, usually beginning with the introduction of high school graduation requirements, such as a year of U.S. history in eleventh grade. A few jurisdictions grew more specific. The public schools of California, Texas, and Florida, for example, could only use (at state expense, anyway) textbooks that state-level boards had vetted and approved. (State-wide textbook adoption is now the practice of twenty-two states.) New York's powerful Board of Regents, via its famed "Regents exams," spelled out the actual content of particular courses. Across most of the land, however, curricular decisions still remained with locally run school systems, individual schools, and teachers.

This situation began to mutate during the 1970s as America awakened to the troubling fact that some of its high school graduates could barely read and many were ill-prepared for college and work. One by one, states responded by enacting "minimum competency" tests that young people had to pass as part of demonstrating their fitness for a diploma. This had the effect of intruding the state directly into the specification of academic skills that all students must learn and show that they possess. It had the further effect of beginning to centralize and standardize such decisions, though almost exclusively with regard to basic skills such as the "three Rs."

But the centralizing did not stop there. After the National Commission on Excellence in Education warned us in 1983 that the nation was at risk due to the weak academic attainments of our students, states and, increasingly, the federal government began to get more precise about what pupils must learn at various grade levels. The "excellence movement," as some termed it, evolved into what is now called "standards-based reform," wherein (typically) the state prescribes a body of skills and knowledge that all schools are supposed to teach; administers tests designed to give everyone feedback on how well those standards are being met; and imposes rewards and sanctions intended to prod children and educators into doing better. Under NCLB, all states must now set academic standards for their public schools in three core subjects (reading, math, and science); give annual tests to monitor progress; and devise "accountability" schemes that seek, via a combination of carrots and sticks, to alter the behavior of students, teachers, and schools so as to foster the attainment of these standards.

One might suppose that this more centralized curriculum would make it easier for "the government" to do something about civic education, too, but that turns out, so far at least, not to be so. Because almost all the pressure and resources today are focused on basic skills, other worthy subjects—art, music, and languages, as well as social studies—risk marginalization. And to the extent that decisions about curricular content are centralized, they grow more remote from the consensual values of local communities and more vulnerable to state-level and national politics. This is a particular problem in the messy field of social studies, where state academic standards, for example, are now as subject to political pushing and tugging as textbooks already were. The result, as with textbooks, is apt to be safe, boring, and vanilla.

A school's curriculum is the obvious place to augment "book learning" about civics—how a bill becomes a law, and so on—with a fit concern for citizenship, values, and morals. When this succeeds, children come to understand not just how the government works and what it means to live in a democracy, but also how to behave in the public square (obey the traffic laws, pay your taxes, vote, wait your turn for the bus, engage in volunteer work, etc.) and in the privacy of one's home and neighborhood.

As one's conception of citizenship expands from knowledge to action, however, and from "understanding" to "participating," the formal curriculum's inherent limits become manifest. The recent and much-discussed Carnegie report on *The Civic Mission of Schools*, for example, spells out four goals for civic education, all denominated in terms of "competent and responsible citizens." The first one says such citizens are "informed and thoughtful," which meshes well enough with a classically curricular view of the school's role. But the other three—"participate in their communities," "act politically," and "have moral and civic virtues"—are harder to instill through books and classroom lessons.[4]

The Carnegie team was undeterred by that challenge. In its view, today's schools are doing a weak job with their "civic mission," but their doorstep is where this responsibility properly lodges, if only because society's other institutions "have lost the capacity or will to engage young people. . . . Schools can help reverse this trend."[5]

But can they really, especially as the definition of civic education stretches beyond the mundane facts of history and government functioning and addresses children's values and behavior? Will public schools be allowed to do much in this space? Do they know how? Have they the leverage?

Close scrutiny by fierce watchdog groups that scan the education horizon for the slightest hint of bias, religiosity, or sensitivity has made schools and educators wary, even as many of the professors who train them abjure fixed distinctions between right and wrong. How, then, can the schools reasonably be expected to mold young citizens? If all judgments depend upon one's unique perspective or background rather than universal standards of truth, beauty, or virtue, if every form of family, society, and polity is deemed equal to all others, and if every group's morals and values must be taught (along with its culture, food, music, etc.), who is there (in school) to help children determine what it means to be an upstanding American or moral adult?

Further complicating this picture is the embrace by many civic education reformers of what we may term the "political activism" view of their mission. This was crystal clear in the Carnegie study, which sees influencing public policy and engaging in political activity as the highest—maybe the only legitimate—form of civic participation and gives short shrift to being a good parent, dependable neighbor, and conscientious member of the nongovernmental institutions that comprise civil society. (It even faults school-based "service-learning" programs that are nonpolitical on the grounds that they may encourage "students to volunteer in place of political participation."[6])

Civic education is also roiled by overwrought political correctness and hypersensitivity to the possibility of controversy, beginning but not ending with the content of textbooks. This problem arises on both the left and the right. As the education historian Diane Ravitch explains, "The content of today's textbooks and tests reflects a remarkable convergence of the interests of feminists and multiculturalists on one side and the religious Right on the other. No words or illustrations may be used that might offend the former groups, and no topics can be introduced that might offend those on the other side of the ideological divide."[7]

Hence, much gets omitted from even the most straightforward instructional materials, and much of what remains has been so sanitized that it cannot possibly offend any person, group, cause, or viewpoint. This solves one problem but it also deprives schools and teachers of many of the very stories, books, poems, plays, and legends from which children might best learn the difference between good and evil, right and wrong, hero and villain, patriot and traitor. Because this peculiar paranoia has now been internalized by curriculum writers and textbook publishers, it causes new instructional materials to be value-free from the outset. Escalated to the level of state standards and district curricula, it substitutes mushy generalities for specifics. Nowhere is this clearer than in the troubled territory known as "social studies."

THE SOCIAL STUDIES MESS

The man in the street doubtless believes that social studies is mainly about history and civics, leavened with some geography and economics and that, at the end of a well-taught K–12 social studies sequence, young people will know who Abraham Lincoln and Theodore Roosevelt were, why World War II was fought, how to find Italy and Iraq on a map, what "supply and demand" mean, and how many senators each state sends to Washington for terms of what duration.

If that were so, school-based social studies would contribute to the forging of citizens, at least on the cognitive side. But that is not what animates the experts who dominate this field, shape its academic standards and textbooks, and signal to future primary-secondary teachers what is important for children to learn.

The main professional organization in this field is the National Council for the Social Studies (NCSS). Here is its view of what schools should accomplish:

> A well-designed social studies curriculum will help each learner construct a blend of personal, academic, pluralist, and global views of the human condition in the following ways: Students should be helped to construct a *personal perspective* that enables them to explore emerging events and persistent or recurring issues, considering implications for self, family, and the whole national and world community. . . . Students should be helped to construct an *academic perspective* through study and application of social studies learning experiences. . . . Students should be helped to construct a *pluralist perspective* based on diversity. This perspective involves respect for differences of opinion and preference; of race, religion, and gender; of class and ethnicity; and of culture in general. . . . Students should be

helped to construct a *global perspective* that includes knowledge, skills, and commitments needed to live wisely in a world that possesses limited resources and that is characterized by cultural diversity. A global perspective involves viewing the world and its people with understanding and concern. This perspective develops a sense of responsibility for the needs of all people and a commitment to finding just and peaceful solutions to global problems.[8]

Reading this statement, one can see that American education has a problem with the field of social studies itself, a field that is endlessly devoted to multiple "perspectives," manifests scant interest in students' basic knowledge of civics and history, and seems oblivious to the formation of Americans committed to the values of civic society.

If the Carnegie group has its way, I believe, the NCSS and its allies will have even more clout and civic education will be slanted even more in the direction of their idiosyncratic political values—and away from the kinds of book learning that may at least ground children in important information. (*The Civic Mission of Schools* report is schizophrenic about "knowledge," first admonishing educators to do better at instructing students in "government, history, law, and democracy," then deprecating "rote facts" on grounds that these "may actually alienate [pupils] from politics.") Thus we face a true conundrum: our schools have not done well at forging character, values, or civic consciousness in young Americans. But neither have they succeeded in imparting fundamental information to children about their country's history and the workings of its government and civil institutions. This ignorance was on massive display in May 2004 when innumerable articles about the new World War II memorial revealed how little the grandchildren and great-grandchildren of those brave warriors know about the causes, course, or consequences of that immense conflict. Yet those who rule this part of the curriculum today, and prominent reshapers of it for tomorrow, do not seem half as interested in closing the knowledge gap as in turning children into Americans with multiple perspectives.

CAN ANYTHING BE DONE?

Suggestions for strengthening school-based civic education take many forms and come from many directions. Six deserve brief mention:

• Redoubling and reorienting "civic education" in the schools along the lines suggested by Carnegie and "CIRCLE" or the Center for Civic Education.

There is some merit here, as well as plenty of curricular precedent, but I doubt that the "activist" side of this curriculum is healthy or that it can command wide political support.

- Introducing explicit "character education" programs into the schools. Many individuals and organizations are working at this, and they may do some good, especially if schools have a menu of such programs to select from. As with reading programs, however, sooner or later they have to demonstrate their efficacy via formal evaluations—the genuine kind, complete with control groups—or they're not worth bothering with.[9]

- Inclusion of civics in standards-based reform. If states required students to develop a certain level of knowledge and skill in civics and related subjects before being promoted or given a high school diploma, there is little doubt that schools and pupils would take this more seriously. But states are already encountering plenty of resistance to their high-stakes demands for basic skills. It is hard to picture many of them extending the list anytime soon.

- Increased leadership from Washington. Especially since September 11, the federal government has boosted its support for civic and history education through such agencies as the National Endowment for Humanities, the Department of Education, and the Corporation for National and Community Service. The White House established an office to spearhead and coordinate this.[10] Some have suggested that all such initiatives be housed in a new agency. Others urge that the No Child Left Behind Act be revised to include civics and history, along with reading and math, among the subjects that states must address. Certainly, Washington can supply modest funding streams for worthy projects, but it is awfully clumsy with so politically charged a topic—the more so after abortive efforts in the early 1990s to develop "national standards" for history and other subjects—and I see scant prospect that Uncle Sam is going to shift his focus away from the three Rs.

- Wholesale overhaul of social studies. A plucky band of historians and social studies reformers—self-styled "contrarians"—insists that the field itself is wrong-headed and needs a top-to-bottom reshaping that centers on more specific knowledge of history, geography, and civics.[11] I share this view. But it does not yet have much traction.

- School choice. Advocates of greater diversity, competition, and choice in K–12 education suggest (and can cite some evidence) that "schools of choice" are more apt to function as coherent communities with powerful norms and values and that their graduates are likelier to be civically engaged. Choice also provides a means of accommodating American pluralism without reducing everything to its least common denominator. In effect, it restores the "village school" that was able to harmonize its curriculum with its community's values—albeit with some risk that the cause of generally accepted civic values may not be served because the values taught in one school may differ from those taught a few blocks away.

At day's end, I am not confident that any of these reform strategies will succeed, but neither have I abandoned hope. We simply do not yet have sufficient evidence to put all our eggs into a single basket. Let us, therefore, not force ourselves to select among them. Rather, let us embark upon a period of serious experimentation on multiple fronts, including those just noted and combinations of them. But let it be serious experimentation, the kind that demands proof of efficacy, not just pious hopes and warm feelings.

Let me, finally, repeat this solemn but inconvenient truth: our schools would be far better able to succeed with their part of the task of socializing the young if our families and other institutions also did their parts—and if we curbed the negative influences at work on young Americans. Nothing I have seen or learned leads me to think that schools can handle this weighty assignment by themselves.

NOTES

1. http://www.state.nj.us/njded/cccs/11socintro.html.
2. Steve Farkas and Jean Johnson, *Different Drummers: How Teachers of Teachers View Public Education* (New York: Public Agenda, 1997). This was the first comprehensive survey of the views of education professors from U.S. colleges and universities ever undertaken. Their vision of education and the mission of teacher education programs are explored, including their attitudes toward core curriculum, testing, standards, and the public's parameters.
3. One can easily calculate this. The numerator consists of 180 (the typical number of days in the school year, assuming perfect attendance) × 13 (the number of years of schooling from kindergarten through high school (assuming full-day kindergarten) × 6 (the number of hours in the typical school day, with no discount taken for recess, lunch, gym or study hall). The denominator is 365 (days in the year) × 18 (years on earth) × 24 (hours per day). The quotient is .09. If you want to allow for sleep, change the number of hours per day in the denominator to 16. Then the quotient is 13.3. But keep in mind that few youngsters have perfect attendance in school and that few schools devote a full six hours a day to academics.

4. Carnegie Corporation of New York and CIRCLE: The Center for Information and Research on Civic Learning and Engagement, *The Civic Mission of Schools* (February 2003): 10.

5. Carnegie, *Civic Mission*, 5

6. Ibid., 26.

7. Diane Ravitch, "Education After the Culture Wars," *Daedalus* (Summer 2002): 15. Also see Diane Ravitch, *The Language Police: How Pressure Groups Restrict What Students Learn* (New York: Knopf, 2003).

8. http://www.socialstudies.org/standards/1.2.html.

9. For a recent journalistic account, see Valerie Strauss, "For More Schools, Teaching Morals is Right," *Washington Post* (June 1, 2004), A12. Good bibliographies of books in this field are available from the Josephson Institute, at http://www.josephsonin stitute.org/books/bookchar.htm, and Boston University, at http://www.bu.edu/educa tion/caec/files/CElist.htm. My own trusted guide is Stanford education professor William Damon, whose books include *Bringing in a New Era in Character Education* (Stanford, CA: Hoover Institution Press, 2002); and *The Moral Child* (Cambridge, MA: Harvard University Press, 1988).

10. You can learn more at http://www.usafreedomcorps.gov/.

11. See, for example, James Leming, Lucien Ellington, and Kathleen Porter, eds., *Where Did Social Studies Go Wrong?* (Thomas B. Fordham Foundation, August 2003).

Chapter 11 Citizenship, Civic Unity, and National Service

William A. Galston

The concept of "civic society" encompasses both the ensemble of voluntary associations and informal social attachments known as "civil society" and the official institutions and processes of political life.[1] Citizenship is the name we give to formal membership in a particular civic community. It is a legal status carrying with it a bundle of legal rights and duties. While informal membership in civil society does not have a generally accepted name, and its defining characteristics are fuzzy, it involves a special sense of identification with other members and the belief that in some important respects their fate is intertwined with one's own.

During the past decade, many scholars have argued that civic membership, both formal and informal, is weaker than it once was. I do not intend to recapitulate those arguments here.

CITIZENSHIP AND THE ALL-VOLUNTEER FORCE

The Vietnam-era military draft was widely regarded as arbitrary and unfair, and it was held responsible for dissension within the military as well as the wider society. In the immediate wake of its disaster in Vietnam, the United States made a historic decision to end the draft and institute an All-Volunteer Force (AVF). On one level, it is hard to argue with success. The formula of high-quality volunteers plus intensive training plus investment in state-of-the-art equipment has produced by far the most formidable military in history. Evidence suggests that the military's performance, especially since 1990, has bolstered public trust and confidence. For example, a recent Gallup survey of public opinion trends since the end of the Vietnam War in 1975 indicates that while the percentage of Americans expressing confidence in religious leaders fell from 68 to 45 and from 40 to 29 for Congress, the percentage expressing confidence in the military rose from under 30 to 78. Among eighteen- to twenty-nine-year-olds, the confidence level rose from 20 to 64 percent. (Remarkably, these figures reflect sentiment in late 2002, before the impressive victory in Iraq.)

While these gains in institutional performance and public confidence are significant, they hardly end the discussion. As every reader of Machiavelli (or the Second Amendment) knows, the organization of the military is related to larger issues of citizenship and civic life. It is along these dimensions that the decision in favor of the AVF has entailed significant costs. First, the AVF reflects, and has contributed to the development of, what I call "optional citizenship," the belief that being a citizen involves rights without responsibilities and that we need do for our country only what we choose to do. Numerous studies have documented the rise of individual choice as the dominant norm of contemporary American culture, and many young people today believe being a good person—decent, kind, caring, and tolerant—is all it takes to be a good citizen. This duty-free understanding of citizenship is comfortable and undemanding; it is also profoundly mistaken.

Second, the AVF contributes to what I call *spectatorial citizenship*—the premise that good citizens need not be active but can watch others doing the public's work on their behalf. This spectatorial outlook makes it possible to decouple the question of whether *we* as a nation should do X from the question of whether *I* would do or participate in X. In a discussion with his students during the Gulf War, Cheyney Ryan, professor of philosophy at the University of Oregon, was struck by "how many of them saw no connection between whether the country should go to war and whether they would . . . be willing to fight in it." A similar disconnect exists today. Young adults have been more supportive of the war against Iraq than any other age group (with more than 70 percent in favor), but recent surveys have found an equal percentage would refuse to participate themselves.

As a counterweight to this decoupling, Ryan proposes what he calls the Principle of Personal Integrity: you should only endorse those military actions of your country in which you yourself would be willing to give your life. The difficulty is that integrity does not seem to require this kind of personal involvement in other public issues. For example, a citizen of integrity can favor a costly reform of the welfare system without being required to serve as a welfare caseworker. Presumably, it is enough if citizens are willing to contribute their fair share of the program's expenses. So one might ask: Why is it not enough for citizens to contribute their fair share to maintain our expensive military establishment? Why should integrity require direct participation in the case of the military but not in other situations? This raises the question, to which I shall return, of when monetary contributions are morally acceptable substitutes for direct participation, and why.

Finally, the AVF has contributed to a widening gap between the orientation and experience of military personnel and that of the citizenry as a whole. This is an empirically contested area, but some facts are not in dispute. First, since the inauguration of the AVF, the share of officers identifying themselves as Republican has nearly doubled, from 33 to 64 percent. (To be sure, officers were always technically volunteers, but the threat of the draft significantly increased the willingness of young men to volunteer for officer candidacy.) Second, and more significantly, the share of elected officials with military experience has declined sharply. From 1900 through 1975, the percentage of members of Congress who were veterans was always higher than in the comparable age cohort of the general population. Since the mid-1990s, the congressional percentage has been lower, and it continues to fall.

Lack of military experience does not imply hostility to the military. Rather, it means ignorance of the nature of military service, as well as diminished capacity and confidence to assess critically the claims that military leaders make. (It is no accident that of all the post–World War II presidents, Dwight Eisenhower was clearly the most capable of saying no to the military's strategic assessments and requests for additional resources.)

For these reasons, among others, I believe that as part of a reconsideration of the relation between mandatory service and citizenship, we should review and revise the decision we made thirty years ago to institute an all-volunteer armed force. I hasten to add that I do not favor reinstituting anything like the Vietnam-era draft. It is hard to see how a reasonable person could prefer that fatally flawed system to today's arrangements. The question, rather, is whether feasible reforms could preserve the gains of the past thirty years while more effectively promoting active, responsible citizenship across the full range of our social, economic, and cultural differences.

AN INFRINGEMENT OF LIBERTY?

My suggestion faces a threshold objection, however, to the effect that any significant shift back toward a mandatory system of military manpower would represent an abuse of state power. In a recent article, Judge Richard Posner drafts John Stuart Mill as an ally in the cause of classical liberalism—a theory of limited government that provides an "unobtrusive framework for private activities." Limited government so conceived, Posner asserts, "has no ideology, no 'projects,' but is really just an association for mutual protection." Posner celebrates the recent emergence of what he calls the "Millian center"—a form of politics that (unlike the left) embraces economic liberty and (unlike the right) endorses personal liberty, and he deplores modern communitarianism's critique of untrammeled personal liberty in the name of the common good. High on Posner's bill of particulars is the recommendation of some (not all) communitarians to reinstitute a draft.

Before engaging Posner's own argument, I should note that his attempt to appropriate Mill's *On Liberty* to support an anti-conscription stance is deeply misguided. To clinch this point, I need only cite a few of the opening sentences from Chapter Four, entitled "Of the Limits to the Authority of Society over the Individual:"

> Everyone who receives the protection of society owes a return for the benefit, and the fact of living in society renders it indispensable that each should be bound to observe a certain line of conduct toward the rest. This conduct consists, first, in not injuring the interests of one another, or rather certain interests which, either by express legal provision or by tacit understanding, ought to be considered as rights; *and secondly, in each person's bearing his share (to be fixed on some equitable principle) or the labors and sacrifices incurred for defending the society or its members from injury and molestation. These conditions society is justified in enforcing at all costs to those who endeavor to withhold fulfillment* [emphasis added].

Posner's view of Mill would make sense only if Mill had never written the words I have italicized.

It is not difficult to recast Mill's position in the vocabulary of contemporary liberal political thought. Begin with a conception of society as a system of cooperation for mutual advantage. Society is legitimate when the criterion of mutual advantage is broadly satisfied (versus, say, a situation in which the government or some group systematically coerces some for the sake of others). When society meets the standard of broad legitimacy, each citizen has a duty to do his or her fair share to sustain the social arrangements from which all benefit, and society is justified in using its coercive power when necessary to ensure the performance of this duty. That legitimate society coercion may include mandatory military service in the nation's defense.

A counterargument urged by the late Robert Nozick is that we typically do not consent to the social benefits we receive and that the involuntary receipt of benefits does not trigger a duty to contribute. Mill anticipated, and rejected, that thesis, insisting that the duty to contribute does not rest on a social contract or voluntarist account of social membership. Besides, the argument Socrates imputes to the Laws in the *Crito* is not bad: if a society is not a prison, if as an adult you remain when you have the choice to leave, then you have in fact accepted the benefits, along with whatever burdens the principle of social reciprocity may impose.

Robert Litan has recently suggested that citizens should be "required to give something to their country in exchange for the full range of rights to which citizenship entitles them." Responding in a quasi-libertarian vein, Bruce Chapman charges that this proposal has "no moral justification." Linking rights to concrete responsibilities is "contrary to the purposes for which [the United States] was founded and has endured." This simply is not true. For example, the right to receive G.I. Bill benefits is linked to the fulfillment of military duties. Even the right to vote (and what could be more central to citizenship than that?) rests on law-abidingness; many states disenfranchise convicted felons for extended periods. As Litan points out, this linkage is hardly tyrannical moralism. Rather, it reflects the bedrock reality that "the rights we enjoy are not free" and that it takes real work—contributions from citizens—to sustain constitutional institutions.

Now on to the main event. Posner contends that "conscription could be described as a form of slavery, in the sense that a conscript is a person deprived of the ownership of his own labor." If slavery is immoral, so is the draft. In a similar vein, Nozick once contended that "taxation of earnings from labor is on a par with forced labor." (If Nozick were right, then the

AVF that Posner supports, funded as it is with tax dollars, could also be described as on a par with forced labor.)

Both Posner's and Nozick's arguments prove too much. If each individual's ownership of his or her own labor is seen as absolute, then society as such becomes impossible, because no political community can operate without resources, which must ultimately come from someone. Public choice theory predicts, and all of human history proves, that no polity of any size can subsist through voluntary contributions alone; the inevitable free riders must be compelled by law, backed by force, to ante up.

Posner might object, reasonably enough, that this argument illustrates the difference between taxation and conscription: while political community is inconceivable without taxation, it is demonstrably sustainable without conscription. It is one thing to restrict self-ownership of labor out of necessity, but a very different matter to restrict it out of choice. The problem is that this argument proves too little. Posner concedes that "there are circumstances in which military service is an obligation of citizenship." But there are no circumstances in which slavery is an obligation of citizenship. Moreover, it is not morally impermissible to volunteer for military service. But it is impermissible, and rightly forbidden, to voluntarily place oneself in slavery. Therefore, slavery and military service differ in kind, not degree. And if there are circumstances in which military service is an obligation of citizenship, then the state is justified in enforcing that obligation through conscription, which is not impermissible forced labor, let alone a form of slavery.

Quod est Demonstratum. For the purposes of this chapter, then, I will suppose that a legitimate government would not be exceeding its rightful authority if it chose to move toward a more mandatory system of military recruitment.

But this is not the end of the argument, because Posner has another arrow in his quiver. He rejects the claim, advanced by Michael Sandel and other communitarians, that substituting market for nonmarket services represents a degrading "commodification" of social and civic life. Indeed, Posner celebrates what communitarians deplore. "Commodification promotes prosperity," he informs us, "and prosperity alleviates social ills." Moreover, commodification enables individuals to transform burdensome obligations into bearable cash payments: middle-aged couples can purchase both care for their children and assisted living for their parents, and so forth.

Posner charges that communitarian theory is incapable of drawing a line between matters that rightly belong within the scope of the market and those that do not. Posner's celebration of the cash nexus is exposed to precisely the same objection. Rather than scoring rhetorical points, I will offer a series of examples designed to help delimit the proper sphere of non-market relations.

CIVIC DUTY AND THE LIMITS OF THE MARKET

Paying people to obey the law. Suppose we offered individuals a "compliance bonus"—a cash payment at the end of each year completed without being convicted of a felony or significant misdemeanor. It is not hard to imagine situations in which the benefits of this policy (measured in reduced enforcement costs) would outweigh the outlays for bonuses. What (if anything) is wrong with this?

My answer: at least two things. First, it alters for the worse the expressive meaning of law. In a legitimate order, criminal law represents an authoritative declaration of the behavior the members of society expect of one another. The authoritativeness of the law is supposed to be a sufficient condition for obeying it, and internalizing the sense of law as authoritative is supposed to be a sufficient motive for obedience. To offer compliance payments is to contradict the moral and motivation sufficiency of the law.

Second, payment for compliance constitutes a moral version of Gresham's law: lower motives will tend to drive out higher, and the more comfortable to drive out the more demanding. When those who are inclined to obey the law for its own sake see others receiving compensation, they are likely to question the reasonableness of their conduct and to begin thinking of themselves as suckers. Most would end up accepting payment and coming to resemble more closely those who began by doing so.

Paying citizens for jury duty. Consider the analogy (or disanalogy) between national defense and domestic law enforcement. The latter is divided into two subcategories: voluntary service (there is no draft for police officers) and mandatory service (e.g., jury duty). Our current system of military manpower is all "police" and no "jury." If we conducted domestic law enforcement on our current military model we would have what might be called "The All-Volunteer Jury," in which we would pay enough to ensure a steady flow of the jurors the law enforcement system requires to function.

There are two compelling reasons not to move in this direction. First, citizens who self-select for jury duty are unlikely to be representative of the population as a whole. Individuals who incur high opportunity costs (those who are gainfully employed, for example) would tend not to show up. The same considerations that militate against forced exclusion of racial and ethnic groups from jury pools should weigh equally against voluntary self-exclusion based upon income or employment status. (We should ask ourselves why these considerations do not apply to the composition of the military.)

Second, it is important for all citizens to understand that citizenship is an *office*, not just a *status*. As an office, citizenship comprises matters of both rights and duties—indeed, some matters that are both. Service on juries is simultaneously a right, in the sense that that there is a strong presumption against exclusion, and a duty, in the sense that there is a strong presumption against evasion. To move jury duty into the category of voluntary, compensated acts would be to remove one of the last reminders that citizenship is more than a legal status.

Paying foreigners to do our fighting for us. Consider: we might do as well or better to hire foreigners (the All-Mercenary Armed Forces) as kings and princes did regularly during the eighteenth century. The cost might well be lower, and the military performance just as high. Besides, if we hire foreigners to pick our grapes, why should we not hire them to do our fighting?

There is of course a practical problem, discussed by Machiavelli among others: a pure cash nexus suggests the mercenaries' openness to opportunistic side-switching in response to a better offer, as happened in Afghanistan. In addition, what Abraham Lincoln called the "last full measure of devotion" would be less likely to be forthcoming in the handful of extreme situations in which it is required.

Beyond these practical considerations lies a moral intuition: even if a mercenary army were reliable and effective, it would be wrong, even shameful, to use our wealth to get noncitizens to do our fighting for us. This is something we ought to do for ourselves, as a self-respecting people. I want to suggest that a similar moral principle does some real work in the purely domestic sphere, among citizens.

Paying other citizens to do our fighting for us. Consider military recruitment during the Civil War. In April 1861, President Lincoln called for, and quickly received, 75,000 volunteers. But the expectation of a quick and easy Union victory was soon dashed, and the first conscription act was passed in March 1863. The act contained two opt-out provisions: an individual facing conscription could pay a fee of $300 to avoid a specific draft notice; and an individual could avoid service for the entire war by paying a substitute to volunteer for three years.

This law created a complex pattern of individual incentives and unanticipated social outcomes, such as anti-conscription riots among urban workers. Setting these aside, was there anything wrong in principle with these opt-out provisions? I think so. In the first place, there was an obvious distributional unfairness: the well-off could afford to avoid military service, while the poor and working class could not. Historian James McPherson observes that the slogan "a rich man's fight, but a poor man's war" had a powerful impact, particularly among impoverished Irish laborers already chafing against the contempt with which they were regarded by the Protestant elite. Second, even if income and wealth had been more nearly equal, there would have been something wrong in principle with the idea that dollars could purchase exemption from an important civic duty. As McPherson notes, this provision enjoyed a poor reputation after the Civil War, and the designers of the World War I–era Selective Service Act were careful not to repeat it.

CIVIC DUTY AND SOCIAL SOLIDARITY

We can now ask: What is the difference between the use of personal resources to opt *out* of military service and the impact of personal resources on the decision to opt *in*? My answer as both a practical and a moral matter is less than the defenders of the current system would like to believe. To begin with, the decision to implement an AVF has had a profound effect on the educational and class composition of the U.S. military. During World War II and the Korean War—indeed, through the early 1960s—roughly equal percentages of high school and college graduates saw military service, and about one third of college graduates were in the enlisted (that is, nonofficer) ranks. Today, enlisted men and women are rarely college graduates, and elite colleges other than the service academies are far less likely to produce military personnel of any rank, officer or enlisted. As a lengthy *New York Times* feature story recently put it, today's military "mirrors a working-class America." Of the first twenty-eight soldiers to die in Iraq, only one came from a family that could be described as well-off.

Many have argued that this income skew is a virtue, not a vice, because the military extends good career opportunities to young men and women whose prospects are otherwise limited. There is something to this argument, of course. But the current system purchases social mobility at the expense of social integration. Today's privileged young people tend to grow up hermetically sealed from the rest of society. Episodic volunteering in soup kitchens does not really break the seal. Military service is one of the few experiences that can.

The separation is more than economic. The sons and daughters of the upper-middle classes grow up in a cultural milieu in which certain assumptions tend to be taken for granted. Often, college experiences reinforce these assumptions rather than challenge them. Since Vietnam, many elite colleges and universities have held the military at arm's length, ending ROTC curricula, and banning campus-based military recruitment. As a Vietnam-era draftee, I can attest to the role military service plays in expanding mutual awareness across cultural lines. This process is not always pleasant or pretty, but it does pull against the smug incomprehension of the privileged.

In an evocative letter to his sons, Brookings scholar Stephen Hess reflects on his experiences as a draftee and defends military service as a vital socializing experience for children from fortunate families. His argument is instructive: "Being forced to be the lowest rank . . . serving for long enough that you can't clearly see 'the light at the end of the tunnel,' is as close as you will ever come to being a member of society's underclass. To put it bluntly, you will feel in your gut what it means to be at the bottom of the heap. . . . Why should you want to be deprived of your individuality? You should not, of course. But many people are, and you should want to know how this feels, especially if you someday have some responsibility over the lives of other people." It is a matter, not just of compassion, but of respect: "The middle-class draftee learns to appreciate a lot of talents (and the people who have them) that are not part of the lives you have known, and, after military duty, will know again for the rest of your lives. This will come from being thrown together with—and having to depend on—people who are very different from you and your friends."

A modern democracy, in short, combines a high level of legal equality with an equally high level of economic and social stratification. It is far from inevitable, or even natural, that democratic leaders who are drawn disproportionately from the upper ranks of society will adequately understand the experiences or respect the contributions of those from the lower. Integrative experiences are needed to bring this about. In a society in which economic class largely determines residence and education and in which the fortunate will not willingly associate with the rest, only nonvoluntary institutions cutting across class lines can hope to provide such experiences. If some kind of sustained mandatory service does not fill this bill, it is hard to see what will.

A PROPOSAL FOR MANDATORY SERVICE

The concept of universal service with civilian as well as military components is hardly revolutionary. In a major comparative study, Donald Eberly and Michael Sherraden identified policies of this sort in postwar Germany and Israel, among others. In other cases, such as Mexico, university students are required to perform a significant period of service as a condition of graduation. (Without referring to Mexico, author David Eggers has recently proposed just such a plan for U.S. university students.) The question is not whether it is technically feasible for the United States to move in this direction. Nor (if you accept the argument I have made this far) is it an issue of moral legitimacy. The question, rather, is whether it would be effective and wise to do so.

To explore this question, let me put a concrete proposal on the table. To the extent that circumstances permit, we should move toward a system of universal, eighteen-month service for all high school graduates (and in the case of dropouts, all eighteen-year-olds) who are capable of performing it. Within the limits imposed by whatever ceiling is imposed on military manpower, those subject to this system would choose either military or full-time civilian service. (If all military slots are filled, then some form of civilian service would be the only option.) The cost of fully implementing this proposal (a minimum of $60 billion per year) would certainly slow the pace of implementation and might well impose a permanent ceiling on the extent of implementation. The best response to these constraints would be a lottery to which all are exposed and from which none except those unfit to serve can escape.

There is evidence suggesting that movement toward a less purely voluntary system of military and civilian service could pass the test of democratic legitimacy. For example, a 2002 survey sponsored by the Center for Information and Research on Civic Learning and Engagement (CIRCLE) found

60 percent-plus support for such a move across lines of gender, race and ethnicity, partisan affiliation, and ideology. Still, it is plausible that intense opposition on the part of young adults and their parents could stymie such a change. Assuming that this is the case, there are some feasible interim steps that could yield civic rewards. Let me mention three.

First, we could follow the advice of former secretary of the navy John Lehman and eliminate the current bias of military recruiters in favor of career personnel and against those willing to serve for shorter periods. As Lehman puts it, we should "actively seek to attract the most talented from all backgrounds with service options that allow them to serve their country . . . without having to commit to six to ten years' active duty." He makes a strong case that this change would markedly increase the number of young men and women from elite colleges and universities who would be willing to undergo military service. Coupled with a more accommodating stance toward the military on the part of academic administrators, this new recruitment strategy could make a real difference.

Second, the Congress could pass legislation sponsored by senators John McCain (R-AZ) and Evan Bayh (D-IN) that would dramatically expand AmeriCorps (the Clinton-era national and community service program) from its current level of 50,000 to 250,000 full-time volunteers each year. Survey evidence shows overwhelming (80 percent-plus) support for the basic tenet of this program, that young people should have the opportunity to serve full-time for a year or two and earn significant post-service benefits that can be used for higher education and advanced technical training. As Senator McCain rightly puts it, "one of the curious truths of our era is that while opportunities to serve ourselves have exploded . . . opportunities to spend some time serving our country have dwindled." In this context, the ongoing resistance to AmeriCorps in some quarters of Congress verges on incomprehensible.

Third, we could follow the blueprint that the Progressive Policy Institute's Marc Magee has recently sketched. That is, we could shift the current Selective Service registration requirement toward a system that provides young people incentives to choose among three options: military service, civilian homeland security service, and service in international civic programs focused on "reducing the conditions that support terrorism." Controversially, but I believe correctly, Magee argues that with such a shift, the current exclusion of women from participation in the Selective Service System "is no longer practical or philosophically justifiable."

It would be wrong to oversell the civic benefits that might accrue from the revisions to the AVF that I propose, let alone the more modest alternatives I have just outlined. Still, enhanced contact between the sorts of young people who provide the bulk of today's volunteers and the sons and daughters of the privileged upper-middle class would represent real progress. Moreover, some of our nation's best social scientists see a link between World War II–era military service and that generation's subsequent dedication to our nation's civic life. If reconsidering a decision about military manpower made three decades ago could yield even a fraction of these civic dividends while preserving the military effectiveness of the current system, it would be well worth the effort.

NOTE

1. A somewhat different version of this chapter appeared in *The Public Interest* no. 154 (Winter 2004).

Chapter 12 The Fair Society

Amitai Etzioni

We must work together for a fair society: a society in which everyone is treated with full respect, recognizing that we are all God's children. A society in which no one—adult or child—is left behind. A place in which such moral commitments are truly honored rather than served up as hollow promises. A society in which one's race, ethnicity, country of origin, religion, gender, and sexual preference matter not. A society in which every person is treated with the dignity they are entitled to by merely being human.

A fair society is one in which no one is above the law and all play by the same rules. It is a society in which no one is demonized as a result of exercising his or her right to free speech, even (and especially) when that speech criticizes those in power; a society in which knowingly selling defective drugs, toys, cars, or any other product or service is treated as the serious offense that it is. In a fair society, the promises made, in the form of pensions and health care plans, to those who have worked all their lives are not retroactively watered down. Hard-working women and men can earn a living wage in a fair society, and no one dies in a parking lot because he or she has no health insurance. In such a society, senior citizens do not have to choose between dinner and medication, and the families of those serving their country in harm's way need not live on food stamps. It is a society that is fair to all—a society in which we are all proud to be counted among its members.

I drafted the preceding lines in 2003, trying to find a communitarian vision that would appeal to Americans in both red and blue states—a vision that would help to overcome the polarization that is said to afflict the American society. Several distinct lines of deliberation led me to focus on a fair society rather than, say, a just one or one of ownership. However, before I spell these out, I report on the results of a nationwide public opinion poll that I commissioned from Greenberg Quinlan Rosner Research. The poll was conducted from June 28 through July 1, 2004—that is, at the height of the presidential election campaign. The sample pool consisted of 1,000 randomly selected likely voters. For some questions, this pool was split into smaller groups.

THE FAIR SOCIETY POLICIES AND VISION

To introduce the concept of a fair society and to test the extent to which it speaks to the values important to Americans from many different backgrounds, I both connoted and denoted the concept, first providing a list of key examples (policies to be assessed as fair or unfair) and then defining the concept directly. This distinction presumes that people think in gestalts or contexts (sometimes referred to as subtexts, or the music behind the words), as well as in terms of specific policies or issues—as long as these find a home within one gestalt or another. These specifics can also serve as kinds of pegs on which to hang the more generalized conception of a fair society or through which to introduce the vision it contains. I first illustrate the seven policies used to introduce the fair society and the responses that they elicited, and then turn to the reactions given to the more generalized concept of a fair society.

SEVEN SOCIETAL FEATURES

Here follow the responses to the seven societal policies that 500 likely voters from the pool of 1,000 were asked to assess in terms of how fair they considered them to be (very fair, fair, unfair, and so on).[1] One of the optional responses was the category of "A Little Unfair." After consideration, I determined not to include this category in this analysis for two reasons. First, if this response is included, we would be counting three responses for unfairness, compared to only two for fairness. Second, I felt that "A Little Unfair" was a weak categorical response; the people who responded that way may also have thought that the policies described were "a little fair." However, if it were included, the results would favor even more strongly respondents' sense of unfairness. Additionally, the category of "Don't Know/Refused" has not been included, which explains why the percentages do not add up to 100.

Before being read the policy statements, which reveal various societal features, the respondents first heard the following:

> I'm going to read you another series of statements. After hearing each statement, please tell me if you would describe that situation as very fair, fair, a little unfair, unfair, or very unfair.

At this point, the respondents were asked to respond to each of the seven statements in sequence.[2]

QUESTION 1: Millions of American workers spent their entire careers with one company on the basis of a contract that promised them a pension plan to provide for them and their families in retirement, only to have the company cut their pension pay and benefits after they retired.

Nearly six out of ten respondents (58 percent) considered such a policy very unfair, with another 24 percent perceiving it as unfair. Only about one out of twelve (8 percent) considered such policies very fair to fair (very fair 1 percent and fair 7 percent).

QUESTION 2: Health insurance companies have avoided paying an insured person's bills when costly illnesses occur even after that person has fully paid health insurance premiums for years.

Roughly two out of three Americans (65 percent) considered such actions by insurance companies to be very unfair, and another 23 percent saw them as unfair. Only one out of twenty respondents (5 percent) considered such a policy to be fair (2 percent very fair and 3 percent fair). These two questions (Questions 1 and 2) elicited the most one-sided and clearest responses of unfairness. It seems to me that the reason for this is that most Americans, if not all, can imagine themselves on the receiving end of the unfair treat-

214 Character, Citizenship, and Values

ment described in the two statements. These statements do not concern only minorities or the poor, or immigrants or any other subgroup, nor do they entail reducing the assets, income, and/or power of one group in order to assist another.

QUESTION 3: The federal government has created the largest deficits in U.S. history, with deficits on the horizon for many years, leaving the debts to be paid by our children and grandchildren.

With their responses to this question, Americans continued to demonstrate a considerable sensitivity to unfair policies, with more than two-thirds regarding the deficit's burden on future generations as unfair (very unfair 44 percent and unfair 24 percent) and only 17 percent claiming it fair (very fair 4 percent and fair 13 percent). Given that this question was asked during an election campaign in which the Democrats accused the Bush administration of recklessly increasing the deficit, some respondents may have allowed their political affinities to override their sense of fairness or may have accepted Bush's promise to scale back the deficit in coming years. Still, the overwhelming majority, including many Independents and Republicans, viewed such policies as unfair.

QUESTION 4: The IRS now audits a higher percentage of tax returns of those making low incomes, less than twenty-five thousand dollars a year, than it does those making higher incomes, above one hundred thousand dollars per year.

The responses to this question are similar to those of the preceding one with over two-thirds of all respondents considering such a policy unfair (40 percent very unfair and 28 percent unfair), as well as a similar proportion for those who considered it fair (2 percent very fair and 15 percent fair). Granted, Question 4 did not garner quite as strong a response of unfairness as did Questions 1 or 2, perhaps because of respondents' inability to apply this policy to their own lives—a concept previously discussed. However, this is precisely why the overwhelming reaction of unfairness to the policy regarding IRS audits is here so important. Wealthy respondents or those who hope to gain affluence could have viewed such a policy as having little to do to with their own situations and therefore ignored its implications for those in different financial circumstances. However, as we see, their sense of fairness clearly prevailed, attesting to the strength of the concept of a fair society.

QUESTION 5: Today, the average CEO makes more than 500 times the salary of his or her average employee.

This question provides for an even stronger test for the power of a sense of fairness than does the previous one because it directly addresses wealth differentiations. Indeed, in many ways, the policy statement in Question 5 could well have resonated with those who hold various pro-capitalism or pro-business viewpoints and believe that CEOs should be paid what the market bears because by running large businesses they provide employment to hundreds of thousands of people. Still, roughly two-thirds of Americans— including, as we shall see, a considerable number of conservatives and Republicans—viewed such salary differences as unfair (45 percent very unfair and 21 percent unfair). Only one out of five respondents considered these wage differences fair (3 percent very fair and 17 percent fair), which is only a slightly higher proportion of the sample in comparison to the responses of fairness for the previous questions. Perhaps even more telling for the force of fairness is that over half (57 percent) of those making $75,000 and upwards a year, those who could stand to benefit the most from such policies, still found such earning discrepancies unfair.

QUESTION 6: The vast majority of government tax breaks go to large corporations, in the form of export subsidies, low-interest loans, or offshore tax havens, rather than small businesses or individuals.

In many ways, the "tilt" of this question and its responses parallel the previous one. Almost seven out of ten Americans considered this policy unfair (41 percent very unfair and 27 percent unfair), while only 14 percent of respondents viewed it as fair (2 percent very fair and 12 percent fair). Thus, these responses serve as additional evidence for the power of the concept of fairness.

QUESTION 7: The Patriot Act, passed in the aftermath of the 9/11 attacks, allows the government to perform wiretaps or review your financial and medical records without a warrant.

When the concept of fairness conflicted with that of homeland security, it did not fare quite as well but still carried the day, with more than half of all respondents considering this part of the USA Patriot Act unfair (31 percent very unfair and 21 percent unfair) and less than one out of three fair (8 percent very fair and 21 percent fair).[3]

Table 12.1 provides a summary of the responses to the seven policy statements (here abbreviated).[4]

As the table demonstrates, the majority of respondents registered a per-

Table 12.1 Rating of Seven Policy Statements (Percent)

	Very Fair	Fair	Unfair	Very Unfair	Total Fair	Total Unfair
1. Pension	1	7	24	58	8	82
2. Insurance	2	3	23	65	5	88
3. Deficits	4	13	24	44	17	68
4. IRS Audits	2	15	28	40	17	68
5. CEO Salaries	3	17	21	45	20	66
6. Tax Breaks	2	12	27	41	14	68
7. Patriot Act	8	21	21	31	29	52

ception of unfair practice in relation to each and all of the policy statements presented to test the public's response to the societal features highlighted. These statements also served to introduce respondents connotatively to the general concept of a fair society.

AN OVERARCHING STATEMENT AND A
MEASURE OF SALIENCY

Once the respondents were introduced to the concept of a fair society through connotation by the seven key policies (although the concept applies to many others), a fair society was defined in a few lines, as follows:

> A fair society is one in which nobody is left behind. This is not just a promise, but a new America where anyone who seeks work can get a job, nobody can be cheated out of their pension rights, and all health care is accessible to everyone so nobody will ever have to choose between buying medicine and food.

I wondered how powerful the concept is. Public opinion polls often count noses or responses but rarely measure how strongly people feel about that of which they approve or disapprove. Hence, analysis based solely on the number of positive or negative responses can be misleading. For example, one might find that the majority of the public favors the right to privacy— only to discover later that this number drops dramatically when that same majority realizes that this right clashes with other concerns or has costs associated with it. Thus, saliency measurements, which determine how strongly committed people are to whatever they hold dear, add a great deal to our understanding. For example, some years back, respondents who had been questioned about various policy issues were then asked if they would

Table 12.2 Likelihood of Voting for a Candidate Supporting a "Fair Society" (Percent)

Much More Likely	Somewhat More Likely	A Little More Likely	No More Likely	Less Likely
36	22	13	12	12

still support their preferred presidential candidate knowing that he agreed with them on all of the issues except one. It turned out that for numerous issues only 3 percent or less of the respondents would abandon their favorite candidate for the sake of this or that specific policy—except for Social Security. This was the only issue in the poll where 25 percent said that they would change sides. I used a similar measure of saliency here.

The respondents were asked to rate their likelihood of voting for a presidential candidate based on his or her support of a fair society as defined above. The responses are shown in Table 12.2, demonstrating the great saliency of the fair society concept. Here again, the category of "Don't Know/ Refused" has not been included, which explains why the percentages do not add up to 100.

WHO FAVORS A FAIR SOCIETY?

The vision of a fair society appeals to people from many different backgrounds and affiliations. True, it does not appeal to all groups in equal measure. However, in a nation said to be highly polarized, the concept of a fair society has found significant support across the aisle, so to speak— indeed, across many aisles. This point is best highlighted by an assessment along party lines of responses to the two policy statements that elicited both the greatest sense of unfairness and the least, Question 2 (insurance coverage) and Question 5 (CEO salaries).[5] The behavior of the insurance companies prompted very similar levels of outrage from Democrats, Independents, and Republicans. Ninety percent of Democrats and Independents found such actions to be very unfair to unfair. The proportion of Republicans was only 7 percent lower, with about four out of five (83 percent) agreeing with Democrats and Independents that this policy was very unfair to unfair. When asked in Question 5 about the salary disparity between CEOs and their employees, respondents did not react quite as strongly (in terms of unfairness) as they did when questioned about the practices of insurance companies. But they still demonstrated a considerable sense of indignation and agreement over the unfairness of the policy. Again, Democrats reacted the most strongly with about three out of four (78 percent) finding the statement very unfair to unfair. Independents followed closely on their heels by a percentage difference of less than ten points with 69 percent perceiving the policy as very unfair to unfair. And over half of the Republican respondents (52 percent) agreed with them. Pollsters like to focus on difference. One should note here that on this issue the largest difference between the three groups amounted to 26 percent (between Democrats and Republicans). That is, about two out of three Americans (66 percent) saw this policy in the same light, and all disapproved.

Additionally, those who identified themselves as liberal, moderate, or conservative also demonstrated accord on a perception of unfairness regarding the above policy issues. To the statement about insurance providers turning a cold shoulder to a covered person's medical bills, at least four out of five respondents whether liberal, moderate, or conservative, called the action very unfair to unfair. On this issue, liberals and conservatives differed by only 11 percentage points, with 92 percent of liberals and 81 percent of conservatives interpreting the situation in the same way. When it came to the high salaries of CEOs, the numbers were not quite so close together. However, that said, about two thirds (66 percent) of liberals, moderates, and conservatives combined affirmed that a scenario that permitted such a gap between the salary of a chief executive and those beneath him or her was very unfair to unfair. And liberals and conservatives were separated on their interpretation of this policy as very unfair to unfair by only a little over 20 percent, with 81 percent of liberals and 59 percent of conservatives deeming the practice very unfair to unfair.

The concept of a fair society also reaches across the gender divide. Much has been made lately of how gender influences one's stance on various public policies, leading politicians to cater first to Soccer Moms and then to NASCAR Dads. But on the issue of a fair society, we find no great disparity between the sexes. Returning to the policy statements about insurance companies and CEOs' salaries, the measure of agreement between women and men on the unfairness of these policies far outstrips any differences. Regarding the unfairness of the insurance companies' policy, men and women only differed by 12 percent (women 93 percent and men 81 percent), with 88 percent agreeing that such actions are very unfair to unfair. On the issue of the salaries of CEOs, they were even closer together with a separation of only 8 percent (women 70 percent and men 62 percent). Thus, 66 percent of women and men combined found this kind of wage differential very unfair to unfair.

A fair society speaks as well to Americans from all regions of varying ages and levels of education, as shown by their responses to the questions about insurance companies and CEO pay. Indeed, the largest disparity in regional reaction to the issue of insurance coverage was only 5 percent with 85 percent of those from the South finding the refusal to pay by insurance companies very unfair to unfair and 90 percent espousing a similar feeling in the central states. Furthermore, both the elderly (over 64) and the young (18 to 29) shared a sense of unfairness over the disparity between CEOs' incomes and those of their workers. Well over half of both elderly and young voters felt that such a policy was very unfair to unfair (71 and 63 percent, respectively). And a majority of respondents—regardless of whether they were with or without a high school diploma or a college degree—gave a similar assessment of unfairness in regard to the issues at hand.

In short, the findings of the poll are unmistakable. The demand that society be designed and policies be cast so that they meet the norms of fairness is widely spread, strongly held, and supported—albeit not with equal measure—by Americans of all walks of life and from the various "boxes" into which we tend to place people of different gender, age, state, and so on. It follows then that those who seek to unite Americans and appeal to them on a broad base will find in fairness a bracing theme.

BEYOND THE PUBLIC OPINION POLL

Actually, there is reason to believe that fairness may well hold an even stronger and more universal appeal than thus far indicated. In drafting the questions used in the survey, I ran into the fact that certain kinds of conduct are perceived so strongly by so many people as unfair that it made little sense to include them in the study. For instance, if we had asked: "In a sports event, say a football game, should all of the players be required to abide by the same rules?" people either would have responded practically in unison, "Of course," or suspected that we were asking some kind of trick question. Otherwise, as people told me when I tested such questions informally, why else would anyone ask a question whose answer is so obvious? The same would have happened if we had asked: "Do you agree or disagree that no one is above the law?" These are but two more examples, and examples of considerable import, of how strongly and widely shared a sense of fairness is.

Fairness, especially the applications of it that are broadly endorsed, serves as a critical standard that can be and is often used to chastise those who violate it (or seem to). Hence, favoritism, cronyism, and tribalism are all viewed with disdain precisely because they entail unfair practices. I do not know whether or not Halliburton was accorded favorable treatment by the Department of Defense because its previous CEO, Dick Cheney, was serving as the Vice President of the United States; however, few would have any doubt that if this were the case, Americans from all over the political and ideological spectrum would consider such favoritism grossly unfair to the competitors of Halliburton (and to American taxpayers). And when we read that the company of Kojo Annan, son of UN Secretary General Kofi Annan, has been given a lucrative deal by the UN, we wonder whether such an award is merited—whether other companies might have been equally or better suited for the job. I could go on and on with examples that illustrate the normative and emotive power of the norm of fairness, but precisely because it is so widely held and strongly endorsed, this is hardly necessary. Among the small number of studies that have examined fairness empirically, one, by psychologist Tom Tyler, stands out. Tyler found that when people feel that they have had their day in court—that they have been given the chance to present their case and have then been judged fairly—they are much more likely to accept a ruling against them.[6]

Even more profoundly, there is reason to believe that fairness is one of those few moral values that we treat as what the Founding Fathers called a "self-evident truth." Although there is sure to be disagreement as to what exactly fairness encompasses, the concept itself is rarely challenged. Indeed, I take for granted that the very idea of fairness is a normative one. I believe that fairness compels us not because it offers benefit to the self, as the late John Rawls seems to suggest, but because we consider it to be morally valid. Rawls defined fairness as follows:

> The main idea is that when a number of persons engage in a mutually advanta-geous cooperative venture according to rules, and thus restrict their liberty in ways necessary to yield advantages for all, those who have submitted to these restrictions have a right to a similar acquiescence on the part of those who have benefited from their submission.[7]

Although one can rarely be clear about what Rawls meant to say, this definition sounds rather utilitarian—as if we agree by social contract to accord fairness to others in return for similar treatment.[8] As I have explained my position on this issue elsewhere, for the purpose of this discussion let it suffice to say that I agree with deontologists' assertion that there are moral concepts, like fairness, which are based not on self-interest but on self-evident truths.[9]

Indeed, studies show that even small children have a sense of fairness. I here cite but a few of the findings. William Damon from Stanford reports that "virtually all [the studies] have found four-year-olds already in possession of active, flourishing conceptions of fairness. Most children at this age have firmly internalized the standard of sharing."[10] And UCLA's James Q. Wilson writes, "These principles have their source in the parent–child relationship, wherein a concern for fair shares, fair play, and fair judgments arises out of the desire to bond with others."[11] Wilson also explains that "virtually everyone who has looked has found [the fairness norm] in every culture for which we have the necessary information."[12] Some even believe that this moral judgment is anchored in our very biology.[13]

The fair society as a normative concept has an attribute, which, as Senator Pat Moynihan emphasized, makes for strong political appeal: universality. To demonstrate the sway of universality, Moynihan compared the popularity of Medicare to the limited favor in which Medicaid is held and the laudatory treatment of the Holy Grail of Social Security to the highly critical public attitude toward welfare. Despite the fact that Medicare and Social Security both contain some elements of wealth transfer, people still greatly prefer these programs over Medicaid and welfare, in part because Medicare and Social Security provide benefits to all instead of entitlements to only a select few.[14] (Although wealth transfer was not the main focus of our poll, some of the questions alluded to it.) This is precisely the reason that numerous people find fairness normatively more compelling than a similar term: equality.[15]

If one were to seek through universal terms to address these same issues in the context of fairness rather than equality (or procedural justice rather than social justice), one would not reference the disgraceful statistic that there are 44 million Americans with no health insurance. Instead, one would discuss the need for everyone to receive health care coverage. Likewise, one would not harp on joblessness but rather focus on the promise that in a fair society all Americans who wish and need to work will find employment. One would not frame the normative and political give-and-take in terms of class warfare or reallocation of wealth but through observations that we are all God's children. And finally, one would not speak only to the rights of this or that group but to the vision that all Americans be treated in the same, fair way.

NOTES

1. The other 500 likely voters in the sample pool were given the same policy statements and asked to respond to them in terms of how upset the assertions made them (very upset, upset, not upset, and so on).
2. The seven policies were not randomized; that is, they were read to all respondents in the same sequence. This did not matter for the purposes at hand because I was interested in the halo effect of all seven. However, one should take this fact into account if one seeks to assess which elements provoked the greatest sense of consternation.
3. For further discussion about the USA Patriot Act from a communitarian perspective, refer to Amitai Etzioni, *How Patriotic Is the Patriot Act? Freedom versus Security in the Age of Terrorism* (New York: Routledge, 2004).
4. As earlier noted, the category of "A Little Unfair" has been omitted, and the figures for the "Total Unfair" category have been adjusted to reflect its absence. Again, the category of "Don't Know/Refused" has also been removed. However, as this category had no bearing upon the data listed in the summary categories of "Total Fair" and "Total Unfair," its removal is of little consequence.
5. The policy statement about the USA Patriot Act actually garnered greater affirmations of fairness than the statement about CEOs' salaries. However, the issue of the Patriot Act is one that is politically charged, causing many likely voters to respond according their individual party's position as opposed to what they personally deem fair or unfair.
6. Tom Tyler, *Why People Obey the Law* (New Haven, CT: Yale University Press, 1990): 98–101.
7. John Rawls, *A Theory of Justice* (Cambridge, MA: Harvard University Press, 1971): 96.
8. Among those who have taken issue with a theory of fairness grounded in self-interest, see Norman Finkel, *Not Fair! The Typology of Commonsense Unfairness* (Washington, DC: American Psychological Association, 2001): 47.
9. See Amitai Etzioni, *The New Golden Rule: Community and Morality in a Democratic Society* (New York: BasicBooks, 1996).
10. William Damon, *The Moral Child: Nurturing Children's Natural Moral Growth* (New York: Free Press, 1988): 36.
11. James Q. Wilson, *The Moral Sense* (New York: Free Press, 1997): 70.

12. Ibid., 65.

13. See Wilson, *The Moral Sense*.

14. See John Thibaut and Laurens Walker, *Procedural Justice: A Psychological Analysis* (Hillsdale, NJ: Erlbaum, 1988).

15. See Jonathan Wolff, "Fairness, Respect, and the Egalitarian Ethos," *Philosophy and Public Affairs* 27, no. 2 (Spring 1998).

Part Six Environmental and Electoral Reform

Chapter 13 Toward a Sustainable Environmentalism

Mark Sagoff

The National Environmental Policy Act (NEPA), which authorized the creation of the Environmental Protection Agency (EPA) in 1969, responded to the first of three stages in the development of environmental thought. In the 1960s the environmental movement focused on protecting human health, safety, and welfare from visible harms that were caused by substantial and clearly identifiable industrial, municipal, and other sources of pollution. In its second stage after the passage of NEPA, environmental thought expanded its focus to include less visible and less demonstrable dangers—for example, smaller amounts of hazardous wastes and toxic substances that were possible carcinogens, the sources and effects of which were harder to identify and to quantify. During the 1980s and 1990s, policymakers managed, with difficulty, to sort out the extent to which political deliberation had to supplement scientific inquiry in determining how safe is "safe enough" and which small risks were "acceptable" and which were not.[1]

The third and current stage in environmental thought moves the emphasis from protecting human health, safety, and welfare to maintaining biodiversity and the "health" or "integrity" of biological systems. According to this new wave of conservationist philosophy, intact ecosystems and the biodiversity that supports them provide important life-sustaining services that science can teach society to value and protect. In this third approach to environmental policy, science must play a new role, that is, to determine not only which actions are harmful but also what "harm" to ecosystems means or consists in. Science becomes responsible for identifying not just the means but the ends of policy, in other words, for defining and measuring environmental values—for example, biodiversity, ecological complexity, and ecosystem services—and suggesting ways to protect them. The new conservationism poses essentially what are known as "wicked" problems—questions that so deeply involve normative commitments that no value-neutral science can state, much less answer, them.

FROM SEEN TO UNSEEN HAZARDS

It is easy to understand the broad public support that backed efforts in the 1960s and 1970s to control "visible and demonstrable" environmental problems, such as municipal sewage and commercial effluents in waterways and industrial and automobile pollution in the air. First, the public could easily see (or scientists could easily develop a consensus about) the connection between the source of a pollutant, such as car exhaust, and the harm it caused, such as smog. Second, environmental regulation could be justified as an extension of the common law of nuisance. An individual who is one among many to suffer the ill effects of a polluting industrial or municipal plant may not by himself or herself be able to undertake the costs involved in suing the polluter to cease the nuisance and repair the damage. To protect the public from what were plainly wrongful injuries or torts, the government solved this collective action problem by regulating gross effluents and emissions.

In 1985, William D. Ruckelshaus, then administrator of the Environmental Protection Agency (EPA), described the transition from the first to the second phase of environmental concern:

> There has been a shift in public emphasis from visible and demonstrable problems such as smog from automobiles and raw sewage, to potential and largely invisible problems, such as the effects of low concentrations of toxic pollutants on human

health. The shift is noticeable for two reasons. First, it has changed the way science is applied to practical questions of public health protection and environmental regulation. Second, it has raised difficult questions as to how to manage chronic risks within the context of free and democratic institutions.[2]

By the mid-1980s, as Ruckelshaus suggested, environmental policy had evolved to a second stage, which addressed subtle, chronic, or "statistical" hazards for which causal connections are more difficult or impossible to establish between those who are responsible and those who suffer harm. For example, elevated levels of lead in the blood of children have been correlated with developmental deficits—but a given child may be exposed to lead from water carried by pipes, lead-based paints, emissions from manufacturing or refining operations, food grown on land containing lead, and many other causes as well. Accordingly, the causal path between a particular harm and a particular source of pollution—the link between a plaintiff and a defendant in a tort action—could be impossible to demonstrate by scientific evidence in a court of law.

Alvin Weinberg, who directed the Oak Ridge National Laboratory for many years, described problems regulators face when causal paths are indeterminate. When a car hits a pedestrian, he wrote, the question is not what the cause is but who is at fault. If the lead from the exhaust of a single car is alleged to cause harm, in contrast, the causal path is uncertain. "The two situations are quite different: in the first, the relation between the cause and the injury is not an issue; in the second, it is *the* issue."[3]

Over the decades, scientists have come to terms with the conceptual difficulties involved in measuring the health risks of low levels of pollution from diffuse sources (such as lead in auto exhaust). Policymakers and the general public have come to terms with the normative difficulties involved in determining whether those risks are acceptable in view of compensating benefits or in comparison to other dangers that society has chosen not to regulate. Even though statutes may wrongly suppose, as does the Clean Air Act, that scientists can identify "threshold" doses or exposures beneath which hazardous substances are safe, agencies and courts came to re-conceive the goals of regulation in terms of progress, not perfection. Regulators learned not to make the best the enemy of the good. They settled for what could be achieved, in the form of reduced levels of risk—and searched for inexpensive technical "fixes" to avoid more burdensome policies. For example, the inexpensive catalytic converter installed in cars to reduce smog also removed lead from car emissions, since the converter requires lead-free gasoline. The public and professional discussion of environmental policy acknowledged that while scientific research could discern broad causal relationships, the measurement of smaller, chronic, synergistic, and long-term risks to human health often had to rely on extra-scientific normative assumptions and judgments.

SCIENCE, TRANS-SCIENCE, AND "WICKED QUESTIONS"

Weinberg captured a central lesson of the 1980s in a distinction he coined between science and "trans-science."[4] A trans-scientific question is one that can be stated in scientific or causal terms but cannot be answered by science. For example, it is scientifically meaningful to ask how many people will die as a result of exposure to very low levels of dioxin. Science lacks the ability, however, to answer that question. Risk assessment—the attempt to measure scientifically the likelihood that a given environmental insult will harm human health—proved to be fraught with uncertainties. Because of these uncertainties, the scientific process of assessing the magnitude of a risk confronted many of the normative choices associated with the policy process of managing it.

The regulation of environmental hazards responds, moreover, not just to the extent or magnitude of a risk, however it may be assessed, but at least as much to public concerns about its cultural or moral conditions—whether a risk is voluntary or imposed, dreaded or familiar, intentional or accidental, man-made or naturally occurring, related or unrelated to future generations, controllable or uncontrollable, a threat to children, accompanied with compensating benefits, spread equitably through the population, associated with beneficial or fearful technologies, and so on.[5] The meaning of a risk—its ethical character—appeared to some to be even more important than its magnitude.

By the 1990s, society had absorbed the lesson that, in many instances, its goal was not to eliminate but to reduce risk to an "acceptable" level. For example, the Delaney Clause of the Federal Food, Drug, and Cosmetic Act prohibited, in processed food, any additive, any pesticide, found to induce cancer in humans. Because virtually all processed food contains some trace amount of pesticide that in mega-doses causes cancer in some laboratory animals, EPA skirted the law by allowing pesticide residues that posed only minimum risks. In response to a suit brought by environmental organizations, a federal court proposed to make EPA enforce the actual wording of the Delaney Clause, even if, as a consequence, no food could be manufactured or sold in the United States. Congress responded in 1996 by rescinding the Delaney Clause and affirming the de minimis standard EPA had long used. At some level, environmental risk is unavoidable; to attain "an adequate margin safety," to quote the mandate of the Clean Air Act, society would have to bring the economy to a halt. Instead of seeking to measure and eliminate small, chronic, and synergistic hazards, Congress and the regulatory agencies looked to continued technological innovation to reduce subtle risks while controlling costs. One commentator explained: "The 'BAT' standards for toxics under the Clean Water Act, for example, are based on the 'best available technology economically achievable.' . . . These standards reflect a pragmatic judgment by Congress that a full-blown evaluation of the health and environmental benefits of certain environmental protection measures is too time and resource-intensive to be warranted."[6]

Over about twenty-five years, both regulators and the general public accepted the idea that while pollution had to be dramatically reduced, it could not be eliminated. Most commentators acknowledged that political, cultural, and ethical judgments informed both the scientific task of risk assessment and the political task of risk management so that the assessment and the management of environmental risk—the scientific and the political—were joined at the hip. In the absence of measurements that might provide a convincing scientific basis for risk–benefit analysis, society looked more and more toward improvements in technology to reduce or control environmental hazards at lower or at least bearable costs. By the time of the Clinton administration, the policy of "reinventing regulation" had replaced the quest for a risk-free environment with the search for technological fixes, incentives, and other mechanisms to bring hazards down to minimum levels.

Environmental policy problems may not be susceptible to objective, value-free, or scientific resolution for either of two reasons. First, they may involve what Weinberg called trans-scientific questions—questions that science can pose in objective, value-neutral terms but lacks the ability to answer. An example is the probability of a very rare event, such as the meltdown of a nuclear reactor. Scientists recognize that social values are critical considerations that inform risk assessment in the face of tremendous uncertainty.

Second, as law professor Holly Doremus notes, problems can be "wicked" in that they cannot be objectively characterized; observers with different perspectives and values describe them very differently. Because these problems cannot be objectively defined, no finite set of solutions can be identified, and there is no objectively right or wrong answer. To make matters worse, measures that might be taken to address wicked problems are not readily reversible, so that trial and error is a high-cost, high-risk approach.[7]

For an example of a wicked question, consider the decision the Bush administration announced in May 2004 to consider hatchery-bred salmon that join and survive among stream-bred populations in determining whether the species merits listing under the Endangered Species Act (ESA). The government has long pumped hatchery-raised fish by the hundreds of millions into rivers to maintain commercially valuable stocks that dams, overharvesting, and other activities have damaged. Should hatchery-bred clones of wild fish, if they eventually survive and breed in streams, be deemed as good as wild fish for purposes of conservation?[8] Are we trying to protect simply a biological species or a "wild" population that is independent of human activity?

Consider other examples of wicked questions. A 2002 Department of Agriculture census found that the number of bison raised commercially totaled 231,950 animals, dwarfing the 15,000 wild buffalo, most of which roam in Yellowstone National Park, where they are inspected for disease and their numbers managed. Bison were once almost extinct. Should the commercial herd count in determining the survival of this species?

The influx of nonnative species raises many wicked questions. Nonnative species usually increase the species richness—that is, the number of different kinds of creatures—that make up an ecosystem. Scientists have found that in areas of San Francisco Bay, for example, "exotic organisms typically account for 40 to 100 percent of the common species, up to 97 percent of the total number of organisms, and up to 99 percent of the biomass." Of about 400 species found in Bay waters, 234 are exotic and 125 "cryptogenic," that is, of undetermined origin. No native Bay species is known to have become extinct.[9] "With regard to biological diversity," as ecologist Michael Huston, has written, "invasions potentially lead to an increase in species richness, as invading species are added to the species gene pool." Many ecologists have found that species richness supports what they call ecosystem functioning, productivity, and stability.[10] Do alien species, then, increase or diminish local biodiversity; do they generally support or undermine ecosystem function?

Answers to these wicked questions depend entirely on the values one considers important, for example, whether one wishes to exclude from the concept of "biodiversity" those organisms that come to a place—or that are created—with human assistance. Answers to wicked questions depend on how one defines normative concepts such as biodiversity and ecosystem integrity or health, for example, on whether one considers the presence of nonnative species a per se indicator of environmental decline.

Both scientists and policymakers, when they assess risk, handle transscientific questions by invoking societal values to decide, for example, how conservative to keep their assumptions, what kinds of risks and susceptibilities to consider, and so on. The values that are considered and the normative weights that are attached to each value are explicitly exogenous to the science; they are moral, cultural, and political in character.

To deal with wicked questions, in contrast, the conservation sciences themselves have become normative. In other words, they incorporate into their fundamental concepts and definitions decisions that reflect cultural, ethical, and political values and commitments. The crucial difference is this. During the first two stages of environmental policymaking, scientists deferred to political and other extra-scientific values in making judgments, for example, about how safe is safe "enough." Today, conservation scientists may ask political and other authorities to defer to their science since it is itself normative, that is, conservation science has itself incorporated crucial aesthetic or ethical judgments and thus presents itself as the arbiter of what is good or bad for ecosystems and for the environment.

In its third stage, environmental thought goes far beyond the original objectives of protecting human health, safety, and welfare by introducing the additional objective of maintaining biodiversity and the health or integrity of biological systems. The public is asked to look to science or scientists to understand what it means to keep ecosystems intact—to determine not only which actions are harmful to the environment, but also what "environmental harm" means. Science becomes responsible for identifying not just the means but the ends of policy, in other words, for defining and measuring environmental values—biodiversity, ecological complexity, and ecosystem services—and suggesting ways to protect them.

The last part of this chapter explores the problems and prospects of this latest turn in conservationist thought. Historically, the purpose of environmental regulation—and of the role of the EPA—was not to protect ecosystems, biodiversity, or the environment per se, but to reduce environmental risks to public health, safety, and welfare. The new conservationism relies on normative concepts developed by the new environmental sciences to frame new policy goals, such as the preservation of biodiversity and the maintenance of intact ecosystems. The argument presented here suggests that the new conservationism must adjust its ambitions to the legal framework that supports environmental regulation and tailor its normative commitments to the political context in which they must seek acceptance.

THE PRESERVATIONIST PREDICAMENT

The direction of regulatory policy has traditionally been to protect human beings from the environment—from pollutants and other hazards—rather than to protect the environment from human beings. Since at least the time of John Muir and the founding of the Sierra Club, however, preservationists have challenged the idea that environmental policy should focus only on minimizing changes in the environment that negatively affect human beings, while allowing all those changes that tame, domesticate, and transform nature for human purposes. Historically, the more vigorously Americans have transformed what they considered a natural wilderness for economic reasons, the more vehemently some leaders of the environmental movement have called for its preservation on spiritual and ethical grounds. Muir recognized, for example, that damming the beautiful Hetch Hetchy valley made economic sense because there was no other way to supply San Francisco with water. He railed against the project for spiritual reasons. "Dam Hetch Hetchy! As well dam for water-tanks the people's cathedrals and churches, for no holier temple has ever been consecrated by the heart of man."[11]

Those who seek to protect the "the integrity, stability, and beauty of the biotic community," to quote Aldo Leopold's famous dictum, have confronted at least four obstacles to translating this "land ethic" into a legal and moral basis for regulation.

First, Under Article III of the Constitution, as construed by the Supreme Court, no citizen has standing—the legal ability—to sue on behalf of the environment or to rectify harm to the environment per se. "The relevant showing for purposes of Article III standing . . . is not injury to the environment but injury to the plaintiff." If environmental law is an extension of the common law of nuisance, it protects individuals—and the environment only indirectly—from injury. One commentator notes: "Under this formulation, the environment is relegated to a subordinate role within environmental jurisprudence. . . . The Court's elevation of the plaintiff at the expense of the environment effectively turns the citizen suit provision into an extension of nuisance law."[12]

Second, the courts adjudicate environmental cases in terms of issues of distributive justice that have controlling precedents in other areas of jurisprudence, such as nuisance, natural resources, and property law. Many commentators suggest that environmental protection has largely ceased to exist as a distinct field of law. Not since a famous dissent in 1972 by William Douglas has a Supreme Court Justice proposed a legal theory that makes the environment or nature itself an object of protection. Unlike the right to due process, the separation of church and state, or freedom of speech, environmental protection has no constitutional basis but must tag along under a broad reading of the Commerce Clause. An attempt during the 1970s by legal theorists and philosophers to provide an alternative framework that endows natural objects with legal or moral rights went nowhere; it could not provide a basis for making policy or for resolving disputes.[13]

Third, it seems undeniable that what John Muir wanted to preserve—nature direct from the hand of the Creator—has already been lost, if it ever existed. Before Europeans arrived, aboriginal Americans had transformed the landscape, as environmental historians have shown.[14] Human-induced global changes, such as global warming and invasive species, have dramatically altered the ecological character of the most protected places. Nature, to be preserved, has to be maintained according to a clear definition of "natural." This demands that scientists and environmentalists must, somehow, determine which creatures to countenance as "native" and what to do about all the others—whether, when, and how to suppress forest fires, to re-introduce wolves and other predators, to combat invasive species, to manage "wild" populations that exceed carrying capacity, to allow hatchery-based fish, and so on. There may be no ecologically meaningful "baseline" at which the environment is sufficiently cleansed of human influence to be described as "natural."

Fourth, economies develop by transforming the natural world—by converting savannas to cities, forests to farms, meadows to malls, fields to factories, cozy copses to college campuses, and so on. Economic interests in development tend to trump aesthetic and spiritual motives that inspire preservation. For example, actions undertaken under the ESA (1973), while popular in principle, met ferocious political opposition in practice. Property owners vowed to "shoot, shovel, and shut up"—in other words, quickly to rid their property of endangered species before they could be discovered.[15] Rather than to allow the ESA to serve as an incentive to landowners to sanitize their property from an endangered species point of view, the government failed to list species and centered protection on publicly owned lands. Hard political experience led federal officials to design Habitat Conservation Plans to accommodate politically powerful owners of private property.[16]

Unlike the Civil Rights movement, preservationism did not draw on a fundamental constitutional set of protections or build on a traditional political theory. Courts rarely take the aspirations of environmental stewardship seriously. Environmental lawyers often found that the best they could do was to negotiate settlements and "paper" transactions. By rebuffing the Kyoto protocol and other international "green" initiatives, moreover, the Bush administration has added to the frustration of environmentalists. Many politicians regard the environmental movement as a passion of the 1970s that (like the War on Poverty) has run its political course. Environmental groups now must work hard to defend earlier successes; it is all they can do to hold on to what they have.

THE THIRD WAVE OF ENVIRONMENTALISM

Despite this depressing picture, or perhaps in response to it, a group of scientists, philosophers, and policy professionals have redefined the idea of environmental stewardship—the protection of nature itself—as a basic objective of society. The current view, like that of the 1970s, is revolutionary in that it does not appeal to constitutionally based protections of person and property, yet it seeks a legitimacy beyond the principles of distributional justice associated with traditional nuisance, land-use, and natural resource law. However, the current revolutionary moment in environmentalism differs from the environmentalism of the 1970s in three ways.

First, the new conservationism starts with a scientific project, which attempts to develop or understand ideas such as biodiversity and ecosystems as objects of protection. The goal of environmental protection, in this latest approach, is to explain and preserve the structure and functioning of the ecosystems on which all life on earth, including our own, depends. "The single-species focus of the ESA has not been especially successful in protecting functioning ecosystems," one ecologist observed. Another added, "The highest priority for conservation ought to be relatively intact ecosystems." In their view, the discovery of how ecosystems work becomes the principal project of environmental science. A conservation biologist summarized this point: "By looking at the function of ecosystems, by trying to understand how ecosystems work—if we lose that we've lost the whole ballgame. So this has to be a paramount concern as well as the most challenging scientifically."[17]

During the 1990s, new disciplines, notably Conservation Biology and Ecological Economics, emerged to provide scientific content and direction to the belief that society must protect biodiversity and the integrity of ecosystems to sustain the ecological services on which the economy depends. The challenge to scientific research appeared daunting. As ecologist Peter Raven said, "We cannot even estimate the number of species of organisms on Earth to an order of magnitude, an appalling situation in terms of our knowledge and our ability to affect the human prospect positively. There are clearly few areas of science about which so little is known, and none of such direct relevance to human beings."[18]

Second, the new direction in environmental thinking abandons the assumption associated with John Muir, Aldo Leopold, and other preservationists that nature maintains a "balance" or "equilibrium" as long as it is "untrammeled by man," to quote the Wilderness Act of 1964. The goal of the new conservationists is not to preserve in timeless amber the "Last Great Places," as the Nature Conservancy calls them. Rather it is to understand how human beings interact with ecosystems and to find ways to make that interaction sustainable. The scientific challenge lies in revealing the principles that underlie a sustainable interaction—what NEPA described as a "harmonious" relation between man and nature—when nature itself is not harmonious but discordant. As historian Donald Worster has written, "Many have begun to believe [that nature] is fundamentally erratic, discontinuous, and unpredictable. It is full of seemingly random events that elude our models of how things are supposed to work."[19]

Finally, the new conservationism—unlike both the preservationist ethic of John Muir and the rights-based approach of Deep Ecology—rests on a broadly utilitarian ethic. Its appeal, however, vigorously rejects the traditional utilitarian assumption, of John Locke and John Stuart Mill, that nature "unimproved" by development and domestication has little economic value. The emerging sciences of Ecological Economics and Conservation Biology emphasize, on the contrary, the economic value of "services" that functioning ecosystems provide. Thus, these disciplines take on the additional task of identifying and measuring these ecological services and "pricing" or "costing" damage to ecological systems caused by economic activity.[20] In the absence of a market mechanism to measure these ecological losses, the new conservationists argue that society may invoke a "precautionary principle"[21] to delay industrial projects until scientists are able to measure or assess the ecological risks they present. There is little indication, however, that environmental scientists are anywhere near finding a method to determine which proposed changes to the environment—for example, building schools, hospitals, and so on, in place of undeveloped areas—undermine ecosystems enough on balance to harm rather than help humanity.

WRESTLING WITH THE WICKED

Biological sciences outside of medicine have traditionally eschewed value judgments. Medicine takes its central value—the prevention and alleviation of injury and disease—from a broad social consensus about the importance of human health. It is not clear that analogous social consensus exists about either the meaning or the urgency of ecosystem health. Many ecologists believe that their science, like physics and chemistry, cannot tell what outcomes are "good" or "bad" because this is a social judgment. "The words 'good' and 'bad' constitute value judgments and so lie beyond the bounds of science," Michael Rosenzweig has written. "Were exotic species to reduce diversity by 30 percent, no ecologist could test whether that loss of species would be a bad thing."[22]

On the other hand, many conservation biologists contend that "nature is the norm." The integrity of ecosystems—or the character of biodiversity—depends on the absence of human influence. "Our ability to protect biological resources depends on our ability to identify and predict the effects of human actions on biological systems, especially our ability to distinguish between natural and human-induced variability in biological condition."[23] For the new environmental scientists the *absence* of human influence is the measure of the health, integrity, or functioning of ecosystems. This fundamental normative commitment captures the essence of John Muir's view that Creation presents a kind of perfection—an immaculate gift—that human influence corrupts. Instead of attributing to its obvious spiritual and religious sources the view that human activity corrupts or contaminates nature, however, the new conservation biology entrenches it as a principle of conservation science by embedding this view in central concepts such as biodiversity, intact ecosystems, native species, and so on.

TOWARD A SUSTAINABLE ENVIRONMENTALISM

The new environmental sciences, notably Conservation Biology and Ecological Economics, have reenergized the academic study of the environment. While these sciences have generated interest and excitement in the academic community, the practice and prospects of environmental law and regulation have not improved. There are at least three reasons that explain why the boom in environmental science has not reversed the bust in environmental law.

First, the outreach from conservation biologists and ecological economists to the legal professions has been minimal. Although new disciplines and new journals have developed within ecology and economics to reflect the turn toward "sustainability," the law schools have remained largely unaffected.[24]

Second, the new conservation sciences have had to abandon the "balance-of-nature" or "equilibrium" assumptions that characterized ecological theory in the 1970s.[25] The balance-of-nature theory supported statutes that assumed that nature is best protected when it is left untouched—statutes such as NEPA, the ESA, Section 404 of the Clean Water Act, and the nondegradation provisions of the Clean Air and Clean Water Acts.[26] Today's nonequilibrium approach undermines assumptions on which many of the environmental statutes of the 1970s rest.[27] The new conservationism maintains the conclusion that nature knows best—that "intact" ecosystems are those that show the least human influence. Yet nothing has really replaced the old scientific argument for this view—a justification that referred to a balance of nature and to concepts of equilibrium that no one now accepts.

Third, the new conservationism has been more successful in proposing research programs than regulatory programs. The National Science Foundation has initiated a major initiative in biocomplexity aimed, in part, at identifying the systematic elements, if any, in ecosystems. The U.S. Forest Service has engaged for several years in extensive studies to discover how to manage forests as holistic ecosystems rather than as resources for which interest groups compete. The EPA has convened a Science Advisory Committee to determine how best to measure the value of ecosystem services. The National Research Council has undertaken a related project.[28] Conservation biologists hope that as they discover more about ecosystems as holistic functioning units and as they learn how to identify and quantify the services ecosystems provide, they will know better how to manage them. However, as things stand now, an immense and growing research project, seeking to reveal how ecosystems work, has produced more questions than answers about environmental policy. Perhaps this research program will succeed over time. But so far it has failed to result in a serious regulatory agenda.

CONCLUSIONS

From the 1960s to the year 2000, environmentalism succeeded by appealing to public or societal values closely tied either to human safety and welfare or to the natural beauty of Creation. The effort to protect natural areas and endangered species rested primarily on aesthetic, religious, and historical values that had little or nothing to do with science. While accepting the commitments of the old preservationists, such as Muir, to nature untrammeled by man, the new conservation sciences seek to base this commitment on scientific principles and concepts, such as biodiversity and ecosystem integrity. Thus, environmental science takes on the responsibility of determining ends, not just means; it looks inside itself for the fundamental values it serves rather than responding to the values society proposes or pursues. This may not close but only widen the breach between science on the one hand and law and policy on the other.

In the new millennium, environmentalists must fight to sustain public support for the basic goals and values that gained general acceptance in the 1970s. These goals and values center, first, on protecting human health, safety, and welfare from pollution and other environmental insults and, second, on preserving some of the most beautiful and magnificent aspects of the natural world. Particularly at a time when political forces are attempting to roll back existing environmental regulation, one may wonder if it is wise to anchor the rationale of the environmental movement in a complex and still tentative new scientific framework, largely unfamiliar to public thinking and at odds with the assumptions that have underpinned environmental regulation to date. Concepts that are freighted with normative connotations, such as biodiversity and ecosystem integrity, may seem to bring to environmental causes the legitimacy of science. However, as environmental science itself appears politicized and adversarial, the enormous contribution it can make to environmental causes may eventually become attenuated or lost.

To sustain environmental regulation one must also secure the support of the public and of the legal system. The third wave of environmentalism, which relies on advances in conservation biology as a normative science, is still forming too far out at sea to provide the needed legal and political basis for environmental regulation. While the concepts of biodiversity and healthy ecosystems enrich environmental thought, and may in the long run deepen our understanding of nature, environmentalists would be wise to remain mindful of the roots of their movement that lie in well-understood and widely accepted conceptions of public health, safety, human welfare, and "acceptable risk." At a time when all environmental values are under attack, environmentalists should mount a clear defense of these widely accepted, root principles of the environmental movement. They include a respect for nature and a reverence for its most beautiful and magnificent historical properties—a respect and reverence more associated with aesthetic judgment and spiritual communion than with the concepts of biological science.

NOTES

1. Two classic works are William W. Lowrance, *Of Acceptable Risk: Science and the Determination of Safety* (Los Altos, CA: William Kaufmann, 1976); and Joseph V. Rodricks, *Calculated Risks: Understanding the Toxicity in Human Health Risks of Chemicals in Our Environment* (Cambridge, UK: Cambridge University Press, 1992).
2. William D. Ruckelshaus, "Risk, Science, and Democracy," *Issues in Science and Technology* 1, no. 3 (1985): 19–38.
3. A. M. Weinberg, "Science and Its Limits: The Regulator's Dilemma," *Issues in Science and Technology* 2, no. 1 (1985): 59–82.
4. A. M. Weinberg, "Science and Trans-Science," *Minerva* 10 (1972): 209–222.
5. For discussion, see Paul Slovic, *The Perception of Risk* (Sterling, VA: Earthscan, 2000).
6. Amy Sinden, "The Economics of Endangered Species: Why Less Is More in the Economic Analysis of Critical Habitat Designations," *The Harvard Environmental Law Review* 28 (2004): 186.
7. Holly Doremus, "Constitutive Law and Environmental Policy," *Stanford Environmental Law Journal* 22 (June 2003): 295–378. Doremus attributes the coinage of the term "wicked" to W. J. Horst and Melvin M. Webber, "Dilemmas in a General Theory of Planning,"*Policy Sciences* 4 (1973): 160–167. As Doremus points out, the use of the term "wicked problem" was elaborated in the context of conservation biology by Cathy Geist and Susan M. Galatowitsch, "Reciprocal Model for Meeting Ecological and Human Needs in Restoration Projects," *Conservation Biology* 13 (1999). These authors point to five criteria: "(1) interconnection and complexity of components; (2) uncertainty; (3) ambiguity of definition; (4) controversy; and (5) societal constraints." Of these, "ambiguity of definition" may be the most important.

8. Blaine Harden, "Hatchery Salmon Plan Announced: Fish to Be Used in Stream Rebuilding," *Washington Post* (May 29, 2004), A03. This policy follows a 2001 U.S. District Court decision delisting Oregon coast coho salmon because genetically similar hatchery-bred fish had joined and swelled the wild population. *Alsea Valley Alliance v. Evans*, 161 F. Supp.2d 1154 (D. Or. 2001). Doremus considers this among other examples of "wicked" questions in Holly Doremus, "The Purposes, Effects, and Future of the Endangered Species Act's Best Available Science Mandate," *Environmental Law* 34 (Spring 2004): 397–450.

9. A. N. Cohen and J. T. Carlton, "Accelerating Invasion Rate in a Highly Invaded Estuary," *Science* 279 (1998): 555–558; A. N. Cohen and J. T. Carlton, "Nonindigenous Aquatic Species in a United States Estuary: A Case Study of the Biological Invasions of the San Francisco Bay and Delta," a report for the United States Fish and Wildlife Service, Washington, DC; and The National Sea Grant College Program Connecticut Sea Grant, 1995; available at http://nas.er.usgs.gov/publications/sfinvade.html. M. A. Huston, *Biological Diversity: The Coexistence of Species on Changing Landscapes* (Cambridge, UK: Cambridge University Press, 1994): 318; D. U. Hooper and P. M. Vitousek, "The Effects of Plant Composition and Diversity on Ecosystem Processes," *Science* 277 (1997): 1302–1305, quotation at 1312. See also R. B. Waide, M. R. Willig, C. F. Steiner, G. Mittelbach, L. Gough, S. I. Dodson, G. P. Juday, and R. Parmenter, "The Relationship Between Productivity and Species Richness," *Annual Review of Ecology and Systematics* 30 (1999): 257–300.

10. D. U. Hooper and M. Vitousek, "The Effects of Plant Composition and Diversity." See also R. B. Waide et al., "The Relationship Between Productivity and Species Richness."

11. A. Dan Tarlock, "Is There a There There in Environmental Law?" *Journal of Land Use & Environmental Law* 19, no. 2 (2004): 214–252. Tarlock explains: "Environmental law, as now defined, is primarily a synthesis of pre-environmental era common law rules, principles from other areas of law, and post-environmental era statutes which are lightly influenced by the application of concepts derived from ecology and other areas of science, economics, and ethics." Ibid., 222. See, for example, Perry Miller, *Nature's Nation* (Cambridge, MA: Harvard University Press, 1967). John Muir, "Hetch-Hetchy Valley," *Sierra Club Bulletin* (January 1908): 220.

12. *Friends of the Earth, Inc. v. Laidlaw Environmental Services (TOC), Inc.*, 528 U.S. 167 (2000), at 181; David N. Cassuto, "The Law of Words: Standing, Environment, and Other Contested Terms," *Harvard Environmental Law Review* 79 (2004): 79–128, quotation at 93–94.

13. "An environmental lawyer is likely to find the most important, most relevant precedent elsewhere, precisely because it is elsewhere." Richard J. Lazarus, "Thirty Years of Environmental Protection Law in the Supreme Court," *Pace Environmental Law Review* 19 (2002): 619–652, quotation at 633. In a series of articles, Lazarus shows by a detailed analysis of judicial opinions that the Supreme Court has stripped the concept of the environment from environmental law. See also Richard J. Lazarus, "Restoring What's Environmental about Environmental Law in the Supreme Court," *UCLA Law Review* 47 (2000): 703–772; Sinden, "The Economics of Endangered

Species," 186; *Sierra Club v. Morton*, 405 U.S. 727, 741 (1972) (Douglas, J., dissenting). For a survey of the extent of judicial willingness to accommodate environmental law by stretching the concept of the regulation of interstate commerce, see, for example, Sam Saad, "Commerce Clause Jurisprudence: Has There Been a Change?" *Journal of Land, Resources, & Environmental Law* 23 (2003): 143–172. Tarlock points out: "Even Leopold's most passionate defenders recognize that the whole 'project' of environmental ethics has not succeeded in creating a convincing case for non-human rights and in developing substantive rules which are capable of making the inevitable choices among competing resource use options." Tarlock, "Is There a There There," 242.

14. See, for example, William Cronon, *Changes in the Land: Indians, Colonists, and the Ecology of New England*, 20th anniversary ed. (New York: Hill & Wang, 2003).

15. For discussion of the "shoot, shovel, and shut up" phenomenon among other political and constitutional constraints on the ESA, see, for example, Mark Sagoff, "Muddle or Muddle Through? Takings Jurisprudence Meets the Endangered Species Act," *William and Mary Law Review* 38 (1997): 825–993.

16. Interior Secretary Bruce Babbitt said, "We will continue to aggressively pursue a variety of reforms to make the [Endangered Species] Act less onerous on private landowners." U.S. Department of the Interior, "Secretary Babbitt Welcomes 'Common Sense' Action of Supreme Court Species Ruling; Says It Will Not Alter His Flexibility Push," Press Release, June 29, 1995, available in 1995 WL 386054. For a good survey of federal restraint in applying the ESA on private land, see J. B. Ruhl, "Biodiversity Conservation and the Ever-Expanding Web of Federal Laws Regulating Nonfederal Lands: Time for Something Completely Different?" *University of Colorado Law Review* 66 (1995): 555.

17. For one groundbreaking collection of papers advocating this view, see Kathryn A. Kolm, ed., *Balancing on the Brink of Extinction: The Endangered Species Act and Lessons for the Future* (Washington, DC: Island Press, 1991); the quotation is from Dennis Murphy's essay, "Invertebrate Conservation," 193. David Ehrenfeld as quoted in David Takacs, *The Idea of Biodiversity* (Baltimore, MD: Johns Hopkins University Press, 1996): 69; G. Carleton Ray, as quoted in Takacs, *Idea of Biodiversity*, 71.

18. Peter Raven, as quoted in Walter Reid, Charles Barber, and Kenton Miller, *Global Biodiversity Strategy: Guidelines for Actions to Save, Study, and Use Earth's Biotic Wealth Sustainably and Equitably* (Washington, DC: World Resources Institute, 1989): 1.

19. Wilderness Act of 1964. 16 U.S.C. 1131(c) (2000); Daniel B. Botkin, *Discordant Harmonies: A New Ecology for the Twenty-First Century* (New York: Oxford University Press, 1990); Donald Worster, "The Ecology of Order and Chaos," *Environmental History Review* (Spring/Summer 1990): 13.

20. See, for example, Frances Cairncross, *Costing the Earth the Challenge for Governments, the Opportunities for Business* (Cambridge, MA: Harvard Business School, 1992).

21. According to this principle, "where there are threats of serious or irreversible damage, lack of full scientific certainty shall not be used as a reason for post-poning [sic] cost effective measures to prevent environmental degradation." *Rio Declaration on Environment and Development*, Principle 15, June 14, 1992, U.N. Conference on Env't & Dev., UN Doc. A/CONF.151/5/Rev.1 (1992), reprinted in 31 I.L.M. 874, 879 (1992).

For commentary, see Frank Cross, "Paradoxical Perils of the Precautionary Principle," *Washington & Lee Law Review* 53 (1996): 851.

22. Michael Rosenzweig, "The Four Questions: What Does the Introduction of Exotic Species Do to Biodiversity?" *Evolutionary Ecology Research* 3 (2001): 361–367.

23. J. R. Karr and E. W. Chu, *Restoring Life in Running Waters: Better Biological Monitoring* (Washington, DC: Island Press, 1998).

24. For a more hopeful discussion of the effects ecosystem science, particularly the idea of ecosystem services, may have on environmental law, see James Salzman and J. B. Ruhl, "Currencies and the Commodification of Environmental Law," *Stanford Law Review* 53 (2000).

25. Today, ecosystem scientists do not study the ecological superorganism or equilibrium that Eugene Odum perceived but confront a moving target. Indeed, many biologists believe that ecosystems are not *systems* in any sense but blooming, buzzing confusions of contingency, and that the ecosystem concept should be abandoned as a will-o'-the-wisp. See, for example, W. H. Drury, *Chance and Change: Ecology for Conservationists* (Berkeley: University of California Press, 1998); R. V. O'Neill, "Is It Time to Bury the Ecosystem Concept? (with full military honors, of course!)," *Ecology* 82 (2001); 3275–3284. For discussion, see Mark Sagoff, "The Plaza and the Pendulum: Two Concepts of Ecosystem Science," *Biology and Philosophy* 18 (2003): 529–552; available at http://www.cnr.colostate.edu/class_info/ey505/Sagoff2003.pdf.

26. Lakshman Guruswamy, "Interacting Threats and Integrated Solutions for the Environment: Integration and Biocomplexity," *Ecology Law Quarterly* 21 (2001): 1191–1238, quotation at 1194.

27. Conservation biologists are well aware that their view of the ecosystem as essentially unpredictable conflicts with the view of nature implicit in earlier law. See, for example, C. S. Holling, Fikret Berkes, and Carl Folke, "Science, Sustainability and Resource Management," in Fikret Berkes and Carl Folke, eds., *Linking Social and Ecological Systems: Management Practices and Social Mechanisms for Building Resilience* (Cambridge, UK: Cambridge University Press, 1998): "The system itself is a moving target," Ibid., 347. These authors add: "The inherent unpredictability of ecosystems plays havoc with conventional resource management science, which starts with the assumption of a clockwork, predictable world." Ibid., 352–353.

28. "Biocomplexity is a multi-disciplinary approach to understanding the world's environment . . . [it accounts for] the importance of scale, from micro to macro, and includes social and behavioral sciences into the ecosystem calculus." Jeffrey Mervis, "Biocomplexity Blooms in the NSF's Research Garden," *Science* 286 (1999), quoting Rita Colwell, Director, National Science Foundation. For discussion, see Allen K. Fitzsimmons, *Defending Illusions: Federal Protection of Ecosystems* (Lanham, MD: Rowman & Littlefield, 1999). "Assessing and Valuing the Services of Aquatic Ecosystems," an NRC project in process chaired by Professor Geoffrey Heal.

Chapter 14 Is Reform of America's
Electoral System Possible?

Thomas E. Mann

Since September 11, the self-declared vision of America as "the world's oldest and greatest democracy" has played an increasingly prominent role in supporting an ever more assertive U.S. foreign policy.[1] Many Americans take for granted the proposition—oft articulated in different ways by the George W. Bush administration and by presidents before him—that the United States, acting resolutely to promote its own interests and values, will perforce advance freedom, prosperity, security, and democracy around the world.

Yet this view of the United States as an inherently progressive and benign power, while widely shared among Americans (and not without historical justification), is less universally acclaimed outside the United States. Indeed, particularly since the war in Iraq, large majorities in both allied and other nations around the world have developed a decidedly negative view of America's impact on world peace and security.[2] Equally troubling, perhaps, many outside the United States have come to question the very integrity, performance, and legitimacy of our democratic political institutions.

Sadly, events of the last several years have done little to enhance (and much to detract from) the reputation of American democracy around the globe. The 2000 presidential election, the closest and arguably most controversial in American history, unmasked a highly decentralized, underfunded, inequitable, error-prone, and potentially chaotic system of election administration. That George W. Bush won the presidency even though Al Gore received more votes nationwide was startling to many observers, though fully consistent with constitutional and statutory provisions for the electoral vote. The disjunction between popular and electoral votes has appropriately raised once again the question of whether we should abandon the Electoral College for direct election of the president.

More shocking than the functioning of the Electoral College was how ill-prepared Florida was to deal with a disputed, dead-heat election, one whose outcome would determine the presidency. Many factors that contributed to the chaos and errors on election day—egregious ballot design, improper purging of registered voter lists, the unavailability of provisional ballots, inadequate training for poll workers and instructions for voters—could not have been corrected after the fact with a proper recount. The absence of statutory provisions for a statewide recount opened the way to a thirty-six-day, post-election political struggle that ended with a five-to-four decision by a conservative majority on the Supreme Court halting the recount and effectively declaring Bush the winner.[3]

Most Americans came to accept Bush as the legitimate president, an inclination later strengthened by the events of September 11 and their aftermath. Regardless, many at home and abroad continue to view the entire experience of Bush's election and tenure of office as a failure of American democracy. How could the United States tolerate such an uneven and politicized system of election administration? How could so slender and questionable an electoral victory produce so radical a change in domestic and foreign policy, especially in light of the much-fabled checks and balances in the American political system?

GROWING POLARIZATION

Part of the answer to the latter question lies with changes in the party system. Razor-thin majorities in Congress and the parties' increasing ideological polarization have produced a level of party unity seldom seen in American politics.[4] With Republicans controlling both ends of Pennsylvania Avenue for the first time since the 1950s, party loyalty has trumped fealty to basic institutions. As the center of gravity in each party has shifted to its ideological pole, the majority leadership has used every procedural lever to hold its members together on behalf of a president whose agenda was skewed to his conservative base. The few remaining moderates in Congress have been under enormous pressure to toe the party line.

How American politics came to be so polarized is a fascinating and complicated story, one that can be only briefly summarized here. The seeds of this polarization were planted in the 1965 Voting Rights Act, which led to the electoral mobilization of blacks in the South and an eventual regional party realignment in which conservative white Southerners found their way to the Republican Party. Ronald Reagan reshaped the party as a champion of tax cuts, cultural conservatism, and a muscular national defense. Intense conflict in Washington over this agenda in turn reinforced and accelerated the shifts already underway among voters toward their more ideologically compatible party.

The point here is not that the electorate itself became more ideologically extreme but rather that voters sorted themselves in a way that produced fewer conservative Democrats and moderate Republicans.[5] Voters became more predictable partisans in their voting patterns, which in turn encouraged politicians to appeal more explicitly to the values, interests, and policies of the base of their party. Interest groups, especially those concerned mainly with cultural issues, increasingly aligned themselves with one or the other major party and became enforcers of the party creed. Media outlets, most importantly talk radio and cable news channels, sharpened party differences on policy and routinized the demonization of one's political adversaries. The so-called "permanent campaign"—in which the line between governing and campaigning has become blurred—has ensured that these pitched and often bitter partisan battles would be just as intense after the election as before.[6]

This party polarization has taken on a distinct geographical cast, with huge implications for electoral competition and public engagement in the political process. One of the ironies of contemporary American politics is that a more competitive and high-stakes struggle for control of government is decided by fewer and fewer voters. All discussions of presidential elections must begin with the red states and the blue states—those that absent a landslide are safely in the Republican or Democratic camps. A substantial majority of states and their citizens (including California, Texas, and New York, the three largest) are largely ignored by the presidential candidates in allocating their campaign resources. The number of reliable "battleground" states—those truly up for grabs in a presidential election—has declined over time, with the result that fewer voters are exposed to the presidential campaigns.

The concentration of like-minded partisans can also be seen within states. Over the past several decades, counties have become much more one-sided in their partisan composition.[7] Most inner-city neighborhoods are now overwhelmingly liberal and Democratic, while developing suburbs, exurbs, and rural areas are distinctively conservative and Republican. Over time, decisions by citizens about where to reside have promoted an ever-increasing political homogeneity. Natural social processes have worked to further reinforce a nexus of ideology, partisanship, and voting behavior. The very geographical building blocks for local governments and legislative districts have thus facilitated a pattern of uncompetitive elections, producing incumbents who tend to operate at the ideological poles of their respective parties.

Nor are politicians content to let these patterns develop on their own. They work aggressively to gain a structural advantage from the electoral rules of the game. A prime opportunity to seek such an advantage arises after each decennial census when states must redistrict their House constituencies. Unlike the practice in many other democracies, where nonpartisan authorities redraw legislative district lines, redistricting in almost all of the states in this country is lodged with political bodies. Americans traditionally have been reluctant to cede this authority to bureaucratic officials or nonpartisan agencies. Not surprisingly, the redistricting process is a deeply political one, with incumbents openly seeking to minimize the risk to themselves (via bipartisan gerrymanders) or to gain additional seats for their party (via partisan gerrymanders).

Evidence from the latest round of redistricting suggests that the Republican Party and incumbents of both parties have gained a significant advantage.[8] The 2002 congressional elections were remarkably stable, all the more striking because the first election after districts are redrawn typically witnesses a surge in retirement, incumbent defeats, and membership turnover, as well as a decline in the percentage of incumbents reelected by landslides. This time, just the opposite occurred. Voluntary retirements declined. Only four House incumbents were defeated by challengers, the smallest number in U.S. history. The freshman class in the new 108th Congress was unusually small. Fewer than four dozen House contests were hotly contested by both parties, leading to an increase in the number of incumbents (338) who won handily.

Republicans increased the size of their majority and in so doing bucked the historic pattern of the president's party losing seats at midterm.

While a number of factors contributed to this pattern of results in the 2002 elections, the post-2000 round of redistricting succeeded in strengthening the Republican advantage, shoring up the position of marginal incumbents in both parties, and reducing the overall number of competitive seats. House Republicans were not content to rest on their laurels, however. After gaining control of both legislative chambers as well as the governorship in Texas and Colorado in the 2002 elections, national Republican leaders orchestrated a brazen move to take a second bite of the redistricting apple. Violating a century-long norm, each state pushed through a second post-2000 set of House district maps, designed solely to elect more Republican representatives. The partisan gerrymander in Colorado was reversed by the state supreme court, which found that it violated an implicit provision in the state constitution limiting redistricting to only once per decade. But the Texas gerrymander succeeded, putting seven Democrats in the state delegation at severe risk. As one U.S. House staffer working on the Texas redistricting plan put it in an e-mail not designed for public consumption: "The maps are now official. I have studied them and this is the most aggressive map I have ever seen. This has a real national impact that should assure that Republicans keep the House no matter the national mood."[9] So much for democratic accountability and responsiveness.

The mid-decade Texas partisan gerrymander worked like a charm in the 2004 elections. One Texas Democratic incumbent switched parties before the election, a second retired, a third lost a primary challenge, and four were defeated by Republicans in the general election. The four defeated Texas Democrats comprised a majority of the seven House incumbents who lost nationwide and more than accounted for the net pickup of three seats for the Republican Party. The 2004 House elections revealed a fortress of stability and incumbent protection, with a little partisan mischief at the margin.

PROBLEMS OF CAMPAIGN FINANCE

If America's reputation as the very model of a vibrant constitutional democracy has been tarnished by shoddy, politicized administration of elections and brazenly self-interested legislative redistricting, recent campaign finance practices have made matters still worse. Fund-raising abuses in the Clinton White House, part of an aggressive effort to avoid the spending limits tied to the presidential public financing system, ushered in an era of blatant disregard for federal campaign finance law. Long-standing prohibitions on corporate and union treasury financing of federal election activity were rendered obsolete. Elected and party officials avidly solicited soft-money contributions from sources and in amounts otherwise proscribed by federal law, a practice replete with conflicts of interest if not outright corruption. Million-dollar-plus contributions to parties became commonplace. Those funds were then used to finance communications intended to influence federal elections. Independent groups discovered that they could circumvent disclosure requirements and contribution limitations by disguising campaign communications as "issue ads." By the 2000 election, parties and groups geared their fund-raising efforts and campaign strategies to take full advantage of these loopholes in federal law.[10]

Financing of congressional elections, meanwhile, suffered from feast and famine. Incumbents had little difficulty filling their campaign coffers, whether or not they faced serious competition in the November election, while challengers found ever more daunting the task of raising the money needed for the escalating costs of campaigns.[11] This reinforced a broader pattern of uncompetitive elections, depriving most voters of a meaningful electoral choice and undermining democratic accountability.

Americans have been embarrassed and disturbed by revelations of the huge gap between the historical reputation and current reality of their electoral institutions. In two cases—election administration and campaign finance—Congress in 2002 passed legislation designed to deal directly with the well-publicized breakdowns. The third issue—legislative redistricting—has attracted little reform interest in Congress. The only signs of life on this problem are to be found in a handful of states.

Of course, enacting a law in Washington or in the states is no guarantee that the problems addressed by the legislators will be remedied. The ultimate success of the Help America Vote Act (HAVA)—the major 2002 piece of legislation aimed at reforming election administration—would be determined by a difficult implementation process in the fifty states. Similarly with campaign finance reform, the ability of the Bipartisan Campaign Reform Act of 2002 to abolish party soft money and to regulate electioneering communications would be critically shaped by administrative rulings and enforcement actions by the Federal Election Commission and by the responses of political actors to the regulatory regime that emerges from judicial and administrative actions. Meanwhile, efforts in a handful of states to depoliticize the redistricting process with nonpartisan commissions face myriad practical and political hurdles. And even if these initiatives meet with measured success, a host of challenges will remain.

REFORMING ELECTION ADMINISTRATION

Congress was slow to move on election reform in the months following the 2000 Florida debacle. President Bush conveyed little sense of urgency on the subject, preferring to focus his initial agenda on a tax cut and thereby avoid calling public attention to the circumstances of his election. The political parties viewed the broader set of problems through distinctive lenses. Democrats saw election administration reform largely as a means of expanding the franchise to underrepresented minorities, while Republicans sought primarily to remove irregularities from the voting process and to prevent unqualified voters (for example, felons barred from voting) from casting a ballot. In the words of ABC correspondent Cokie Roberts, "Democrats wanted every vote to count, while Republicans wanted votes to count only once." Moreover, no consensus existed in the policy community on precisely what needed to be done. Federal elections are administered in the United States in a highly decentralized fashion, with counties assuming most of the responsibility for electoral financing and administration. This decentralized system has its virtues and advantages, but it has encouraged an underinvestment in election administration (for voting equipment, registration systems, poll worker recruitment and training, and voter education); relatively little systematic monitoring of and research on spoiled ballots; few minimum standards across the country; and less uniformity within states than the post-2000 citizenry was willing to tolerate.

While Congress dragged its feet in the early months of 2001, essential work was proceeding elsewhere. A number of commissions and study groups released reports with strikingly similar diagnoses and prescriptions for election reform.[12] Essentially, the reports suggested the following: a federal system to administer federal elections, one that includes uniform national ballots, voting equipment, and counting procedures, is infeasible. Improvements to voting technology, including equipment upgrades, are desirable but far from sufficient to deal with the many problems that plague the administrative system. The federal government should share the cost of administering elections by providing subsidies to states for upgrading their systems, link these subsidies to some minimum standards, and sponsor research and development on—as well as the dissemination of—best practices on all aspects of the casting and counting of votes. The states should give priority to statewide registration systems, provisional balloting, precinct-level capacity for error detection and correction, standards for determining valid votes and for conducting recounts, poll worker recruitment and training, and voter education.

After months of study, debate, and uncertainty, Congress passed the Help America Vote Act, just days before the November 2002 midterm elections. HAVA authorized $3.86 billion to help states meet new requirements for voter registration, voting systems, and voter safeguards; to replace punch card and lever voting machines; and to improve election administration. The act relies largely on the states to achieve uniform and nondiscriminatory administration of federal elections by arming them with resources, information, and authority to implement new federal requirements. Uniformity is sought within rather than across states, which are given broad discretion to implement the new requirements to fit their existing electoral systems, intergovernmental arrangements, and political contexts.

HAVA implementation has been halting.[13] With delays in Washington on appropriations and the appointment of the new Elections Assistance Commission, states were left with insufficient funding and guidance in developing plans for meeting new federal requirements and upgrading their election systems. Few states had statewide voter registration databases in place for the 2004 election. Most took advantage of a waiver to postpone implementation until 2006. Many states had new voting machines in some of their polling places, but only a handful eliminated entirely their punch card machines and just two—Georgia and Maryland—adopted statewide touch-screen voting systems. The latter have become an object of intense controversy. Critics have raised serious questions about the security and integrity of paperless, direct recording electronic voting machines.[14] This controversy has delayed or altered the acquisition of new voting equipment in some states and has led others to consider requiring voter-verified paper audit trails and open-source software codes revealing how votes are stored and counted.

The exceptions to the pattern of gradual implementation concern provisional voting and voter identification, both of which were required by the new law to be in place in 2004. Individuals arriving at polling places but not appearing on voting rolls were issued provisional ballots, which were then to be counted only if it was determined the voters were properly registered. First-time voters who registered by mail without providing verification of their identity were required to show identification for the first time in a presidential election. These two requirements reflect the delicate partisan compromise needed to enact the new law. Yet even these seemingly straightforward requirements were the focus of controversy in the 2004 elections. States adopted widely disparate rules for determining which provisional ballots were to be counted. As a consequence there was a huge variance among the states in the percentage of provisional ballots that were counted. And some states applied the new voter identification requirement to all voters, raising questions about vote suppression.

Fortunately, the margin of victory in the 2004 presidential election exceeded the margin of litigation.[15] That is, resolving the problems that arose would most likely not have changed the outcome. But another vote counting debacle was barely avoided. A swing of fewer than 60,000 votes in Ohio would have resulted in post-election chaos.

In sum, the United States has made a constructive if uneven start at addressing the flaws in election administration that contributed so much to the controversy and conflict over the 2000 presidential election. We now have a much clearer sense of what went wrong and what needs to be done to see that it does not happen again. But implementing these objectives in a highly decentralized administrative system during a time of great fiscal stress and partisan distrust is no simple task. Most voters saw relatively little change in the registration and voting process when they cast their ballots in 2004 and public confidence in the electoral process remains shaky.

THE FATE OF THE ELECTORAL COLLEGE

Moreover, no serious consideration whatsoever has been given to the larger structural issues surrounding presidential elections. For example, should the Electoral College (and its backup system of election by House state delegations in the event no candidate wins a majority of the electoral votes) be replaced by some form of direct popular vote? Disagreement over such weighty matters as federalism, the two-party system, minority influence, incentives for popular participation, and electoral legitimacy makes that question difficult to answer.[16] But the national failure to deliberate on it reflects the high constitutional hurdle faced by proponents. The small-state bias of the Senate and, therefore, the Electoral College appears to have doomed direct election (or a revision of the allocation of electoral votes to reward the winner of the national popular vote) absent a national crisis and subsequent popular demand.

States could, of course, move on their own to alter the rules under which popular votes are converted into electoral votes. Two states—Maine and Nebraska—already reject the otherwise universal practice of awarding all of a state's electoral vote to the candidate who wins a plurality of the popular vote. But their alternative—awarding electoral votes to candidates who win each congressional district as well as the statewide vote—is limited by the uncompetitiveness and partisan bias of congressional district lines. Another possibility is for states to make their allocation of electoral votes proportional to the votes cast for each candidate. Under this system, to discourage a proliferation of third-party candidates and nonmajority national electoral vote outcomes, states could use instant runoff voting, limiting the allocation of electoral votes to the top two candidates in each state. Here again, however, the political obstacles are formidable. Individual states would be reluctant to dilute their potential influence by dividing their electoral votes between the major candidates. In 2004 the citizens of Colorado rejected an initiative to require proportional allocation of the state's electoral votes. And even if states were to adopt proportional allocation, the bias in the allocation of electoral votes among states would still allow for a disjunction between the national popular vote and electoral vote.

CAMPAIGN FINANCE PROGRESS

The seven-year battle to enact the Bipartisan Campaign Reform Act of 2002 (otherwise known as McCain-Feingold) was an extraordinary legislative odyssey.[17] Critical to its eventual enactment were several factors: the tenacity of the congressional sponsors, the steadfastness of a small group of moderate Republicans who supported reform, and a decision by proponents to pursue a scaled-down agenda after the 1996 elections. Also important were the availability of new, policy-relevant research that helped define specific regulatory approaches, Senator John McCain's emphasis on reform during his quest for the Republican presidential nomination in 2000, Democratic gains in the Senate later that year, and the surprising and consequential efforts by Democratic leaders Tom Daschle and Richard Gephardt to pass the legislation. Finally, the reform community demonstrated an unusual level of pragmatism. Ultimately, support for a filibuster in the Senate eroded to the point where the will of the majority prevailed and the bill was finally adopted.

The Act bans the raising of soft money (funds subject only to state, not federal, restrictions) by national parties and federal officeholders and candidates. It restricts soft-money spending by state and local parties on what are defined as "federal election activities." The act also regulates a class of issue-advocacy broadcast ads, labeled "electioneering communications." Political advertisements that refer to a clearly identified candidate for federal office, are targeted on the constituency of that candidate, and are broadcast within thirty days of a primary or sixty days of a general election must be financed and disclosed in a manner consistent with existing federal election law. Corporations and unions are prohibited from spending treasury funds, directly or indirectly, for such electioneering communications. The Reform Act also treats coordinated electioneering communications as contributions to and expenditures by a candidate or party, increases the hard-money amounts individuals can contribute to candidates and parties, and raises limits on individual and party support of any candidate whose opponent exceeds certain levels of personal campaign spending (known as the Millionaires' Amendment).

Proponents of the new law view it as a long-overdue package of reforms designed to restore the system of campaign finance envisioned by Congress when it adopted and amended the Federal Election Campaign Act in the 1970s. The legislation's purpose, they argue, is to repair the tears in the regulatory fabric that rendered ineffective disclosure requirements for federal electioneering as well as long-standing prohibitions on corporate and union treasury financing of federal elections.

Opponents see the law as much more ambitious and ominous, a wholesale assault on protected First Amendment speech and rights of political association. They argue the law's restrictions would unconstitutionally limit the rights of individuals and groups to participate in federal elections and undercut the ability of national, state, and local parties to work cooperatively to promote candidates and issues at all levels of the political process.

These opposing views clashed in a titanic legal struggle over the constitutionality of McCain-Feingold.[18] A highly diverse set of individuals and groups, spanning the political spectrum from the Republican National Committee to the California Democratic party and ranging in political ideology from the National Rifle Association and various right-to-life groups to the

AFL-CIO and the American Civil Liberties Union, rushed to court to challenge the law as soon as it was signed by President Bush. The law was defended by the Department of Justice, the Federal Election Commission, and the Act's principle congressional sponsors, who were accorded the status of "intervenor-defendants" in the litigation.

On December 10, 2003, the Supreme Court upheld the major provisions of the new law in its ruling in *McConnell v. Federal Election Commission*.[19] The majority opinion was notable for its heavy reliance on the evidentiary record assembled by Congress and McCain-Feingold's defendants, its strikingly pragmatic view of money and politics, and its surprising willingness to defer to Congress's "ability to weigh competing constitutional interests in an area in which it enjoys particular expertise."

As dramatic as the Court's decision was, it would be a mistake to conclude that the United States has entered a new world of campaign finance. Changes in the law are best viewed as incremental repairs, not new departures. Campaign finance law and jurisprudence continue to heed the free speech imperatives of the First Amendment. Long-standing prohibitions on corporate and union financing of federal election campaigns have been restored after years of leakage, and disclosure regimes have been strengthened. Ample scope remains for candidates, parties, and interest groups to engage in relatively unlimited campaign communications.

Not surprisingly, the intense battle over campaign finance reform in Congress and the courts extended to the law's implementation and assessment of its impact in the 2004 election cycle.[20] Critics have pointed to the explosion of fund-raising in presidential and congressional elections, the decision of both major party presidential nominees to opt out of the presidential public financing program in the primaries, and the formation of party "shadow committees" designed to provide a new outlet for unregulated political funds in federal elections. Defenders responded that McCain-Feingold was not designed to reduce the overall amount of money in federal campaigns but rather to reduce the potential for corruption by breaking the nexus among officeholders, party officials, and large donors. While banning soft money, the new law actually increased the amount individuals can contribute to candidates as well as the total sum individuals can contribute to candidates, parties, and PACs during a two-year cycle. The surge in fund-raising by candidates and parties in 2004 reflects the intensely competitive and combative political environment and the new and successful emphasis on small-donor fund-raising. Parties have adapted well to the ban on soft money, more than matching in hard money alone what they had raised in hard and soft money combined in the previous presidential cycle. Some of the new so-called "527 organizations"—denounced by critics as party "shadow committees"—may well have skirted the law by failing to register as federal political committees or to use the requisite hard-money funds to finance their federal election activities. But these groups accounted for a modest share of the funds raised and spent to influence federal elections in 2004. Candidates and parties dominated fund-raising in 2004. In addition, the 527 groups do not appear to be drawing from the old party soft-money contributors, and they must adhere to the coordination and electioneering communications regulations of the new law—so that they cannot cooperate directly with the campaigns.

McCain-Feingold is far from the last word on campaign finance reform. As the majority opinion in *McConnell* concluded: "We are under no illusion that BCRA will be the last congressional statement on the matter. Money, like water, will always find an outlet. What problems will arise, and how Congress will respond, are concerns for another day." Struggles over the implementation of the new law, and experience with its application in the real world of campaigns, will likely lead Congress back to the legislative drawing board at some point.

Beyond this need for regular maintenance and repair of existing regulations, substantial problems surrounding money and politics remain. BCRA was designed to plug the most glaring loopholes in federal election law. Now reformers have to turn to other measures to enhance electoral competition; increase the quantity and quality of information about candidates, parties, and issues available to citizens; and reduce the conflicts of interest in public policymaking. High on the agenda for future reform are repairing the presidential public financing program (such as by raising the overall spending limit and increasing the value of the public matching funds), providing free or subsidized broadcast time for parties and candidates, reinstituting tax credits for small donors, and restructuring the Federal Election Commission.[21] None will be achieved without enormous difficulty, but the saga of McCain-Feingold suggests that reformers need not despair.

BEYOND GERRYMANDERING?

The pathologies associated with legislative redistricting—incumbent protection, noncompetitive elections, partisan bias, and polarization—have prompted frequent efforts to establish redistricting standards and to alter the process by which boundaries are redrawn.[22] There is a long history at the federal and state levels of attempts to constrain the choices of congressional district mapmakers by imposing redistricting standards. Between 1842 and 1929, Congress established various national standards for congressional redistricting, including contiguity, compactness, and equality of population. Out of this experience came the widely accepted view that Congress has the constitutional authority to impose on the states specific requirements governing congressional redistricting. That experience also demonstrated that states could ignore those requirements with impunity, as Congress had no means of enforcing redistricting standards, short of refusing to seat members elected in districts drawn in violation of them, a major step that no Congress has taken.

Since 1929, many proposals for setting national redistricting standards have been offered, but with the voting rights exception discussed below, none have survived the legislative process. Proposed standards have ranged from contiguity, compactness, equal population, adherence to local political boundaries, and respect for communities of interest, to neutrality with regard to any political party or candidate. The latter was of course designed to counter partisan and incumbent-protection gerrymandering. Today, the one national standard that has attracted attention in Congress would prohibit more than a single round of congressional redistricting after the decennial apportionment. A bill introduced by Representative Gene Green and other Democratic members of the Texas delegation in the U.S. House, whose ranks were decimated by the recent Republican gerrymander, would formalize what had been a long-standing norm. Of course, as long as Representative Tom DeLay, the chief architect of the Texas redistricting plan, remains a Republican leader, that bill will go nowhere. The more interesting question is how a Democratic majority in Congress might react to it.

One federal mandate on redistricting by states—prohibiting minority vote dilution—has its roots in the Voting Rights Act of 1965 and subsequent amendments, but the courts have taken the lead in fleshing out its application in the redistricting arena. Over time that jurisprudence has evolved from maximizing the number of majority-minority districts, to prohibiting race as the predominant factor in redistricting, to sanctioning the creation of minority-influence districts.

Another federal mandate—equal population districts—is entirely a creature of the courts. In a series of decisions from *Wesberry v. Sanders* (1964) to *Karcher v. Daggett* (1983), the Supreme Court developed a standard of absolute population equality in determining whether a congressional redistricting plan is constitutional. Any departure from precise mathematical equality of district populations within states must be justified by some compelling state interest. While the equal population standard has eliminated gross disparities associated with malapportioned districts and has constrained somewhat the ability of politicians to rig electoral outcomes, it has also provided an excuse and a cover for mapmakers seeking to extract every possible benefit from partisan and bipartisan gerrymanders. Easing somewhat the equal population standard (which is unlikely to do much damage to any reasonable conception of representation) might actually reduce the level of mischief by allowing more stability in district composition and respect for local political and social boundaries.

In *Davis v. Bandemer* (1986) the Court appeared to be moving toward the imposition of yet another standard when it ruled that partisan gerrymandering is justiciable under the Equal Protection Clause. Yet by setting a high threshold for successful challenges—"evidence of continued frustration of the will of a majority of the voters or effective denial to a minority of voters of a fair chance to influence the political process"—the Court rendered this standard ineffectual. Only one successful partisan gerrymandering claim—in a judicial election—has been litigated under *Bandemer*. The Court's 2004 decision in *Vieth v. Jubelirer* appears to have maintained this status quo. All nine justices acknowledged that partisan gerrymandering could be unconstitutional, but the Court majority despaired of finding workable standards for determining precisely when it was. While *Vieth* dealt exclusively with partisan gerrymandering, some legal scholars look to the courts to constrain what they see as the more problematic bipartisan gerrymanders (where the two parties collude to protect their respective incumbents). Others argue against any further judicial intervention to counter bipartisan as well as partisan gerrymanders. In the past the Court has sanctioned the protection of incumbency as a legitimate redistricting objective. It is not easy to see how the Court might reverse itself and develop a workable standard to mitigate incumbent-protecting gerrymanders.

On the state level, redistricting standards for congressional and state legislative mapmaking are written into constitutions and codified by statute. The most common are contiguity, compactness, adherence to existing political and geographical boundaries, and respect for communities of interest. The logic of these largely aesthetic criteria is that they are both desirable in their own right and likely to constrain partisan and incumbent gerrymandering. Contiguity is the only standard that is almost universally applied (assuming one accepts two land masses joined by a body of water as contiguous). The others more nearly approach general values to be sought rather than strict tests to be met. They often suffer from ambiguity (for example, how to define compactness) and from conflict with other standards. Compactness can work against natural communities of interest, especially racial minorities, and existing political boundaries. The equal population standard often requires mapmakers to split existing political and geographical communities.

Some states, typically those using nontraditional redistricting processes, have adopted more explicitly political standards for redistricting. Mapmakers might be instructed to avoid favoring incumbent officeholders or one political party over another. This might be done by blind procedures—denying them certain information (the location of incumbents' homes or election data)—or by requiring them to draw districts that are demonstrably competitive or treat both parties "fairly." Each of these approaches has its own set of complications, and they too can lead to conflict among standards. Protecting racial and ethnic minorities, an overriding federal requirement, can reduce the number of competitive seats and diminish the responsiveness of legislative elections to shifts in public sentiment.

Congressional redistricting plans are typically drawn and approved through the normal state legislative process. Control of both chambers of the legislature (or one in the unicameral Nebraska) and the governorship gives a political party an enormous advantage in crafting a plan that advances its partisan interests. Split-party control, on the other hand, tends to reduce opportunities for partisan gains within states and to facilitate bipartisan gerrymanders. It is no surprise that the national parties invest substantial resources in state legislative and gubernatorial elections leading up to each decennial reapportionment.

To be sure, unified party control of a state government is no guarantee of partisan gains. Many states are too small or too homogeneous to produce such opportunities. Parties in other states are constrained by intraparty differences, the perceived risks to majority party incumbents from maximizing partisan gains, and the geographical distribution of state residents. For example, although Democrats dominated California government at the time of the post-2000 congressional redistricting, they chose to consolidate their gains in the previous election and engage in a bipartisan incumbent gerry-mander with the minority Republicans.

Some states remove authority and responsibility from the legislature and place it in the hands of another group of actors, a panel usually referred to as an independent redistricting commission. Commissions—the most am-bitious and potentially most effective reform of redistricting procedures—are invested with a primary role in congressional redistricting by seven states (Arizona, Hawaii, Idaho, Maine, Montana, New Jersey, and Washington) and in state legislative redistricting by twelve states. They are used as backups if the legislative process fails in drawing congressional plans in two states (Connecticut and Indiana) and state legislative plans in seven states. Addi-tional states employ advisory commissions as inputs to the legislative process. And one state—Iowa—delegates authority for drafting congressional and state legislative redistricting plans to a nonpartisan legislative support staff. The Iowa legislature, however, retains the authority to put its own mark on the ultimate plans.

Commissions presently in use for congressional and state legislative redis-tricting vary according to several different factors: their size, whether they have an even or odd number of members, the criteria and method used to appoint members, the state redistricting standards they must follow, the limits on information they can use in drawing plans, the degree of their independence from the legislature and governor, whether their plans need approval by majority or supermajority rule, the provisions for judicial review, their timetable for action, their staff, their funding, and whatever backup provisions exist if the commission fails to approve a plan. Not surprisingly, commissions usually produce redistricting plans that reflect their structure and rules. Those with partisan majorities and simple majority rules tend to produce partisan plans. Those with evenly divided bipartisan memberships or supermajority rules are more likely to produce plans that protect both parties and their incumbents. Designing a commission that is neutral toward or that dampens the influence of both incumbents and parties is a challenge with which few states have successfully grappled.

Independent commissions operating under rules of transparency and con-strained by criteria of advancing electoral competitiveness probably offer the most promising direction for state-based redistricting reform. The Arizona independent redistricting commission, adopted by popular initiative in 2000, represents the latest and most ambitious exercise in this regard. Washington state and New Jersey have adopted alternative models of commission redistricting whose experience may well prove valuable to other states. But self-interested politicians and parties are unlikely to pursue these reforms on their own. It will take popular initiatives (in those states where they exist) and widespread public revulsion at the self-dealing by elected officials if any progress is to be made. Such efforts are now underway in California, Florida, Ohio, and several other states.

CONCLUSION

Is reform of America's electoral system possible? In one sense, the answer is obvious. We are constantly tinkering with our electoral institutions—in Washington and in the states, often in the wake of scandal or controversy that helps overcome the normal political obstacles. These incremental reforms, however, are no panacea for the ills that weaken American democracy and diminish our standing around the globe. Upgrading election administration is an important step toward avoiding another Florida 2000 fiasco but does not address the wisdom of maintaining the Electoral College in presidential elections. Banning party soft money and enforcing long-standing prohibitions on corporate and union financing of federal campaigns helps restore some legitimacy to campaign finance regulation and counters the most egregious conflicts of interest but does not address the escalating fundraising demands on challengers and the appalling decline of competitive elections at all levels of office. Shifting redistricting authority from state legislatures to independent commissions constrains the ability of elected officials to choose their voters rather than vice versa but cannot alone make elections competitive and parties more centrist and less polarized.

Broader forces—including the geographical dispersal of voters, the regional realignment of parties, and the parity in party strength—limit the effectiveness of these structural fixes. So, too, does our inability to entertain seriously more fundamental changes in the electoral system, ranging from direct election of presidents and proportional representation of representatives in multimember districts to full public financing of federal elections. Set aside the question of whether or not these latter proposals are wise. Our failure to include them in the mix of deliberation on electoral reform means we are fated to fall short of heightened expectations at home and abroad for improving American democracy.

On the other hand, muddling through has its own advantages. Modest improvements in how elections are administered, campaigns financed, and legislative boundaries redrawn can collectively constitute substantial, if not optimal, advances in our political system. Such efforts on a range of governance problems have helped keep American constitutional democracy afloat for well over two centuries; no mean accomplishment.

NOTES

1. Parts of this chapter are adapted from the author's "The United States of America: Democratic Exemplar?" *National Civic Review* 92, no. 3 (Fall 2003): 3–11.
2. The Pew Research Center for the People and the Press, "A Year after Iraq War: Mistrust of America in Europe Ever Higher, Muslim Anger Persists," March 16, 2004; available at http://people-press.org/reports/sedisplay.php3?ReportID=206 (viewed June 30, 2004).
3. E. J. Dionne Jr. and William Kristol, eds., *Bush v. Gore: The Court Cases and the Commentary* (Washington, DC: The Brookings Institution Press, 2001); The National Commission on Federal Election Reform, *To Assure Pride and Confidence in the Electoral Process*, Final Report of the Commission, July 31, 2001; available at http://www.reformelections.org/data/reports/99_full_report.php (viewed June 30, 2004).
4. Gary C. Jacobson, "The Bush Presidency and the American Electorate," in Fred I. Greenstein, ed., *The George W. Bush Presidency: An Early Assessment* (Baltimore, MD: Johns Hopkins University Press, 2003): 197–227.
5. Larry M. Bartels, "Partisanship and Voting Behavior, 1952–1996," *American Journal of Political Science* 44, no. 1 (January 2000): 35–50; Jacobson, "The Bush Presidency," 197–198; and John Tierney, "A Nation Divided? Who Says?" *New York Times* (June 13, 2004), Week in Review section.
6. Norman J. Ornstein and Thomas E. Mann, eds., *The Permanent Campaign and Its Future* (Washington, DC: AEI Press, 2000).
7. Bill Bishop, "The Schism in U.S. Politics Begins at Home," *Austin American-Statesman* (April 4, 2004).
8. Sam Hirsch, "The United States House of Unrepresentatives: What Went Wrong in the Latest Round of Congressional Redistricting," *Election Law Journal* 2, no. 2 (2003): 179–216; and Gary C. Jacobson, "Terror, Terrain, and Turnout: Explaining the 2002 Midterm Elections," *Political Science Quarterly* 118, no. 1 (2003): 16–18.
9. Joby Fortson, "R's will pick up 6-7 seats now in Texas," personal e-mail message to multiple recipients, October 9, 2003.
10. Thomas E. Mann, "The Rise of Soft Money," in Anthony Corrado, Thomas E. Mann, and Trevor Potter, eds., *Inside the Campaign Finance Battle: Court Testimony on the New Reforms* (Washington, DC: The Brookings Institution Press, 2003): 17–39.
11. Norman J. Ornstein, Thomas E. Mann, and Michael J. Malbin, eds., *Vital Statistics on Congress 2001–2002* (Washington, DC: AEI Press, 2002), chapter 3.
12. Caltech-MIT Voting Technology Project, "Voting—What Is, What Could Be," re-

port, July 2001; available at http://www.vote.caltech.edu/Reports/july01/July01_VTP
_%20Voting_Report_Entire.pdf (viewed June 30, 2004); The Constitution Project,
"Building Consensus on Election Reform," A Report of The Constitution Project's
Forum on Election Reform, August 2001; available at http://www.constitutionproj
ect.org/eri/CPReport.pdf (viewed June 30, 2004); Thomas E. Mann, "An Agenda for
Election Reform," Policy Brief #82, The Brookings Institution, June 2001; available
at http://www.brook.edu/comm/policybriefs/pb82.htm (viewed June 30, 2004); The
National Commission on Federal Election Reform, *To Assure Pride*.

13. electionline.org, "Election Reform 2004: What's Changed, What Hasn't, and Why,"
January 2004; available at http://www.electionline.org/site/docs/pdf/ERIP_AR2004
.pdf (viewed June 30, 2004).

14. electionline.org, "Securing the Vote," Election Reform Briefing, April 2004; available
at http://www.electionline.org/site/docs/pdf/EB7.pdf (viewed June 30, 2004).

15. electionline.org, "Election Reform Briefing: The 2004 Election," December 2004;
available at http://www.electionline.org/site/docs/pdf/ERIP%20Brief9%20Final.pdf
(viewed March 1, 2005).

16. John C. Fortier, ed., *After the People Vote: A Guide to the Electoral College*, 3rd ed.
(Washington, DC: AEI Press, 2004).

17. Anthony Corrado, "The Legislative Odyssey of BCRA," in Michael J. Malbin, ed.,
Life after Reform: When the Bipartisan Campaign Reform Act Meets Politics (Lanham,
MD: Rowman & Littlefield, 2003): 21–39.

18. Anthony Corrado, Thomas E. Mann, and Trevor Potter, eds., *Inside the Campaign
Finance Battle: Court Testimony on the New Reforms* (Washington, DC: The Brookings
Institution Press, 2003).

19. See "Symposium: *McConnell v. Federal Election Commission*," *Election Law Journal*,
3, no. 2 (2004): 113–369.

20. Anthony Corrado and Thomas E. Mann, "In the Wake of BCRA: An Early Report
on Campaign Finance in the 2004 Elections," *The Forum* 2, no. 2 (2004): article 3;
available at http://www.bepress.com/forum/vol2/iss2/art3 (viewed July 1, 2004).

21. Thomas E. Mann, "Reform Agenda," in Anthony Corrado, Thomas E. Mann, Daniel
R. Ortiz, and Trevor Potter, eds., *The New Campaign Finance Sourcebook*, Internet
Edition (May 2004); available at http://www.brookings.edu/gs/cf/sourcebk01/Inter
netChap11.pdf (viewed July 1, 2004).

22. This section draws on the author's "Redistricting Reform: What Is Desirable? Possible?," paper prepared for The Brookings Institution/Institute of Governmental Studies Conference on "Competition, Partisanship, and Congressional Redistricting,"
April 16, 2004, The Brookings Institution, Washington, DC; available at http://
www.brook.edu/gs/crc_Mann.pdf (viewed July 1, 2004).

Conclusion: The Impact of Fateful Trends

What future is there today for a centrist agenda in American politics? At present neither major party can lay undisputed claim to the vital center. But there are important trends at work that may eventually compel our political leaders to soften their partisan stance and cooperate to shape a more pragmatic middle course.

The first is the aging of the population. Demographic shifts of the magnitude of the Baby Boom's retirement are the political equivalent of climate change: it is we who must adjust to them, rather than vice versa. Neither major party at present has a formula capable of coping with a change of this magnitude. The dream of a laissez-faire society, with minimal government, where every individual is expected to accept his or her economic fate will prove unacceptable to an aging and increasingly medically dependent population that relies heavily on government help for both retirement income and medical care. At the same time, the position that the New Deal or Great Society programs must not be altered will prove unsustainable in the face of these programs' eventual overwhelming costs. Attempts to preserve Social Security and Medicare in their present form without tax increases are unrealistic. Yet the scale and scope of the new taxes required to preserve Medicare alone will likely choke the U.S. economy. We must therefore expect both tax increases and benefit adjustments, along with new approaches to make these programs more cost-effective.

A key question is how this burden of tax increases and benefit cuts will be distributed; it is unlikely that the middle class will tolerate both higher taxes and benefit cuts while taxes are being reduced or held to a minimum for the highest-income Americans.

A new solution will also have to be found for the U.S. health care system as a whole. More than a decade ago, Republicans resisted Democratic plans for health care reform at least partly on the grounds that there was no health care "crisis." Now most experts agree the crisis is upon us. Whether the Democratic plans of the 1990s would have proved successful is for the history books to decide. But one thing is clear: as employers find medical insurance increasingly unaffordable—and more and more middle-class families are forced off the insurance rolls—politicians will be under pressure to revisit our methods of paying for and delivering health care.

All these issues will require better balancing between the needs of

• aging Americans versus younger workers,
• high-income Americans versus those with middle and lower incomes, and
• the rights of individuals versus the common good of society.

The future of American democracy hinges on achieving these balances with fairness and transparency.

A second major trend is in foreign affairs. Events of September 11 gave the term "globalization" a new and unsettling meaning. It showed Americans how vulnerable we are to attitudes toward America that take shape in regions very distant from our shores. Voters were highly supportive of military action in response to terrorism, especially in Afghanistan and also in Iraq. But most sensible people understand that military action, airport screenings, and homeland security alerts cannot by themselves solve the problem. In particular, the American-led invasions of two Muslim nations carry substantial costs for the United States. Whatever advances democracy may have made in the Middle East, hostile attitudes toward the United States in that region have also intensified, and the United States has alienated many nations throughout the world.

Foreign policy is the issue that most sharply divides Republicans and Democrats today. Republicans put a greater emphasis on the use of force than on diplomacy; Democrats emphasize diplomacy more than the use of

force. But clearly an effective foreign policy requires the right balance between the two. The United States cannot allow other nations to veto its
legitimate efforts to ensure its own security. At the same time, meeting the
global threat of terrorism and nuclear weapons proliferation and fostering
global economic development clearly requires close cooperation with other
nations. The United States has a great deal of work to do to restore the
good will it once enjoyed throughout the world and to recreate the conditions for other nations to accept American leadership.

We may be at an important turning point in our history. In many ways,
the paradigms that our two major parties currently bring to policymaking
are inadequate to address these new challenges. In domestic policy, we are
re-fighting the battles of the New Deal and Great Society. In foreign policy,
we are re-fighting the battles of Vietnam and the Cold War. The force of
public opinion may give rise to a new centrism that will recognize that it is
time to lay these old weapons and old arguments aside and find pragmatic
new tools and ideas to meet our new challenges.

Contributors

Tsung-mei Cheng is the host of *International Forum*, a Princeton University television program on international affairs.

Amitai Etzioni is University Professor at George Washington University and director of the university's Institute for Communitarian Policy Studies.

Chester E. Finn, Jr., is Senior Fellow at Stanford's Hoover Institution and president of the Thomas B. Fordham Foundation and Thomas B. Fordham Institute, and senior editor of *Education Next*.

Francis Fukuyama is Dean of Faculty and Bernard L. Schwartz Professor of International Political Economy at the Paul H. Nitze School of Advanced International Studies of Johns Hopkins University.

William A. Galston is Saul I. Stern Professor of Civic Engagement and director of the Institute for Philosophy and Public Policy at the University of Maryland School of Public Affairs.

Norton Garfinkle is chairman of the Future of American Democracy Foundation.

Thomas E. Mann is the W. Averell Harriman Chair and Senior Fellow in Governance Studies at The Brookings Institution.

Will Marshall is president and founder of the Progressive Policy Institute.

Uwe E. Reinhardt is James Madison Professor of Political Economy at the Woodrow Wilson School of Public and International Affairs at Princeton University.

Mark Sagoff is a Pew Scholar in Conservation and the Environment at the University of Maryland School of Public Affairs and president of the International Society of Environmental Ethics.

Peter H. Schuck is Simeon E. Baldwin Professor of Law at Yale University Law School.

Peter Skerry is Professor of Political Science at Boston College and Nonresident Senior Fellow at The Brookings Institution.

Michael Vatis was the founding director of the U.S. National Infrastructure Protection Center and is a consultant in private practice.

Alan Wolfe is Professor of Political Science and director of the Boisi Center for Religion and American Public Life at Boston College.

Daniel Yankelovich is founder and chairman of Public Agenda, Viewpoint Learning, Inc., and DYG, Inc., and chairman of the advisory board of the Future of American Democracy Foundation.

Index